EX AUDITU

An International Journal for the Theological Interpretation of Scripture

VOL. 35   2019

Ex Auditu is published annually by Pickwick Publications, an imprint of
Wipf and Stock Publishers, 199 West 8th Avenue, Suite 3, Eugene, Oregon 97401, USA

SUBSCRIPTIONS

Individuals:
U.S.A. and all other countries (in U.S. funds): $20.00
Students: $12.00

Institutions:
U.S.A. and all other countries (in U.S. funds): $30.00

This periodical is indexed in the ATLA Religion Database, published by the American Theological Library Association, 300 S. Wacker Dr., Suite 2100, Chicago, IL 60606, Email: atla@atla.com, www: http://www.atla.com/; *Internationale Zeitschriftenshau für Bibelwissenschaft; Religious and Theological Abstracts; and Old Testament Abstracts.*

Please address all subscription correspondence
and change of address information to Wipf and Stock Publishers.

©2020 by Wipf and Stock Publishers
ISSN: 0883-0053
PAPERBACK ISBN: 978-1-7252-6238-6
HARDBACK ISBN: 978-1-7252-6239-3
E-BOOK ISBN: 978-1-7252-6240-9

EX AUDITU

An International Journal for the Theological Interpretation of Scripture

Stephen J. Chester and Dennis R. Edwards, Editors

D. Christopher Spinks, Associate Editor

Klyne R. Snodgrass, Editor Emeritus

Dennis R. Edwards
Associate Professor of New Testament
North Park Theological Seminary
3225 West Foster Avenue
Chicago, Illinois 60625-4987
USA

Tel: (773) 244-6238
email: dredwards@northpark.edu
Web site: http://wipfandstock.com/catalog/journal/view/id/12/

EDITORIAL BOARD

Terence E. Fretheim, Luther Seminary, St. Paul, MN

Richard B. Hays, The Divinity School, Duke University, Durham, NC

Jon R. Stock, Wipf & Stock Publishers, Eugene, OR

Miroslav Volf, Yale Divinity School, New Haven, CT

John Wipf, Wipf & Stock Publishers, Eugene, OR

THE EDITORIAL BOARD MEMBERS AND CONSULTANTS represent various disciplines and denominations. Theological interpretation of Scripture is a task to be taken seriously by scholars who are committed to the Christian faith and tradition. However, as one editorial consultant stated: "Let people gradually get used to the idea that a sane hermeneutics is both oriented in advance toward agreement/consent and is simultaneously exigent, discriminating, critical."

EDITORIAL CONSULTANTS

M. Daniel Carroll R.
Wheaton College
Wheaton, Illinois

Simon Gathercole
University of Cambridge
Cambridge, England

Nijay Gupta
Northern Seminary
Lisle, Illinois

Robert Johnston
Fuller Theological Seminary
Pasadena, California

R. Walter L. Moberly
University of Durham
Durham, England

Sujin Pak Boyer
The Divinity School
Duke University
Durham, N. Carolina

Iain Provan
Regent College
Vancouver, B.C.

Kevin J. Vanhoozer
Trinity Evangelical
Divinity School
Deerfield, Illinois

William H. Willimon
The Divinity School
Duke University
Durham, N. Carolina

N. T. Wright
Wycliffe Hall,
University of Oxford
Oxford, United Kingdom

EX AUDITU

CONTENTS

Abbreviations vi

Introduction vii
Stephen J. Chester

The Church and the Hermeneutical Challenge of Zionism 1
Philip Alexander

Response to Alexander 33
William Andrews

Another Look at "Early" Ideologies of the Land in the Hebrew Bible
in Light of Recent Study 39
Lawson Younger

Response to Younger 76
J. Nathan Clayton

Reading the Gospel of John in the Palestinian Context 80
Yohanna Katanacho

Response to Katanacho 101
Madison N. Pierce

The Jewish People and *Eretz Israel*:
A Jewish Evaluation of Selected Christian Theological Perspectives 106
Yehiel E. Poupko

Response to Poupko 119
Robert Cathey

CONTENTS

Communities of Forgiveness: A Palestinian Christian Perspective 122
Rula Mansour

Response to Mansour 148
Jeff Anderson

The Unknown Path: Martin Buber's Zionism
and the Making of a Vexed, Atypical Christian Zionist 151
Joel Willitts

Response to Willitts 186
Michael Walker

Returning to the Heart of the Gospel: A Practical Evangelical Theology of Liberation and Call to Action for Christians Engaged in Peacebuilding in Israel and Palestine 190
Mae Elise Cannon

Response to Cannon 204
Robert Hostetter

Teach Us Your Ways, Lord (Micah 4:1-3) 208
Jack Y. Sara

Annotated Bibliography on The Holy Land:
Biblical Perspectives and Contemporary Conflicts 214

Presenters and Respondents 219

ANNOUNCEMENT OF THE 2020 SYMPOSIUM

North Park Theological Seminary in Chicago, Illinois, regrets to announce that the thirty-sixth Symposium on the Theological Interpretation of Scripture will not take place in 2020 due to issues arising from the COVID-19 pandemic. We anticipate the symposium's return in September 2021 and publication of a new volume of *Ex Auditu* the following year.

ABBREVIATIONS

Unless listed here, all abbreviations are as specified in *The SBL Handbook of Style: For Biblical Studies and Related Disciplines*, 2nd edition (Atlanta: Society of Biblical Literature, 2014).

AT	Alalaḫ Text
BAH	Bibliothèque archéologique et historique
BTAVO	Beihefte zum Tübinger Atlas des Vorderen Orients
KRI	Kenneth A. Kitchen. *Ramesside Inscriptions: Historical and Biographical*. Oxford: Blackwell, 1979–.
Urk	*Urkunden des ägyptischen Altertums*. Edited by Georg Steindorf. Leipzig: J. C. Hinrichs, 1905–1957.
ZDPV	*Zeitschrift des deutschen Palästina-Vereins*

INTRODUCTION

One of our respondents in this edition of the journal, Professor Robert Cathey of McCormick Theological Seminary, shares an anecdote about public dialogue and controversial issues. A friend directing a program concerned to promote such dialogue found that it was possible in relation to all issues except abortion and the Israeli-Palestinian conflict. Attempts to foster good dialogue in relation to these issues led only to alienation and disengagement. I am glad to be able to report that this was not our experience at the 2019 symposium. Despite some tense and passionate moments our conversations about the Holy Land were constructive and were marked by good will. Nevertheless, Professor Cathey's anecdote was apposite, because, having been involved in one capacity or another in fourteen symposiums at North Park, I had not before experienced so many of our presenters and respondents explaining to me how emotionally difficult and costly their participation was for them. There is something about this issue, from its very practical dimension of who controls what territory to its theological implications in relation to the identity of the people of God, that makes good dialogue profoundly difficult and challenging. I therefore want to express deep thanks to all those who were willing to take part and to engage in this dialogue. For those, like me, who were coming new to sustained theological reflection upon this theme, it was a profound learning experience. Our hope is that it will prove to be the same for readers of this edition of the journal.

This symposium was different and special in another way. It was the first time that North Park has run the symposium in partnership with other institutions. We are extremely grateful for this collaboration with our friends at Bethlehem Bible College and Nazareth Evangelical College, who not only provided presenters (represented in the journal by the articles written by Yohanna Katanacho and Rula Mansour), and our preacher (Jack Sara, the President of Bethlehem Bible College), but some of whose students also attended the event and whom it was a privilege to have present with us at North Park. The vision for a symposium on the theme of the Holy Land grew out of visits to Bethlehem by Max Lee, Professor of New Testament at North Park Theological Seminary, and David Kersten, Dean of North Park Theological Seminary, and their consequent exposure to the challenges and injustices faced by the Palestinian people. Part of our purpose was that the voices of our Palestinian brothers and sisters, which often go unheard in the context of the American church, might be heard more clearly. However, neither our intention nor theirs was an event

Introduction

at which only Palestinian Christian perspectives and those sympathetic to them would be articulated. Readers of the journal will also find articles and responses from very different perspectives. We are especially grateful to Rabbi Yehiel Poupko of the Jewish United Fund in Chicago who became the first non-Christian presenter at the symposium and contributor to *Ex Auditu*. As a journal for the theological interpretation of Scripture we are committed to doing theological interpretation for the church and we felt that on this topic to do that task for the church demanded the inclusion of a Jewish perspective. The dangers of the church considering issues profoundly connected to Jewish identity without the participation of Jewish voices should be clear from the long and tragic history of Christian anti-Semitism. Finally, we are also grateful for the support of the church in the form of Serve Globally of the Evangelical Covenant Church. They provided assistance with the expenses of this year's symposium and their Middle East and North Africa regional coordinator, Jeff Anderson, kindly participated as a respondent.

This symposium has turned out to be my last as its organizer and as editor of *Ex Auditu*. In 2019 I was appointed to the position of Lord and Lady Coggan Professor of New Testament, Wycliffe College, at the University of Toronto. I would like to take this opportunity to thank those who have done so much to make the success of the symposium and journal possible, especially Luke Palmerlee, who cheerfully and efficiently undertakes the administration of the symposium, and Chris Spinks of Wipf & Stock, who is unfailingly kind and helpful in all of his advice and support. I am delighted to report that the new editor of *Ex Auditu* and Associate Professor of New Testament at North Park Theological Seminary is Dennis Edwards. Dr. Edwards brings to the role both expertise in the task of theological interpretation (he is the author of a commentary on 1 Peter in the *Story of God* series) and significant experience in urban ministry. Like all other events of its nature, the symposium now faces a period of uncertainty due to the COVID-19 pandemic, but I am confident that its leadership is in excellent and capable hands.

Stephen Chester
formerly Professor of New Testament
North Park Theological Seminary

THE CHURCH AND THE HERMENEUTICAL CHALLENGE OF POLITICAL ZIONISM

Philip Alexander

The Shoah and the State of Israel

Two events have shaped Judaism in our time, two events that are now inextricably linked in the Jewish imagination in a potent *Heilsgeschichte* of catastrophe and redemption—the Shoah and the founding of the State of Israel. Those same two events have shaped Christian attitudes towards Jews and Judaism; they challenge Christianity as much as they challenge Judaism. There has been much soul-searching within the Church as to whether traditional Christian anti-Judaism, the long centuries of the "teaching of contempt," contributed in any way to the attempted Nazi genocide of the Jewish people. Some theologians argue that the challenge of the Shoah is so profound that it can be met only by a radical reconfiguration of Christianity. Christian responses to the State of Israel have not been lacking. Since 1948 there has been a flood of books and articles and declarations from different churches, particularly as the Israel-Palestine conflict has intensified, but I think it is fair to say that they lack the theological depth, the theological "bite" of the responses to the Shoah. They do not engage adequately with Political Zionism, the Zionism that underpins the Jewish State, and the fundamental reasons for this failure is that they basically accept the view of the historians and the political commentariat that Political Zionism is a secular nationalism, and the founding of the State is the outcome of *Realpolitik*—nothing more. They do not grasp the central fact that from a religious-historical standpoint Political Zionism has to be construed as a *Jewish theology* and critiqued in theological terms. It is a theology that over the last one hundred years has transformed Judaism into a land-centered religion in a way that was not true before it came on the scene. It has been the engine for a profound theological revolution within Judaism.

Reform Judaism and Political Zionism

Let me try and sketch the history of this transformation. I begin with Reform Judaism. This emerged in Europe in the 19th century. As a child of the European

Enlightenment, Reform argued that Judaism was a religion of reason and it therefore rejected those aspects of faith and practice which were deemed not to accord with reason. It also rejected Jewish nationalism. The Jewish people had gone through their national phase in preparation for their role in history to spread the knowledge of the one true God to humankind. In the providence of God their dispersion to the four corners of the earth had helped to achieve their mission. Once the knowledge of God has been imparted to humanity at large (not only by the Jewish people, but by their proxies Christianity and Islam) and the promised era of universal peace and justice is inaugurated, Israel, mission accomplished, can merge into the mass of enlightened and redeemed humanity. There is absolutely no room in this vision of Israel's destiny for an end-time restoration of the Jewish State, and it is explicitly rejected. The Pittsburgh Platform of 1885 avers: "We consider ourselves no longer a nation but a religious community, and therefore expect neither a return to Palestine, nor a sacrificial worship under the administration of the sons of Aaron, nor the restoration of any of the laws concerning the Jewish state." In keeping with this stance Reform Judaism purged its prayerbook of all references to a return to Zion. To return to Zion would be to go in quite the wrong direction.

Today, however, many Reform Jews are supporters of the State of Israel. They tend to be "peaceniks," politically on the left, and to be more inclined to voice criticism of Israel's policies particularly towards the Palestinians, but many support its right to exist. What happened to change their minds? The short answer is that Political Zionism happened, and facts were created on the ground which they could not ignore. The change of attitude is reflected already in the Columbus Platform of 1937, issued to update Pittsburgh. Columbus for the most part fleshed out and tweaked Pittsburgh, save in one area— the return to Zion. It states: "In all lands where our people live, they assume and seek to share loyally the full duties and responsibilities of citizenship and to create seats of Jewish knowledge and religion. In the rehabilitation of Palestine, the land hallowed by memories and hopes, we behold the promise of renewed life for many of our brethren. We affirm the obligation of all Jewry to aid in its upbuilding as a Jewish homeland by endeavouring to make it not only a haven of refuge for the oppressed but also a centre of Jewish culture and spiritual life." The phrasing is careful, and every word deserves careful parsing.

By 1937 the Zionists in Palestine had essentially laid down the infrastructure of a state, and were beginning to press Britain, the Mandatory power, for independence. This is described as "the rehabilitation of Palestine." The form that independence would take, however, was contested. The Platform speaks of "a Jewish homeland." There is surely an echo here of the Balfour Declaration of 1917 in which the British Government promised "the establishment in Palestine of a national home for the Jewish people." The Zionists saw this as a promise of independent statehood. The British government by 1937 was arguing that it was compatible with some political arrangement short of statehood, which nevertheless guaranteed the Jews in Palestine a high degree of cultural and political self-determination. The Platform is non-committal. It also dodges the messianic question, that is to say the question of how the establishment of the new homeland related to the prophetic promises of a return to Zion. There is a nod in this direction in the description of Palestine as "the land hallowed by memories and hopes," but the two functions identified for the new homeland are strictly pragmatic, dictated by the needs of the hour, and theoretically reversible, should circumstances change. They are (1) to be a refuge for persecuted Jews. Already conditions in Germany had become very hostile to Jews and many were seeking to flee. And (2) to be "a centre of Jewish culture and spiritual life." The Platform here aligns itself with the Cultural Zionism of Ahad Ha'am (Asher Ginsberg, 1856–1927) who argued that the priority for Zionism was not the political process of founding a state but the cultural renewal of Judaism. The implication is that if the founding of a state leads to the renewal of Judaism then it may be embraced as instrumental in helping to fulfil the universal Jewish mission envisaged by Pittsburgh.

Orthodoxy and Political Zionism

The Theological Challenge

The impact of Zionism on Reform Judaism has been profound, but it has had an equal if not more profound impact on Orthodox Judaism. Political Zionism challenges Orthodoxy. Ever since the destruction of the Temple in 70 Jews have been praying for a return to Zion. Now that they have returned and built again a sovereign state, does this represent the fulfilment of these prayers? What is this state's relationship to the end-time promises of the Hebrew prophets? Can it in any way be seen as the promised messianic kingdom? There are clear grounds for rejecting the present State of Israel as the prayed-for redemption.

1. First it does not match the descriptions of the messianic kingdom. That had been depicted in idealized, even utopian terms. Some aspects of this are easier to deal with than others. The prophecies speak of the miraculous fertility of the soil: the desert will rejoice and blossom like a rose (Isa 35:1) the reaper will follow in the footsteps of the sower. Israeli agriculture has been startlingly successful in wresting crops from semi-arid land, and the biblical prophecies are often quoted in this context. Perhaps the most lyrical of the traditional descriptions of nature's fecundity in the messianic age have not been met, but still the

success has been spectacular, and it is not too difficult to put the remaining gap down to poetic licence. But one shortfall cannot be easily explained away, and that is the deficit in Torah-observance. Maimonides's description of the messianic state is famously mundane; there is nothing miraculous or utopian about it (see *Yad: Hilkhot Melakhim* 1–4). Nevertheless, for him the state will be Torah-observant. For Maimonides the reason the Temple will have to be rebuilt is because so many of the *mitzvot* in Torah involve the Temple, and so if the Torah in all its fulness is to be observed in the messianic age, then there needs to be a Temple in which to perform those *mitzvot*. But although there were some Rabbis who supported Political Zionism from the start, the vast majority of the founders, and particularly the young Zionist pioneers, were aggressively secular. They gloried in their *non-observance* of Torah. They saw themselves as creating a new Jewish identity, which was precisely *not* Torah-observant.

2. There was a second problem with the state founded in 1948. Where is the Messiah? The traditional messianic scenario foretold the coming of the Messiah at the beginning of the redemption. It would be he who would get the whole process going. Political Zionism produced able, even charismatic leaders, some of whom were sometimes spoken of in messianic language (one thinks here of Herzl) but it was done knowingly and ironically, and any of the founding fathers would have greeted being hailed as Messiah in any literal sense with a mixture of amusement and horror, and none of them came close to fulfilling the conditions for holding this office.

3. The third mismatch between the state of 1948 and the messianic state was, theologically speaking, the most serious of all. It was that the founding of the State in 1948 involved "forcing the redemption." This was a grave charge, because the classic sources of Jewish messianism specifically forbade any activity that could be construed as "forcing the end." From the earliest stages of the development of Jewish Messianism, the stress had been on *God's* agency in redemption. *God* would redeem Israel in his own good time. He would send his Messiah at the time of *his* choosing. There were things that Jews *could* do to hasten the end, but they were all spiritual. They could repent and scrupulously keep the *mitzvot*. They could pray and long for the restoration, and maybe move God to pity them and bring them consolation. But the one thing they could not do was take any concrete action that could be construed as beginning to set the kingdom up—emigrating to the Land and establishing settlements, fighting for its independence. Some even classified saying too many prayers, being *too* importunate with God, pressing him *too* hard, so to speak, as forcing the redemption. All Jews could do was wait expectantly on God—precisely the stance adopted

by the Amidah. The Zionists, however, had set out very deliberately to create a Jewish state. The politicals, led by Herzl, tried to do it diplomatically in one fell swoop, by eliciting the help of the great powers to set it up. The practicals, like Weizmann, adopted the more pragmatic approach of putting all the infrastructure of statehood in place— agricultural settlements, industries, transport systems, educational institutions, hospitals, law courts, security services and so forth—and then trying to call the state into existence. But both were blatantly and brazenly forcing the end.

Orthodox Rejectionism

Political Zionism split Orthodox Judaism down the middle. Some Haredi traditionalists vehemently rejected the new state as a godless entity, born in sin. Their opposition began long before statehood was ever achieved, when Political Zionism was in its infancy, and beginning to send out settlers and encourage *aliyah*. The opposition was particularly fierce among the Hasidim. Two of the most vehement critics were Rabbi Ḥayyim Eleazar Shapira of Munkács (1872–1937) the Munkaczer Rebbe, a prominent Hungarian Hasidic leader, and Rabbi Joel Moshe Teitelbaum (1914–2006) the Satmarer Rebbe. Both of them had a huge influence on the Neturei Karta movement, which emerged in the Haredi community of Jerusalem in 1938 and has continued actively and intemperately to oppose the State of Israel down to the present day. The language of Teitelbaum was by any standards extreme and alienated some Haredim in Israel. He demonized Israel and saw it as an agent of Satan. The reason he did so was simple. It was always open to argue pragmatically that actually the state proclaimed in 1948 had nothing to do with messianism. It was a practical measure—a refuge for those Jews who were persecuted, and particularly the traumatized survivors of the Shoah. It was a lodging for the night, so there was no reason to get too religiously worked up about it. This was, by and large, the line taken by the Rabbis who were involved in early Political Zionism. They were scared stiff of any suggestion that it was messianic. But Teitelbaum would have none of this. He argued that setting up a Jewish state in the Land could never be a matter of indifference, or pure pragmatism, because it stood in the way of founding the true messianic state. Far from bringing the redemption, it was preventing it. On this view the present State of Israel functions like the Kingdom of the Antichrist in some Christian scenarios of the end.[1]

---

1. The best introduction to Orthodox Jewish responses to the State remains Aviezer Ravitsky, *Messianism, Zionism and Jewish Religious Radicalism* (Chicago: University of Chicago Press, 1996). Ultra-Orthodox Jewish rejection of the present State of Israel is sometimes conveniently forgotten by present-day Jewish apologists. The Chief Rabbi of the United Synagogue of Great Britain, Ephraim

Orthodox Accommodation

But rejectionism was not the only response from within the Orthodox camp. There have been Orthodox thinkers who have found an accommodation with Political Zionism. By far the most influential of these was Avraham Isaac Kook, Rav Kook (1865–1935). His son, Zvi Yehudah ha-Cohen Kook (1891–1981) was to take the father's views and develop them in a deeply radical way. He ended up in a position which was the polar opposite of Teitelbaum's, and just as extreme. Where Teitelbaum saw the State of Israel as demonic, Kook the younger saw it as holy and divine. All its actions were messianic and above criticism. Everything it did was furthering the redemption. Zvi Yehudah Kook became the ideologue of Gush Emunim, and more broadly of the settler movement.

Rav Kook started from a theological hermeneutic of experience. He watched the growth of Political Zionism. He met with and befriended the idealistic young pioneers in Palestine, and he was impressed. He simply could not believe that God was not at work somewhere in all this. Whether they realised it or not, the Political Zionists were acting as the agents of God's purpose in history. There was a real danger that the religious, who claimed to be yearning so deeply for the redemption, would miss the tide, and be found opposing God's will. The activism of Political Zionism was not a case of forcing the end, because God was using human agents to further his purpose. God never intended to break into history like a *deus ex machina* and arrange everything miraculously: it was always his intention to work through the historical process, and this meant employing human agents to do every day, human things. But human agency and action that is within the purposes of God simply cannot, by definition, be "forcing the redemption."

In an essay written in 1898, but not published till some time later, Kook addressed head on the charge that Political Zionists were forcing the end. "Nothing in our faith," he wrote, "either in its larger principles or in its details, negates the idea that we can begin to shake off the dust of exile by our own efforts, through natural, historical processes … that we have a sacred duty to try and do so by whatever means are at our disposal." He rejected the claim that "we cannot hope for the salvation of Israel except through palpable miracles, such as the coming of Elijah,

---

Mirvis, posted on 3rd May 2016 on the *Daily Telegraph* website an opinion piece affirming unequivocally that Zionism is integral to Judaism. "One can no more separate it from Judaism than separate the City of London from Great Britain." As proof he exhorted the reader to "open a Jewish daily prayer book used in any part of the world and Zionism will leap out at you. The innumerable references to the land of Israel are inescapable and demonstrative." But you would be hard put to find them in Reform Jewish prayer books (but maybe Reform Judaism doesn't count as authentic Judaism in Rabbi Mirvis's book). And what about ultra-Orthodox rejection of the present State as the longed-for redemption? Such tendentiousness and inaccuracy does nothing to advance the Chief Rabbi's credibility or his cause.

upon which our own efforts have no bearing."[2] He was troubled by the secularism, indeed the godlessness, of the young Zionist pioneers, but he believed things would change, and he turned it rhetorically to good effect against his Orthodox opponents. Wouldn't it be an irony, a tragedy even, if God had to use unbelievers as the instruments of his purpose, because the religious were sulking in their tents, failing to read the signs of the times. But where was the Messiah? Kook believed he would come eventually, but there was no reason to suppose he had to be there from the start. He appealed to a postmillennial type of Jewish messianism,[3] in which the process of redemption is inaugurated by a host of human agents, and the Messiah arrives only as the consummation of the process. In short— to use his famous phrase—Political Zionism and a Jewish State, though not the full redemption, are "the beginning of the redemption (*'athalta di-ge'ullah*)." This accommodation with Political Zionism allowed many Religious Zionists to enter the political arena in Israel, to engage in the political process and try and nudge things in the direction of Torah observance and full redemption.

The Secularity of Political Zionism

This entry of theology into politics has had a profound effect on Political Zionism. It has exposed how shallow, how wafer-thin, its trumpeted secularity was. It has shown that for all its socialism and anti-religion, Political Zionism is locked into a symbiosis with traditional messianism from which it simply cannot escape. Initially Political Zionism tried to present its efforts as having nothing to do with messianism. Max Nordau in 1897 wrote in *Die Welt*: "Zionism has nothing to do with theology; and if a desire has been kindled in Jewish hearts to establish a new commonwealth in Zion, it is not the Torah or the Mishnah that inspire them but hard times."[4] Modern Political Zionism is usually presented in the textbooks as the result of two interlocking causes: first, the growing sense among European Jews in the late 19th century that emancipation had failed. Far from integrating Jews smoothly and uncontroversially into the countries where they had been granted civil rights, it had led to a new, virulent political antisemitism.

The second cause was the upsurge in the late 19th century of nationalism across Europe. Stressing the particularity of nations against the cosmopolitan ideals of the Enlightenment had encouraged some Jews to explore their own national identity,

---

2. See Ravitzky, *Messianism*, 79–144.

3. For different types of Jewish messianism see my "Towards a Taxonomy of Jewish Messianisms," in John F. Ashton, ed., *Revealed Wisdom: Studies in Apocalyptic in Honour of Christopher Rowland* (Leiden: Brill, 2014) 52–72.

4. See Ravitzky, *Messianism*, 93.

and to begin to dream of founding a Jewish State. Many of those Jews strongly rejected their religious heritage. They wanted to negate not just the *Galut*, the exile, but the *Galut*-mentality, which they associated specifically with Rabbinism, and which had left Jews sitting around in exile passively accepting their fate as the butt of anti-Semitism. So, there is a widespread sense that Political Zionism had arisen *outside* the religious tradition; it had come from another place, and only later collided with the long-standing tradition of Religious Zionism and Messianism. This model of how things developed lies behind Gershom Scholem's famous concept of "the price of messianism." "Can Jewish history," he asked, "manage to re-enter concrete reality without being destroyed by the messianic claim which [that re-entry] is bound to bring up from its depths?"[5] But this convergence model is possibly too simplistic. If one reads carefully the founding documents of Political Zionism it becomes clear how much the religious tradition is bubbling away just below the surface or is even explicitly referenced. True, Herzl's *The Jewish State* is a very secular document, in keeping with the non-religious upbringing of its author, but translate it into Hebrew and its secularity is much less clear. And it was soon immersed in a wider Political Zionist discourse where religious echoes were more easily heard.

The fact is that Political Zionism needs religious tradition to make its secular political case. The Declaration of the State of Israel makes this point. Strategically placed in it is language straight out of the lexicon of Religious Zionism. Take the following: "The State of Israel will be open for Jewish immigration and for the *Ingathering of the Exiles*; it will foster the development of the country for the benefit of all its inhabitants; it will be based on *freedom, justice and peace as envisaged by the prophets of Israel*" (my emphasis). Or again: "We appeal to the Jewish people throughout the Diaspora to rally round the Jews of Eretz-Israel in the tasks of immigration and upbuilding and to stand by them in the great struggle for the realisation of the age-old dream— *the redemption of Israel*" (again my emphasis). And it was placing their trust "in the Almighty" that the signatories put their names to the declaration. "In the Almighty" is the official English translation of the Hebrew "in the Rock of Israel" (*be-Tzur Yisra'el*). The story of the last-minute controversy that raged around this phrase has often been told, but it is worth telling again. Rabbi Fishman-Maimon wanted some acknowledgement of God in the text of the declaration. There was precedence for this in the American Declaration of Independence, whose signatories had appealed to "the Supreme Judge of the world" and placed their "firm reliance on the protection of divine Providence." Rabbi Maimon proposed, "Placing our trust in the Rock of Israel and its Redeemer," an echo of Ps 19:15, "O Lord, my Rock and my Redeemer (*Ha-Shem Tzuri ve-Go'ali*)." The secularists, led by Aharon Zisling of

---

5. See Ravitzky, *Messianism*, 3.

Mapam, would have none of this, and refused to sign if this reference was left in. Zisling roundly declared he didn't believe in God, but the secularists were also probably concerned that it would compromise the separation of religion and the state. It took Ben Gurion several hours of tense negotiation to reach a compromise to which both parties could agree. It was simply to drop "and its Redeemer," and so disguise the religious reference. Ben Gurion himself in later life remarked that for him "the Rock of Israel" could mean the Tanakh and its traditions, or the Israel Defence Forces!

It is interesting that the secularists, while objecting to an overt reference to God, did not balk at the religious language of "ingathering of the exiles" or "redemption of Israel." It is usually thought that they were happy to include such emotive phrases for purely cynical reasons; it was a tug at the heartstrings of the religious Jews in the Diaspora, an emotional appeal for their support. But in fact, that religious sentiment was integral to the secular, political argument that was being made. It wasn't enough that Jews had once lived in numbers, and had an independent state, in Palestine in the past. The last time they had exercised any political control over the Land, and short-lived and disastrous it was, had been nearly two thousand years earlier under Bar Kokhba. Equally important was the fact that *they had never lost the aspiration to return to the Land and re-establish their state there.* But where was the evidence for the latter claim? It was to be found in the religious tradition, in prayers like the Amidah. Texts like the Amidah have to be read as enshrining the continuing national and political consciousness of the Jewish people. *It is, therefore, necessary for the case of modern Political Zionism that it builds Religious Zionism into its argument.*

Moreover, it became increasingly clear that the culture that would make the Jewish State *Jewish* would have to be based in some way on Rabbinic tradition, as Cultural Zionists like Ahad Ha'am had argued. The movement known as Canaanism tried briefly to construct a pre-Rabbinic identity for the State, but it failed.[6] There just wasn't enough culture recoverable from ancient Israel, even when set by archaeologists in the wider context of the Ancient Near East, to forge a cultural identity for a modern Jewish state. And anyway, even the Tanakh was really only a *Jewish* document when read through the lens of Rabbinic Midrash. Its Jewish character derived from its reception by Rabbinic Judaism. And so the Bible as read by the Rabbis and indeed the whole panoply of Rabbinic Judaism, have become the foundation of Israeli Jewish cultural identity, whether accepted as Torah from Heaven or simply as a cultural heritage, and Political Zionism has had to swallow this. Religious Zionism was, therefore, enshrined at the heart of Israeli identity. It could not be ignored. The

---

6. On Canaanism see James S. Diamond, *Homeland or Holy Land: The "Canaanite" Critique of Israel* (Bloomington: Indiana University Press, 1986); Yaacov Shavit, *The New Hebrew Nation: A Study in Israeli Heresy and Fantasy* (London: Frank Cass, 1987).

entry of the Religious Zionists into the political arena called the secularists bluff and put them on the back foot. Purely secular Political Zionism had a problem with establishing its *Jewish* authenticity, with establishing its *Jewish* credentials.

Political Zionism and Antisemitism

It is hard to imagine a more striking example of the radical and fundamental transformation that Judaism has undergone under the influence of Political Zionism than the recent International Holocaust Remembrance Alliance definition of antisemitism.[7] I do not know whether this has generated the same level of controversy in the US as it has in the UK. The definition, described rather modestly as a "non-legally binding working definition," was adopted by the IHRA at a Plenary in Bucharest on 26 May 2016. It consists of two parts: the short definition itself, and a set of examples of actions which, "taking into account the overall context," may constitute antisemitism. Since its publication there has been pressure from within the Jewish community for governments, political parties, public agencies, churches, and universities to accept it, together with all its examples. The British Government has accepted it, and the definition can be found on the UK government website. The Church of England has accepted it. There was initially strong resistance within the British Labour party to accepting it in full, and it published a slightly modified version of it, but in the end it too, under pressure from the leadership of the British Jewish community, accepted it in its entirety.

Now it is not my aim to go into this debate here, which so far in the UK has generated more heat than light. For present purposes what I want to highlight is the astonishing fact that of the eleven examples of antisemitism it gives, no less than seven relate to the State of Israel, or to the relationship of the Jews to that state. The most contentious is the third: "Denying to the Jewish people their right to self-determination, e.g. by claiming that the existence of a State of Israel is a racist endeavour." The wording here is unclear, but what it seems to say is that anyone who denies the right of the Jews to *national* self-determination in their own sovereign Jewish State, on the grounds that such a state would be by definition racist, is an anti-Semite. But where does this leave a one-stater, who argues for a federal solution to the Israel-Palestine problem, whereby the maximum rights to self-determination are guaranteed to both communities within a single federal state? That state would no longer be a sovereign Jewish State, in that Jews would no longer have absolute control over it. Would such a position be antisemitic? Arguably so, on this definition.[8] The definition explicitly

---

7. See the IHRA website: https://www.holocaustremembrance.com/working-definition-anti semitism.

8. This would lead to branding some famous Zionists "anti-Semites," e.g., Martin Buber, who

allows criticism of the State of Israel, but what it denies as antisemitic is questioning the legitimacy of the state *per se* in any way shape or form. There is no doubt that this goes a long way towards collapsing anti-Zionism into antisemitism, and there are those who applaud this and try to exploit it for political advantage.[9] But scroll back one hundred years and imagine this definition being proposed then. It would have been greeted with utter astonishment by many within the Jewish community who vehemently opposed emerging Political Zionism.[10] These people no longer saw statehood as part of the future of the Jewish people and opposed it as undesirable. Indeed, if the definition had received a sympathetic hearing then it is more likely to have been among *Christian* Zionists. The change between then and now offers striking evidence for the impact of Political Zionism on Judaism: it has totally transformed the attitude of Jews towards the Land.[11]

---

advocated a federalist position. See Paul Mendes-Flohr, *Martin Buber: A Life of Faith and Dissent* (New Haven: Yale University Press, 2019).

9. There is little doubt that this is already happening. See Kenneth Stern, "I drafted the definition of antisemitism. Rightwing Jews are weaponizing it," *Guardian* online (https://www.theguardian.com/commentisfree/2019/dec/13/antisemitism-executive-order-trump-chilling-effect). This post was reported neutrally by the *Jewish Chronicle* online (https://www.thejc.com/news/us-news/ihra-antisemitism-definition-being-used-by-to-silence-free-speech-at-american-univerisites-1.494352). Stern criticizes Jared Kushner for writing in the *New York Times* that the IHRA definition "makes clear [that] Anti-Zionism is antisemitism."

10. Lucien Wolf (1857–1930) is an obvious case in point. Wolf, a famous journalist in his day, was a prominent member of the Anglo-Jewish community, a community officer, and the founder-president of the Jewish Historical Society of England. Wolf established the Anti-Zionist League of British Jews and wrote tirelessly against Zionism. He argued that far from solving the problem of European antisemitism, as Herzl claimed, it would provoke antisemitism. See his "The Zionist Peril," *JQR* 17 (1904) 1–25, answered by Israel Zangwill in the same journal, "Mr Lucien Wolf on the 'Zionist Peril'" (*JQR* 17 [1905] 397–425). Wolf, like several other Jewish intellectuals of the day, propounded racist theories of Jewish superiority: see Daniel R. Langton, "Jewish Evolutionary Perspectives on Judaism, Anti-Semitism and Race Science in Late 19th Century England," *Jewish Historical Studies* 46 (2014) 37–73.

11. Basically the same point is made, in a rather different way, by the Israeli political scientist Yossi Shain in his book, *Ha-Me' ah ha-Yisraelit ve-ha-Yisraelizatziyah shel ha-Yahadut* (The Israeli Century and the Israelization of Judaism) (Yedi'ot Aharonot: Rishon le-Tziyon, 2019; English translation forthcoming 2020): "Since its establishment in 1948, the State of Israel has gradually situated itself as the most important factor in all areas of worldwide Jewish life … The nation of Israel and Jewish civilization are defined today more than ever through the political, military and cultural power of the sovereign Jewish state" (p. 11). Shain perhaps collapses too completely the distinction between Diaspora Judaism and Israeli Judaism. In many areas there remain two worlds of Judaism (as Charles S. Liebman and Steven M. Cohen argued in *Two Worlds of Judaism: The Israeli and American Experiences* [New Haven: Yale University Press, 1990]) but he makes a compelling case for seeing Judaism as rapidly evolving towards a monopolar world with Israel at its centre.

Christian Responses to Political Zionism

The Challenge to Christian Triumphalism

Since the middle of the last century the Church has faced a transformed and revitalized Jewish people. Its reaction to this new state of affairs—and in particular to Political Zionism and the State of Israel—has been troubled and confused. The problem fundamentally is this: Ever since the time of Eusebius the Church had relied heavily on the degradation of the Jewish people—their wandering, persecuted, landless condition—as evidence that they had lost divine favour: God's covenant with them had been superseded. They were being punished for their obdurate failure to recognize God's Messiah. Since 1948, however, the flag of Christian triumphalism has looked increasingly threadbare. The Christian world has witnessed a rebirth of the Jewish people in their ancient land: the vitality of the State of Israel—on the cultural, scientific, economic, military, political, and religious fronts—is palpable to anyone who visits the country, and Christians are going there on pilgrimage in increasing numbers. How does this new reality fit, from a Christian perspective, into the purposes of God?

Christian Zionism

As within Judaism, so within Christianity, a range of positions has emerged in response to Political Zionism, positions that map rather neatly on to those within Judaism. I begin with the movement now commonly called Christian Zionism. This falls into two phases and two types, Restorationism and Dispensationalism. Both Restorationists and Dispensationalists agree on the cardinal point that a restoration of the Jewish people to statehood in their ancient land remains central to the purposes of God in history, as the Hebrew prophets foretold, but they differ, as we shall see, on important points of detail.

Restorationism

Restorationism is the earlier form of Christian Zionism.[12] It emerges clearly for the first time in late Elizabethan England. A key exponent was Thomas Brightman in his commentaries on Revelation and Daniel. Brightman died in 1607, and his major works were all published posthumously in Latin— the commentary on Revelation

---

12. See: Andrew Crome, *The Restoration of the Jews: Early Modern Hermeneutics, Eschatology and National Identity in the Works of Thomas Brightman* (Cham: Springer, 2014); Andrew Crome, *Christian Zionism and English National Identity, 1600-1850* (Cham: Springer, 2018); Donald M. Lewis, *The Origins of Christian Zionism: Lord Shaftesbury and Evangelical Support for a Jewish Homeland* (Cambridge: Cambridge University Press, 2010).

in 1609 and the commentary on Daniel in 1614. It was not until 1635 and 1644 that English versions appeared. In 1621 Sir Henry Finch (d. 1625) better known as a jurist, also argued for the national restoration of the Jews at the end of history, in his *The World's Great Restauration or Calling of the Jews and with them of all Nations and Kingdoms of the Earth to the Faith of Christ*. Though Restorationism was strongly opposed by some, the idea took root in Puritan circles, and many leading Puritans, such as John Owen, embraced it. It played a part in the readmission of the Jews to England in 1656. Key figures in the entourage of Cromwell, men who took part in the Whitehall Conference, were Restorationists and were open to the arguments deployed by Menasseh ben Israel that the readmission of the Jews to England was a necessary precursor to their eventual ingathering to the Holy Land. There was a significant eschatological convergence between the Sefardi Rabbi from Amsterdam and the Puritan scholars of England. Here was something practical that England could do to hasten the end.

The reasons why Restorationism emerged in England at precisely the time it did are complex and obscure. One factor, however, is clear, and it was the decisive Protestant turn in the 16th and 17th centuries to the *sensus literalis* of Scripture. Restorationists agreed with the Jews that the plain meaning of Scripture *demands* a return of the Jewish people to statehood at the end of time. The prophecies are detailed and explicit, and to read them other than literally is to make a mockery of the Word of God, and opens the door to treating Scripture— to use the famous simile—like a wax nose to be pushed and pulled into any shape we—or the Bishop of Rome—might like.

But scriptural literalism was embraced as an article of faith by all the Protestant churches, not just by the church in England, so the question arises as to why Restorationism arose when it did *in England* and not elsewhere. The answer probably lies in the peculiar political circumstances that prevailed in England in the 17th century. England was seeking to define its national identity, and for some ancient Israel offered a model—a God-sanctioned model—of a national polity. The influence of the example of ancient Israel on English political thought, particularly among the Puritans, was profound. There were two ways in which this position could have been developed. England could have been seen as the New Israel: if it obeyed God's laws *it* would become the elect nation, tasked, like ancient Israel, in a peculiar way, with working out the divine purposes in history. There were some inclined to take this view. The chosenness, the exceptionalism, of England was to have a long history in English patriotism right down to the present day. Its culmination was British Israelism in the 19th and 20th centuries.[13] But it faces the hermeneutical problem

---

13. Tudor Parfitt, *The Lost Tribes of Israel: The History of a Myth* (London: Phoenix, 2003) 41–65,

to which I alluded above: it implies a non-literal reading of the biblical promises to Israel. Where the Prophets said "Israel" you have, in effect, to substitute "England." It is a variation of the classic Christian view that the prophetic promises were fulfilled spiritually in the Church (a view to which I will come presently). The godly, Christian nation takes the place of the Church. The switch is not negligible in that it does allow a more literal fulfilment of the prophecies, but in the end the hermeneutic is fundamentally non-literal and that is a problem.

This was not the line taken by Restorationists. Rather they held that the promises would be fulfilled literally and politically by the ingathering of the Jews to the Promised Land and their founding there of an independent state. England's destiny would lie in facilitating that return. If she did so she could become an instrument in the purposes of God, and thereby garner divine favour and blessing. So by allowing the Jews back into England, if Manasseh was right that this was a necessary step towards the ingathering, England could write herself into the divine scenario of the end. There was Scriptural precedent for such a role in the figure of Cyrus the Persian who in the 6th century BCE enabled the Jews of Babylonia to return to their homeland and rebuild their temple. This Cyrus syndrome became dominant in Christian Restorationism in the early 19th century, when England, now a world power with a mighty navy, was in a position to do something practical about restoring the Jews. The Ottoman Empire was crumbling, and Britain was looking to extend her influence in the Levant and protect her lines of communication with India. The leading spokesman of the Restorationist lobby at the time was Anthony Ashley-Cooper, Lord Shaftesbury (1801–85) a prominent Evangelical, a member of the so-called Clapham Sect. Shaftesbury had impeccable political connections. He spent a lifetime energetically trying to mobilize Britain and other great European powers to sponsor a Jewish return to Palestine. He also tried to stir up leading Jewish businessmen, such as Sir Moses Montefiore, to back the plan, and to take charge of it from the Jewish side. Britain in the end did play a decisive role in the founding of the Jewish State: it issued the Balfour Declaration in 1917 and as the mandatory authority charged after the First World War by the League of Nations with bringing Palestine to independence, it did everything in its power in the twenties and early thirties to advance the Political Zionist cause. But for Britain the State of Israel would probably never have come into being. The Balfour Declaration was crucial. It can be seen as the crowning political achievement of three hundred years of Christian Restorationism in England.[14]

offers a readable survey of British Israelism.

14. See my essay, "Why did Lord Balfour back the Balfour Declaration?" *Jewish Historical Studies* 49 (2018) 188–214.

Dispensationalism

Restorationism, having taken root in England in the 17th century never lost its place in English religious discourse. It had its advocates in the 18th century, one of whom was William Whiston, best known to posterity for his translation of the works of Josephus. Another was the Irish Bishop Robert Clayton. Ireland played a major role in refining Restorationism. The key figure was John Nelson Darby (1880–82) one of the founders of the so-called Plymouth Brethren.[15] Scion of an Anglo-Irish family which had its seat at Leap Castle in King's County (County Offaly) Darby was educated at Trinity College Dublin. He was ordained a priest in the Church of Ireland and served for a time as a curate in a remote area of County Wicklow, before withdrawing from the Anglican communion to throw in his lot with the emerging Brethren movement in Dublin. Over the years Darby developed a form of Restorationism known as Dispensationalism. This was, as already noted, in agreement with the classic Restorationism espoused by Darby's contemporary Shaftesbury on the fundamental point that in the purposes of God the Jews would return at the *eschaton* to their ancient land and form again an independent state, but Darby's position differed in a number of important details. Darby was a premillennialist whereas the Restorationists were postmillennialists. His prophetic scenario was much more fully and systematically worked out. He integrated his eschatology into a complete schema of history which divided the history of the world, from the creation to the consummation, from eternity to eternity, into seven distinctive periods called dispensations. This schema had considerable hermeneutical power. It allowed Darby, for example, to define the relationship between the Church and Israel. The Church is God's heavenly people, Israel was and remains God's earthly people, with a future national destiny. Darby and his followers worked out in painstaking detail the scenario of the end of days. Classic Restorationists were always a bit vague and imprecise. Dispensationalists, though they bicker endlessly about minutiae, are at one in offering blow-by-blow accounts of the *eschaton*. They achieve this by piecing together all the end-time references in the Old and New Testaments into one great coherent narrative. Each discrete reference is treated like pieces of a jigsaw which have to be fitted together without remainder. Scripture already provides two grand narratives—Revelation and Daniel—but these don't by any means exhaust the eschatological traditions of the Bible. There are motifs in the Prophets, in the Gospels and in the letters of Paul which are not mentioned in either text. Daniel has to be meshed with Revelation and then all

---

15. Donald H. Akenson, *Discovering the End of Time: Irish Evangelicals in the Age of Daniel O'Connell* (Montreal and Kingston: McGill-Queen's University Press, 2016); Akenson, *Exporting the Rapture: John Nelson Darby and the Victorian Conquest of North-American Evangelicalism* (Oxford: Oxford University Press, 2018).

the other pieces fitted in in their proper place. The resultant scenarios are a *tour de force*, a major creation of the religious imagination.

The hermeneutical stance behind these scenarios should not be missed. It goes well beyond the biblical literalism that underpins classic Restorationism. It presupposes a very high doctrine of Scripture which stresses Scripture's unity and coherence: what Scripture says in one place has to mesh with what it says in another, even if the passages being meshed are in different biblical books and were composed hundreds of years apart. There are, in fact, possibilities within Dispensationalism for acknowledging the development of doctrine (after all each successive Dispensation goes beyond the preceding Dispensations in the disclosure of truth) but they are not exploited in this case. Each eschatological dictum of Scripture, wherever it is found, points forward timelessly and unerringly to events that will take place at the end of days. Our task is to join up the dots and disclose the full picture.

For Dispensationalism it is not just Scripture that is a source of knowledge. Experience and discernment have a major part to play as well. This is typical of the apocalyptic tradition as a whole—Jewish, Christian, and Muslim. Apocalyptic is much exercised by the "signs of the times." These are events prophesied in cryptic language which will herald the end. The signs are already found in Scripture, but they were massively extended in tradition. There is a whole literature of signs of the end. The problem is whether or not the events we are currently experiencing fulfil the signs and are evidence that the end is near. That requires subjective judgement and discernment. Many apocalyptic scenarios envisage the millennium as being introduced by catastrophes of various kinds—catastrophes known in Jewish tradition as "the birth-pangs of the Messiah," in Christian as "the Great Tribulation." There will be natural disasters, political tyranny and oppression, wars, economic chaos and hardship. Public and private morality will hit an all-time low. This plays into a certain conservative religious psychology. When things are perceived to be going frighteningly awry in the political, moral, economic and natural spheres, end-time watchers start wondering if these are signs that the *eschaton* is at hand. Just how subjective these judgements can be is easily proved from history. Time and again in the past events have been trumpeted as presaging the end, only for history to go merrily on.

One of the major signs of the end according to Christian Zionism was the return of the Jews to their ancient homeland. They predicted this would happen: it heralded the end. Then a return happened and a Jewish State was founded. The challenge was clear: is this the prophesied return? Dispensationalists decided it was. That decision was influenced by a number of factors. They held passionately that the end was imminent: no conditions remained to be fulfilled before the Second

Coming of Christ. They had also predicted that the Jews would return in unbelief. That contrasted with standard Restorationism which saw the return as accompanied by Jewish mass conversion and recognition of the claims of Christ. It accorded well, therefore, with the secular, godless character of Political Zionism. But it remained an act of discernment nonetheless, and deeply subjective.

Comparison with Jewish responses to Political Zionism and the State of Israel makes this abundantly clear. Faced with the same events and starting out from the same premise that the ingathering was part of the purposes of God, some Jews, as we saw, emphatically rejected the State. It was not the promised return. Rather it was a demonic political entity that was hindering the coming of the true Messianic Kingdom. Dispensationalism at this point recalls the position of Rav Kook. Before he emigrated to Palestine, he took the traditional line, criticizing Political Zionism for forcing the end, but when he settled in Palestine and met with the Zionist pioneers, he performed a remarkable *volte face*, and began to argue that unwittingly they were agents in bringing the redemption. The dramatic change can be seen as an act of discernment, based on experience. Kook was prepared to back his reading of the signs, his hunch that in what was happening in Palestine he could hear "the footsteps of the Messiah," against nearly two-thousand years of Jewish tradition, though, being an immensely erudite man, he tried to draw on obscure Jewish sources to justify his stance.

Christian Zionism cannot be separated from Jewish Zionism. The two dynamically interact in the world today, but they have been interacting for centuries. I have already alluded to the convergence of eschatologies in the 1650s that seems to have played a role the readmission of the Jews to England. Puritan scholars read the writings of Manasseh ben Israel, and he was aware of and influenced by Protestant Christian thought with regard to the end of time. The contribution of Christian Zionism to the emergence of modern Political Zionism is only now beginning to be recognized by some historians. If one looks at the three-volumed history of Zionism by David Vital, there is virtually nothing in it about Christian Zionism.[16] The beginnings of modern Zionism are frequently traced back to Zvi Hirsch Kalischer, Judah Alkalai, and the Lovers of Zion (*Hovevei Tziyyon*). This has become the standard Political Zionist *Heilsgeschichte*: it projects a comforting narrative of Jewish self-help, of self-emancipation. But it is lopsided and is actually a comparatively recent point of view. The first comprehensive history of Political Zionism, written by the early Political Zionist Nahum Sokolow and published in 1921 with a preface by Arthur Balfour, devotes hundreds of pages to Christian Zionism as a forerunner of Political

---

16. David Vital, *The Origins of Zionism* (Oxford: Clarendon Press, 1975); *Zionism: The Formative Years* (Oxford: Clarendon Press, 1982); *Zionism: The Crucial Phase* (Oxford: Clarendon Press, 1987).

Zionism.[17] The fact is that Christian Zionism predates Political Zionism by around 250 years. And it anticipated Political Zionism in two crucial ways. First, it insisted that the Jews are a *nation* and that they have a *political* future as a sovereign state, a state with a god-given destiny in the comity of nations. It maintained this view at a time in the 19th century when important sectors of Judaism, as we saw, were de-nationalizing, when there was a real possibility that Jews would abandon their national identity. Second, it had no qualms about taking practical political and even military steps to bring about the restoration of the Jewish state. It did not feel itself constrained, as traditional Jews did, by any Rabbinic embargo on forcing the end. Right from the start a practical, implementable programme was implicit in Restorationism, and Restorationists endlessly urged the British government to implement it.

Restorationism's offshoot Dispensationalism was initially non-activist. Darby would have been well aware of the activism implicit in Restorationism. He must have known the writings of Dean Graves, a luminary of Trinity College Dublin when he was a student. Graves was a leading Restorationist and outlined a plan whereby Britain could return the Jews to Palestine.[18] Darby may even have known of the detailed and highly practical proposals put forward by the Irish heiress, Marianne Nevill, as to how to implement this return, proposals that uncannily presage Herzl's *Der Judenstaat* published some sixty years later. Darby and Marianne Nevill were exact contemporaries and moved in the same social circles. Bizarrely Marianne Nevill's Restorationism landed her in court in a case instigated by her family, who were alarmed that she was about to blow her fortune on actually putting her plans into action.[19] The court declared her insane and deprived her of control of her fortune. It was a *cause célèbre* at the time, widely reported in the Irish and English press, and doubtless a topic of conversation round the dinner table of Darby's brother-in-law, Sergeant Pennefather, an eagle of the Irish bar. Darby must have known also about the politicking on behalf of the Jews by Lord Shaftesbury and his supporters. Against this background his non-activism looks like a very deliberate choice.

The reasons for it lie deep within his theology. His eschatology was a handmaid of his ecclesiology. He was an ecclesiastical revolutionary who was deeply disturbed by the worldliness of the Church, its established position, and the involvement with politics which that entailed. His Dispensationalist hermeneutic, as I hinted earlier, allowed him to define the Church as a heavenly entity, the heavenly Bride of Christ. As members of the Bride of Christ, Christians on earth should have nothing to do

17. Nahum Sokolow, *History of Zionism* (London: Longmans, Green & Co., 1919).

18. Richard Graves, "The Future Conversion and Restoration of the Jews," in his *Lectures on the Last Four Books of the Pentateuch* (2 vols, 2nd edition; London: Cadell and Davies, 1815) vol. 2, 449–77.

19. See my essay, "Christian Restorationism in Ireland in the Early Nineteenth Century: The Strange Case of Miss Marianne Nevill," *Jewish Historical Studies* 47 (2015) 31–47.

with politics: their business is to remain unspotted from the world and await Christ's coming to rapture them to heaven. It is the Jews who are God's earthly people: it is they who are destined to fulfil God's purposes *on earth*. As a result of this teaching the Brethren movement has remained deeply apolitical down to the present day. To get involved in politics is to confuse the two peoples of God. But when Dispensationalism took root in America it became decoupled from Darbyite ecclesiology. It was embraced by non-Brethren churches. It took a leaf out of the Restorationists book, politicized and it now underpins the strong activism of Christian Zionism in the States.[20]

Supersessionist Allegory

For fifteen hundred years the church lived with the prophecies of restoration as part of Holy Writ before anyone seriously thought of applying them literally to the Jewish people. How did it deal with their stubborn concreteness? The standard strategy was to apply them to the Church, the New Israel: what they predicted was the final triumph of Christ's Kingdom on earth. We find this idea all over early Christian literature, not least in the Byzantine apocalypses of the period of the apocalyptic revival in the early centuries of Islam. This apocalyptic revival affected all the major religions of the period (Judaism, Christianity, Zoroastrianism, and Islam) which developed a remarkably similar view as to what would happen at the end of time, a view so structurally congruent as to amount, as I have argued elsewhere, to a common eschatology.[21] For our present purposes it is the parallels between the Jewish and the Christian apocalyptic scenarios that are of interest. Both the Jewish and the Christian texts appeal, explicitly or implicitly, to the same biblical prophecies, but they see them as fulfilled *either* in Israel *or* the Church, or, to be more precise in the latter case, in the Christian Byzantine Empire in which Church and State were effectively fused into one. The roots of this idea lie in the Constantinian settlement, so eloquently championed by Eusebius. It was to have a long afterlife in Christendom and was to allow various subsequent Christian states to claim the biblical prophecies for themselves—the Holy Roman Empire, Czarist Russia, Britain, and other lesser political entities. The Jewish and Christian apocalyptic scenarios were mirror images of each other, but with opposed identifications of key players. So, in the Byzantine

---

20. Victoria Clark, *Allies for Armageddon: The Rise of Christian Zionism* (New Haven: Yale University Press, 2007) gives a readable if impressionistic account of Christian Zionism in the States down to about 2005.

21. See my essay, "The Apocalyptic Revival in Judaism (6th–9th Centuries CE) in its Historical Context," in *Eschatology in Antiquity*, edited by Hilary Marlow, Karla Pollmann, and Helen Van Noorden (London: Routledge, forthcoming).

apocalypses the last Christian Roman emperor would conquer the whole world and then hand over the kingdom to Christ. In the Jewish texts the last Roman Emperor, who is called Armillos (a pun on Romulus, the legendary founder of Rome) is the *Antichrist*, who will have to be defeated in battle by the Davidic Messiah.[22]

The broad scenarios may be very similar, but this should not blind us to the fact that they rest on very different hermeneutical foundations. The Jews could reasonably claim to be interpreting the biblical prophecies *literally*, in that they were the obvious physical heirs of ancient Israel (a claim that Christians did not dispute) and so they could appropriate the prophecies directly in all their concreteness. The Christians, however, had to resort to some sort of allegorizing or spiritualizing of the texts, since they were only the *spiritual* heirs of ancient Israel, and there were many concrete details in the prophecies which could not apply literally to themselves, details which they were obliged to ignore or explain away. Time and again they were forced to take the broad drift of the prophecy, to universalize it and ignore the detail. It was, of course, precisely this allegorizing that Brightman and the Restorationists, with their commitment to biblical literalism, objected to.

This allegorizing of the prophecies of restoration is part of a general allegorical reading which was a major strategy employed by the early Church to appropriate the Tanakh as Christian Scripture. This strategy is found already in the Epistle of Barnabas, composed probably in the 90s of the first century and thus contemporary with some of the later books of the canonic New Testament. Barnabas was influential and nearly made it into the New Testament canon. Barnabas relentlessly adopts the allegorical method, which he ironically almost certainly learned from Jewish exegetes of his time, not only to prophecy but to law. An instructive example for our present purposes is his treatment of the promises of the Land to the ancient Israelites as part of the covenant with God (Barn. 6:8–19). Barnabas argues that a literal land was never God's intention. Rather the land was a symbol, or parable of Christ. The promised patrimony was Christ. His exegesis is markedly forced, as was much early Christian allegorical interpretation, and he knows it. This is why he feels obliged to bolster his extraordinary claim by suggesting that only those who are spiritual, who have been endowed by God with knowledge, will understand this. The Jews, because of their carnal, unspiritual nature, or because they were misled by the devil, misinterpreted the promise, and took it in its literal sense.

A little bit of historical background will be of help here. As I have argued elsewhere, Barnabas's anti-Judaism has to be set in the conditions that prevailed in the

---

22. See Martha Himmelfarb, *Jewish Messiahs in a Christian Empire: A History of the Book of Zerubbabel* (Cambridge: Harvard University Press, 2017); Stephen J. Shoemaker, *The Apocalypse of Empire: Imperial Eschatology in Late Antiquity and Early Islam* (Philadelphia: University of Pennsylvania Press, 2018).

Jewish world in the aftermath of the destruction of the Temple in 70. Historians tend to assume that the Jews gave up the fight after their thumping defeat by the Romans, but there is reason to think that many did not. They regarded the defeat and the loss of the Temple as a temporary setback. They looked for dramatic divine intervention to restore their fortunes. There was a mini-revival of apocalyptic (represented by 2 Baruch, 4 Ezra, Sibylline 5 and the Apocalypse of Abraham) predicting a reversal of the defeat and eventual triumph. This restorationist fervour may have reached fever-pitch under the emperor Nerva (96–98) when he abolished the Jewish tax, an event he thought sufficiently important to merit striking his *calumnia sublata* series of coins. Was Nerva going to play the Cyrus role and restore the Jewish Temple? Barnabas, who probably wrote during the reign of Nerva, would have been aware of these Jewish hopes, and been alarmed by them. The loss of the Temple and the defeat of the Jews were already being seen by Christians as marking decisively and publicly the end of the old covenant. To restore the Temple was going in completely the wrong direction, it was going against the manifest purposes of God in history. God had never intended the promise of the Land to be implemented in a literal sense.[23]

There are intriguing similarities between Jewish aspirations for a return at the end of the first century and Jewish aspirations for a return in the middle of the 20th. In both cases the hope was hope against hope: it was hope expressed in the face of major catastrophe—the destruction of the Temple in the one case, the Shoah in the other. In both cases there were those who were prepared, against all the odds, to force the redemption. Political-military activism remained a force to be reckoned with in the Jewish communities after 70. It was crushed for a time in Palestine, but many "freedom-fighters" seemed to have escaped into the Diaspora where they kept alive the flame of resistance. Josephus makes it clear that in the 90s they were causing problems in the Alexandrian Jewish community. In 115–117, in the reign of Trajan, there were open Jewish revolts in Cyrenaica and Mesopotamia, which were brutally suppressed by Lucius Quietus. Resistance finally exploded into open war in Palestine itself in 132, under the leadership of Bar Kokhba. Bar Kokhba achieved the liberation of Jerusalem but freedom died after three short years at Beitar.[24] This was the last political self-determination that the Jewish people enjoyed till 1948. The bid for freedom in 1948 was more successful and has endured for 70 years. The problem which Barnabas faced vis-à-vis Jewish political aspirations was, then, not dissimilar from that faced by Christians today. Interestingly he saw the problem fundamentally

---

23. See further my essay, "The Image of the Jews and Judaism in the Apostolic Fathers," in *The Cambridge Companion to the Apostolic Fathers,* edited by Michael F. Bird and Scott D. Harrower (Cambridge: Cambridge University Press, forthcoming).

24. See further, William Horbury, *Jewish War under Trajan and Hadrian* (Cambridge: Cambridge University Press, 2014).

as a hermeneutical problem: the Jews cannot claim the land on the basis of divine promises in Scripture, because those promises were never meant to be fulfilled literally. They were fulfilled spiritually in Christ.

Non-literalist and Non-allegorical Responses to Zionism

The allegorical, spiritualizing solution to the problem of Jewish national hopes became standard in the later Church, throughout late antiquity and the middle ages, but it cuts little ice today—certainly not within Protestantism with its agreement on the primacy of the *sensus literalis* of Scripture. This does not mean that Christians who eschew the allegorical approach are thereby locked into some form of Restorationism. A range of Christian positions have been taken up vis-à-vis Political Zionism and Israel which rely neither on biblical literalism nor on allegorization.

A crucial question that has to be posed to any Christian response to Political Zionism is whether or not it envisages the Jews as still having a specific role to play in the purposes of God. Do they remain in any sense *exceptional* among the nations of the world, marked out still for a peculiar destiny. If, for example, one takes a strict supersessionist stance, which implies that the Jews no longer constitute a special case, then, if one wants to construct a response to Political Zionism and Israel, one will have to fall back on general political and moral theological principles. There is nothing specific in Scripture relevant to the case. One would have to apply the principles one would apply to *any* case of national self-determination. This is, of course, how secular political analysis proceeds, but to qualify as a Christian theological response it would have to be grounded in Christian political theology. If the Jews remain in some way exceptional (and many Christian thinkers find this idea hard to resist, given that Paul states it so clearly in Romans 9–11) then one has to decide wherein this exceptionalism lies and how it might affect the response to the State of Israel.

An analogous problem arises within Political Zionism itself. Some Zionists have argued that all Jews ask for is for Israel to be *ke-khol ha-goyyim*—"like all the other nations," neither more nor less, with her share of crooks, pimps, corrupt politicians and other undesirables: she should not be held to higher standards than other nations. But others have argued that she should *or la-goyyim*—"a light to the nations," a paradigm of the good society. This idealist position, though it has obvious biblical antecedents, is deeply entrenched in secular Zionism. Right from Herzl in *Der Judenstaat* onwards many secular Zionists saw the founding of the State of Israel as a chance to build a modern Utopia—a socialist Utopia to be sure, but an Utopia nonetheless. The Kibbutz was offered as the blueprint for that utopia. That socialist vision has rather faded, but there is still a strong competitive ethos within Israel: a desire to be better at things than anyone else, to be a pioneer, a model, a light to the nations. Nowadays the stress is perhaps on technological advance (which is where Herzl put it) but the moral dimension is not entirely absent.

And it is on the moral front that the most trenchant response to Political Zionism has come from the Christian side. Put very simply this approach sets the call of the biblical prophets and indeed the Torah itself for social justice over against the promises of restoration. The one cannot be divorced from the other. Restoration will fail if justice is not implemented. After all it was the lack of justice that led to exile in the past. This approach, which has been adopted in various forms by many of the mainline churches in the west, resonates not only in a religious context, but in a secular as well, because the principles of justice to which it appeals have become universal values of the democratic world. They are foundational to the Judaeo-Christian tradition. And this approach can be claimed as a *Christian* approach, because it was precisely these values of justice for the poor and oppressed that Jesus so powerfully advocated. It is this prophetic message that he endorsed as the heart of the old revelation.

The most authentic form of this response is that developed by Palestinian Christians such as Naim Ateek. I say authentic because it grows out of the Palestinian experience of Jewish restoration—the displacement and loss, the impoverishment and discrimination, the lack of self-determination. Palestinian Christians find themselves theologically in a difficult position; they acknowledge the Jewish Scriptures as Word of God, yet those very Scriptures can be quoted, by other Christians, against them to crush their aspirations. It is deeply important to them that they can root their criticism of Israel in the Old Testament. Ateek and others like him have drawn inspiration form Liberation Theology, but they have tailored it in the light of their own Palestinian experience. The stress in Palestinian Liberation Theology is overwhelmingly on justice—justice as envisaged by the ancient Hebrew Prophets. It dons a prophetic mantle and is less concerned with the nuts and bolts of political process.[25]

This response to Political Zionism from the standpoint of justice resonates within the Jewish community as well. There are secular voices and organizations within the Jewish world and within Israel itself which offer a sustained critique of

---

25. See Naim Ateek, *Justice and Only Justice: A Palestinian Theology of Liberation* (Maryknoll: Orbis Books, 1989); Ateek, *A Palestinian Theology of Liberation: The Bible, Justice, and the Palestine-Israel Conflict* (Maryknoll: Orbis, 2017). Further: Yohanna Katanacho, *The Land of Christ* (Bethlehem: Bethlehem Bible College, 2012); S. Munayer and L. Loden (eds) *The Land Cries Out: Theology of the Land in the Israeli-Palestine Context* (Eugene: Wipf & Stock, 2012); Mitri Raheb, ed., *The Biblical Text in the Context of Occupation: Towards a New Hermeneutics of Liberation* (Bethlehem: Diyar, 2012); Mitri Raheb, *Faith in the Face of Empire* (Bethlehem: Diyar, 2014); Munther Isaac, *From Land to Lands, From Eden to the Renewed Earth* (Carlisle: Langham Monographs, 2015).

Israeli policy towards the Palestinians on the basis of justice, but it is the position adopted by some Reformed Jewish thinkers which I find theologically most interesting. I noted above how in the 1930s the Reform movement swung behind Zionism and supported its aims, and many Reform Jews today are supporters of Israel. This was in stark contrast, as we saw, to their rejection in the 19th century of the idea that the Jewish people had a national future in the Land. It was not, strictly speaking, a *volte-face*, because it can be justified on good Reform hermeneutical principles. Reform Judaism embraces a version of the idea of the development of doctrine. Jewish tradition has and always will develop and change as circumstances change. Reform Jews bought into the 19th century liberal idea of progress and so saw change as by and large positive. The two events that forced a re-evaluation of their position were the rise of the Nazis and the Shoah (which challenged the liberal idea of progress) and the emergence of Political Zionism (which challenged their denationalization of Judaism). Many concluded that while they could not acknowledge it as the Messianic State, a refounded Israel could nevertheless serve the purposes of God in history in two ways. First, it could provide a safe haven for the persecuted Jews of Europe. Second, it offered a platform for Jewish renewal which could further Israel's destiny to mediate the idea of the One God to humanity at large. They are very much on the "light to the nations" side of Zionism. (Interestingly, this position is not dissimilar from that adopted by some Christian Restorationists, who regarded the restored Israel, now, of course, converted to Christ, as the eschatological instrument for the inauguration of the universal Kingdom of God.) The grounds for Reform support for Israel were strictly pragmatic, and involved, yet again, an element of discernment; they did not involve attributing messianic characteristics to the Jewish State. Reform Judaism classically saw the ethical teaching of the great Hebrew Prophets as the core of Tanakh and it is not surprising, therefore, that some of the most trenchant criticism of Israeli policy from within the Jewish world, has been from Reform thinkers.

Ateek's hermeneutical position is most clearly articulated in his most recent book, *A Palestinian Theology of Liberation* (2017). As already noted, the social teachings of Jesus, particularly his call for justice for the oppressed, his social inclusiveness and his love for all humanity, are for Ateek the hermeneutical key to the Scripture. They allow him to affirm the call for justice in the Old Testament. That call is found already in the Torah, but its message was sharpened by the Prophets, and its implications for the covenant and the possession of the Land spelled out. Making the *teachings* of Jesus the *regula fidei* is a well-established principle of liberal Christian biblical hermeneutics, but one has still to decide what those teachings are. Ateek's stress on social justice chimes with a well-known liberal reading of the Gospels. Whether or not it is the essence of Jesus' message (which some would dispute: we should not, surely, forget Christ's *work* as well as his *words*) there is clearly more than enough of it to establish that Jesus cared passionately for the poor and oppressed. Ateek stands in the broad liberal, modernist tradition of biblical interpretation, which sees revelation as progressive, culminating in the revelation in Christ. It broadly accepts but does not rely on the results of modern historical-critical research. What this means in practice is that one cannot take any statement from anywhere in Scripture and assume that it is valid for all time—something which literalists tend to do: the prooftext is their main interpretative tool. Scripture is not simply a quarry for timeless theological propositions. Each statement has to be seen within its context in God's on-going self-disclosure. Scripture contains contradictions and tensions which can only be resolved and transcended from the standpoint of the revelation in Christ. It has to be approached holistically and organically, not atomistically.

But experience also plays a central role in Ateek's position, as it does throughout Palestine Liberation Theology. Much effort is expended in collecting and recording the everyday experiences of Palestinian Christians under Israeli occupation. These testimonies are more than a propaganda device. They are central to the hermeneutics. They are the raw data of the liberation theology. It is in the gap between the lived experience and the demands of justice that the case is made.

Political Zionism and the Politicization of Biblical Studies

I have already ranged far and wide in this brief essay, and am acutely aware of how cursorily I have dealt with vast and complex questions, but if there is one major point that I am trying to make, then it is this: for Jews and Christians behind the question of Israel, behind the Israel-Palestine question, lies a debate over the interpretation of Scripture. That hermeneutical issue applies not only to the religious positions on both sides of the Judaism/Christianity divide but to the most liberal and secular as well. Differences in hermeneutics have generated a broadly similar range of responses within both traditions. The centrality of hermeneutics has also led to the politicization of Biblical Studies. Political Zionism has to be seen as an external ideology like Feminism and Postcolonialism that is having an impact on the academic study of the Bible. Its academic ramifications are well understood on the Jewish side. They are much less understood on the Christian side. This is a huge topic in its own right which I cannot go into here. Two examples, out of many, will have to suffice to illustrate what I mean by the politicization of Biblical Studies in the wake of the rise of Political Zionism. They are small illustrations of how even in the academy Political Zionism has had a significant impact.

The Gospel and the Land

The first example is the debate over the territorial dimension of Judaism. This was sparked off in Biblical Studies by W. D. Davies, *The Gospel and the Land* (1974) and his later, shorter study, *The Territorial Dimension of Judaism* (1982).[26] Davies set out to discover how the New Testament writers dealt with the land-centredness of Judaism. That Judaism is land-centred seems self-evident because the idea is so clearly expressed in the Sinai covenant in which the greatest reward that Israel is offered is to dwell in her own land in peace, prosperity and security, each man under his vine and under his fig tree. Since land-centredness is so embedded in the Torah we would expect that by the first century CE it would have been universally embraced by Jews as an axiom of their faith. But this being the case, what has happened to this land-centredness in the New Testament? Why is the idea not more directly addressed? This was the problem that generated Davies' research.

Davies himself makes clear that he was made aware of the question of Judaism and the Land by the claims of Political Zionism.[27] It was his contacts with Jewish scholars and with Israel that led him to ask what Christianity had done with the Land. That in itself is no bad thing. Inevitably we all read Scripture in the light of the situations in which historically we find ourselves. As I have argued elsewhere, Political Zionism is a *resource* for Christian students of the Bible.[28] I myself cherish my links with Israel, and my understanding of the New Testament has been influenced by my engagement with Jewish colleagues there. The question as to what early Christianity did with the land-centredness of Judaism is a real and valid question. But what Davies, fine scholar though he was, didn't stress enough, in the excitement of his discovery of the centrality of the land, was that the idea was *not* as universal in Judaism as Political Zionism asserted; it was not always normative for all Jews at all times. Much of the far-flung Diaspora in the first century manifested a strong local patriotism. It may, somewhat romantically, have acknowledged Jerusalem as the Mother City (the metropolis) to which once in a lifetime one might go on pilgrimage, but the vast majority of Diaspora Jews seemed to have had no intention of returning to the Land. The Land *as territory* was simply not that central to their Judaism. The point that has to be borne in mind is that even in sources that speak

---

26. W.D. Davies, *The Gospel and the Land: Early Christianity and Jewish Territorial Doctrine* (Berkeley: University of California Press, 1974); Davies, *The Territorial Dimension of Judaism* (Berkeley: University of California Press, 1982). The latter develops and to some extent corrects the former.

27. See especially the Preface to *Territorial Dimension*, p. xiii.

28. See my essay, "Jewish Nationalism from Judah the Maccabee to Judah the Prince and the Problem of 'Continuing Exile,'" in *Exile: A Conversation with N.T. Wright*, edited by James M. Scott (Downers Grove: InterVarsity, 2017) 137–62.

of the Land, land may not be thought of as territory where political sovereignty is exercised. Land may function as a symbol for a range of non-political aspirations.

The complexity of the evidence can be illustrated from Rabbinic sources which contain some of the strongest statements about the centrality of the Land in early Judaism. These need to be read carefully in context. The statements tend to be found in Amoraic sources emanating from Palestine, and this raises the possibility, as Isaiah Gafni suggested, that they represent an attempt by the Palestinian Rabbinate to assert its supremacy against the emerging influence and authority of the Babylonian Yeshivot.[29] The Palestinian Rabbis of the Tannaitic period are not so exercised by the centrality of the Land: they only begin to insist on its primacy when faced with the challenge to their leadership posed by the Babylonian schools. This new stress on the importance of the Land was, then, politically motivated, served a political end, and was internally contested.

In modern Zionist thought one of the arguments used to defend the centrality of the Land is that only in the Land, in independence, can Jews express their full potential as Jews. In the Exile—the *Galut*, that is to say the condition of being outside the Land—they cannot lead a full Jewish life. They live in conditions of constant subservience and deference to hostile non-Jewish cultures, and that fosters a "*galut*-mentality." Only when they return to the Land and negate the exile with all its baleful effects, can they rid themselves of this mindset. Political Zionism set out to create in the Land a new type of Jew, who has cast off the exilic psychology, and stands strong, confident, unafraid. The concept of "*galut*-mentality" owes something to Marxist theories of "false consciousness," but it can also be seen as a secularized restatement of the traditional Religious Zionist claim that one can only live fully as a Jew in the Land because only there can one fulfil the "commandments pertaining to the Land," and so fulfil the whole Torah. It may also owe something to the traditional Christian anti-Judaic trope (mentioned earlier) that evidence for God's rejection of the Jewish people can be seen in their wandering, oppressed, exilic condition. Arguably Jews internalized this charge: exile is in principle bad and has to be negated. The condition in itself is irredeemable: it can only be redeemed through negation and a return to the Land. Exile—*Galut*—to denote the condition of living outside the Land is, of course, already a highly loaded and tendentious term. Diaspora or the Hebrew *Tefutzah* is much more neutral. But the simple fact is that many Jews have lived and continue to live rich and fulfilling lives outside the land, and *outside the Land* have created a stunning Jewish culture, which includes the Babylonian Talmud, the *Mishneh Torah*, and the *Shulhan Arukh*—a culture, as we saw, which has to form the basis

---

29. Isaiah M. Gafni, *Land, Center and Diaspora: Jewish Constructs in Late Antiquity* (Sheffield: Sheffield Academic Press, 1997).

of Jewish culture *within the Land*. Reform Jewish thinkers in the 19th century argued that the dispersion was actually part of the purposes of God, to enable the Jews to fulfil their destiny to be a blessing to the nations. Davies did some excellent work in highlighting the question of the Gospel and the Land, and his detailed discussions of the New Testament references to the Land remain valuable, but his analysis has to be recalibrated to give proper weight to the fact that the Land as territory has not always been central to Judaism in the way that Political Zionism claims that it has.

Minimalism v. Maximalism

It takes a well-trained ear to hear the political undertones in the debate about the Gospel and the Land, but one would have to be very deaf to miss them in my second example, the debate over biblical history. Fundamental to Political Zionism is a particular understanding of the history of the Jews, central to which is the claim that the Jewish people once occupied the Land and exercised sovereignty there but were forcibly expelled from it. They have returned to claim their historical patrimony. "Eretz-Israel" affirms the Declaration of Independence, "was the birthplace of the Jewish people. Here their spiritual, religious and political identity was shaped. Here they first attained to statehood, created cultural values of national and universal significance and gave to the world the eternal Book of Books. After being forcibly exiled from their land, the people kept faith with it throughout their Dispersion and never ceased to pray and hope for their return to it and for the restoration in it of their political freedom." The Zionists were, then, not invaders, not colonizers: they are a people returning to a land that was once theirs. This means that the biblical period is absolutely central to Political Zionist historiography. The biblical account is taken more or less at face value. More secular Zionist historians have, to be sure, rejected the miraculous elements in the biblical stories, but they have treated these by and large as legendary accretions which can be easily stripped away leaving a solid core of historical fact. This biblical history was fully articulated for the first time in Heinrich Graetz's monumental eleven volume *Geschichte der Juden* (1853–1870). Graetz was not a Political Zionist in any precise meaning of that term: he lived at the dawn of modern Political Zionism, but his history, which was widely disseminated in several languages, was highly congenial to Political Zionism. It provided important historical backing for its claims, and its narrative was refined by later Zionist historians.[30]

---

30. Graetz's multivolume *Volkstümliche Geschichte der Juden* was published between 1853 and 1870. The English version (*History of the Jews from the Earliest Times to the Present Day*, first published in 1891) was very popular and often given as a Bar Mitzvah present. On Graetz, see further, Marcus Pyka, *Jüdische Identität bei Heinrich Graetz* (Göttingen: Vandenhoeck & Ruprecht, 2009).

Graetz was important for Zionism because he stressed the *continuity* of Jewish history: he was telling the story of the march through historical time of a single entity—the Jewish people, from their origins in the mists of antiquity to the present day. The Jews *were* a people, a nation, in fact, within accepted 19th century definitions of that term. Their peoplehood, forged in the biblical period, had remained inviolate down to the present day. Historians today take this idea so much for granted (testimony, in part, to the persuasive power of Graetz and the Zionist historians) that it takes an effort to realise that it is in many ways counterintuitive. Jews were scattered all over the world. What linked these dispersed and diverse Jewish communities was not so obviously the attributes of peoplehood as religion. Graetz's most important Jewish predecessor, Isaak Markus Jost, was by no means so clear on the unity of the Jewish people: his history was more a history of scattered, disparate communities that identified themselves as Jewish.[31]

As we have already noted, however, the idea had long been implicit in Christian views of Jewish history, particularly among Restorationists, who emphatically saw the Jews as a unitary people, who would one day be restored to nationhood. Restorationists were as keen as many Orthodox Rabbis that Jews should retain their distinctive national characteristics, and not merge into the other nations of the world, because otherwise they could not fulfil their national destiny. The continuity between the Jews of their own day and the Jews of the Bible was axiomatic in Christian views of Judaism. There were various reasons for this but one of them may have been the influence of Josephus. Josephus in his *Antiquities* of the Jews was the first historian to take for granted that there was linear, genealogical continuity between the Patriarchs and the Jews of his own day. He forged a vital narrative link between what today we would call *biblical* and what we would call *postbiblical* history. It would be hard to overestimate the importance of Josephus for Christian understanding of the history of the Jews. His narrative was carried forward very explicitly by Christian scholars who continued the story of his *Antiquities* down to modern times.[32]

Political Zionism, then, is heavily invested in a view of Jewish history which plays up the continuities between the present and the biblical past and plays down the intervening period of *Galut*. Crucial to biblical history for Political Zionism are the Kingdoms of David and Solomon, and the period of the Maccabees, because it

31. Isaak Markus Jost, *Allgemeine Geschichte des Israelitischen Volkes* (2 vols; Berlin, 1832). See further, Salo W. Baron, *History and the Jewish Historians* (Philadelphia: Jewish Publication Society of America, 1964); Michael Brenner, *Prophets of the Past: Interpreters of Jewish History* (Princeton: Princeton University Press, 2010).

32. The influence of Josephus on Christians' understanding of the Jews and Judaism in England can hardly be overestimated. A copy of William Whiston's translation of his works, first published in 1737, was in the library of most educated Christians in Victorian England, and some later editions brought Josephus's history down to modern times.

was in these eras that Jewish control over the Promised Land and Jewish sovereignty were realized to the fullest extent. Of these, the Davidic Kingdom is the most important because it was the first realization of national self-determination. It offers a kind of ideal expression of statehood. The attitude in Jewish tradition towards the Maccabees is more ambivalent,[33] though they have undergone a massive rehabilitation under Political Zionism. A heroic history of ancient Israel has been constructed which is widely taught in Jewish schools and seen as integral to Israeli Jewish identity.

Archaeology has proved a compliant handmaid to historiography. Graetz was already aware of some of the findings of 19th century exploration of the Holy Land and how they could illuminate the Bible, but the importance of archaeology in underpinning Zionist claims to the Land has grown exponentially. The State of Israel has invested heavily in archaeology and the investment has paid off handsomely: the finds have been spectacular. Many are beautifully displayed in the Israel Museum, which is as iconic a national monument in Israel as the Knesset or Yad Vashem. Archaeology serves many purposes, but politically speaking its most important role has been to uncover material evidence for the presence in antiquity of the Jewish people in the Land. It is important to note yet again the interweaving of Christian and Political Zionist interests: Christians got there first. It was Christian explorers who created the archaeology of the Holy Land long before the rise of modern Political Zionism, and that exploration fired the imaginations of Victorian Restorationists and was seen by them as inextricably bound up with their aims. The Palestine Association was founded in London in 1804 to promote exploration of the Holy Land. It was followed by the Palestine Exploration Fund in 1865, which still survives, and which has sponsored survey work and digs which have helped transform our knowledge of the Holy Land. Note the following statement made by Lord Shaftesbury to the Annual General Meeting of the Fund in 1875: "Let us not delay to instruct our friend the Hon. Secretary, Mr Grove, to send out the best agents he has in his power to search the length and breadth of Palestine, to survey the land, and if possible to go over every corner of it, drain it, measure it, and, if you will, prepare it for return to its ancient possessors, for I must believe that the time cannot be far off before that great event will come to pass. We have there a land teeming with fertility and rich in history, but almost without an inhabitant—a country without a people, and look! scattered over the world, a people without a country. I recollect speaking to Lord Aberdeen, when he was Prime Minister, on the subject of the Holy Land; and he said to me, 'If the Holy Land should pass out of the hands of the Turks into whose hands

---

33. For some reflections on this topic see my essay, "From Poetry to Historiography: The Image of the Hasmoneans in Targum Canticles and the Question of the Targum's Provenance and Date," *JSP* 19 (1999) 103–28.

should it fall?' Why, the reply was ready, 'Not into the hands of other powers, but let it return to the hands of the Israelites.'"

However, voices have been raised challenging this well-told and beguiling narrative of the glorious and heroic biblical past of the Jewish people. Some have been raised within Israel itself, but wider publicity has been achieved by a group of historians associated mainly with the Universities of Copenhagen and Sheffield who are sometimes lumped together under the title of Biblical Minimalism.[34] Minimalism takes a variety of forms, but the common element is that it calls into question whether there is *any* historical reality behind the biblical account of the Davidic monarchy. It argues that the biblical account is a myth constructed for ideological and political purposes centuries after the events which it is supposed to describe. If David even existed, then he would have been at most a petty tribal chieftain who would have controlled a small territory from his obscure stronghold—Jerusalem—tucked away in the hills of Judea. And the unkindest cut of all is that Minimalists have argued that archaeology supports their case: there is no solid archaeological evidence for the existence of a Kingdom of David or Solomon as envisaged in the Bible. In fact, quite the contrary. The Davidic-Solomonic Empire is conspicuous by its absence in the archaeological record.

But does any of this matter? Isn't it enough that Israelite ancestors of the present-day Jews lived in the Land? Well, to judge by the reactions it matters a lot. If the footprint of the ancient Israelites on the Land even in the so-called monarchic period was much smaller than the Bible suggests, then this immediately foregrounds the question of who else was there. Minimalists accuse Maximalists in their pursuit of the chimera of "Ancient Israel" of systematically and tendentiously erasing the presence and history of the non-Israelite peoples of the Land, in order to bolster Jewish claims. To judge by the responses to Minimalism it has struck a nerve. Minimalists themselves are well aware that their work has the potential to subvert the Political Zionist narrative, and at times overtly politicize it by setting it within the context of the Israel-Palestine conflict. They have been ferociously attacked both by conservative Christians and by Political Zionists who agree with each other at least in accepting the biblical account as basically sound. Some have gone so far as to accuse the Minimalists of antisemitism. There is nothing new here. The Political Zionist narrative had already been challenged by the rise of historical biblical criticism in the 19th century, with its deconstruction of the biblical sources, their late dating,

---

34. See e.g. Philip R. Davies, *In Search of Ancient Israel* (London: Continuum, 2006); Keith Whitelam, *The Invention of Ancient Israel: The Silencing of Palestinian History* (London: Routledge, 2001); Niels Peter Lemche, *The Israelites in History and Tradition* (London: SPCK, 1998); Thomas L. Thompson, *The Mythic Past: Biblical Archaeology and the Myth of Israel* (London: Jonathan Cape, 1999).

and its profound scepticism about the historicity of the biblical account. Graetz fiercely attacked Wellhausen and saw his documentary theories as tantamount to antisemitism.

Now it is not my intention here to take sides on either of these issues—the centrality or otherwise of the Land to Judaism, and the historicity of the Davidic kingdom. I cite them in the present context for one purpose and one purpose only and that is to illustrate the impact that Political Zionism has had on academic Biblical Studies. Make no mistake, both issues fall within the competence of academia. They are about evidence and argument, and they should benefit from cool, objective academic analysis. They are debated in academic books and articles, and at academic conferences. But they have ramifications beyond academia, and academia cannot ignore this fact. They have become politically sensitive, and the reason this has happened is clear: it is due to the transformative impact of Political Zionism and the founding of the State of Israel on Biblical Studies. Christians who want to engage seriously with Judaism—and I hope we all do—need to study closely and critically Political Zionism, one of the most complex and powerful ideologies of our times.

My paper, extensive and wide-ranging though it is, still leaves much unsaid. In it I offer no neat solutions. I have simply attempted to analyse and clarify a range of issues, and hopefully indicated the parameters for a measured and informed debate on the important and emotive questions posed to the Church by Political Zionism and the State of Israel.

A RESPONSE TO PHILLIP ALEXANDER: THE CHURCH AND THE HERMENEUTICAL CHALLENGE OF ZIONISM

William Andrews

Introduction

I am grateful for the the privilege and opportunity to participate in this Symposium. I also thank Prof. Alexander for an excellent and challenging paper. He helpfully condenses and organizes a wealth of historical information in a way that will serve as a useful primer for those both in the church and the academy who approach the issues for the first time. For those already familiar with the subject matter, I expect that his methodological approach will also provide a fresh lens as they continue their reflection and it is there—in Prof. Alexander's fourth and fifth theses—that I focus most of my response.

Near the end of his paper, Prof. Alexander offers a summary statement:

> if there is one major point that I am trying to make, then it is this: for Jews and Christians behind the questions of Israel, behind the Israel-Palestine question, lies a debate over the interpretation of Scripture.

That is, the challenge of Zionism to the church is a hermeneutical challenge. Furthermore, in the theological responses to Zionism—from within Christian and Jewish communities—experience is a determinative factor. This resonates with me as a Methodist, working within that tradition that has long recognized the role of experience in the interpretation of Scripture and theological reflection. Therefore, I begin a with a slight digression into my own experience.

When I received Professor Chester's invitation three weeks ago to participate in the symposium I hesitated. I hesitated not only because of the limited time but also because of feelings of inadequacy to address the topic. I also recalled earlier occasions when the questions of Israel and the Holy Land confronted me directly and I felt the same inadequacy. Once as a young, naïve, first-time adjunct instruction in a public university, I worried I might have to ask a Jewish student to leave for a profanity-laden outburst about Palestinians during my lecture on "sacred space" for a "Religious Studies 101" course. Afterwards, I reached out to a senior faculty member—a rabbi—who offered a thoughtful response with suggestions for reading on the issue. However, he opened his response by sharing the story of a family member, murdered by a Palestinian sniper while shopping in Tel Aviv. More recently, most of my teaching takes place inside a maximum-security prison where Dispensationalist theology and a literalist approach to Scripture are common. Questions about Israel's role in God's plan are frequent and my answers are often unsatisfactory to these prisoners. Likewise, the Holy Land is "contested territory" both literally and in public spaces such as this. Fear of misspeaking and finding oneself labeled an anti-Semite is real. These experiences confirm Prof. Alexander's observation about the church's need and mine for serious theological engagement with Political Zionism. Just as Christians have responded theologically to the Shoah, so work remains in considering the significance of the State of Israel.

Methodological Considerations

How, then, should one begin a Christian reflection on Political Zionism? Prof. Alexander's paper is quite helpful here. His approach to the centuries-long engagement of religious communities with Political Zionism organizes that long history and offers a framework to proceed in our own discernment. As he explains, both Jewish and Christian interactions with Zionism have taken the forms of three general responses: rejection, pragmatic accommodation, and acceptance. That the typology of Jewish responses maps neatly onto Christian responses should prove helpful in future Jewish-Christian engagement with the issue. What is essential for our purposes here is the importance of hermeneutics and we might understand this by considering three questions. What is the nature of biblical statements about the Land? How should we read them? And, finally, what is the role of experience in this discernment? What follows is a survey of some of Prof. Alexander's arguments in a manner that highlights these questions.

Jewish Responses

As an ideology, Political Zionism has challenged religious communities—both Jewish and Christian—producing a range of responses from within their own theological systems. Although the history of Christian Zionism predates Political Zionism of the 19th century, Prof. Alexander begins by highlighting how Zionism has shaped Judaism in ways that are nothing less than revolutionary. In fewer than fifty years, Reform Judaism moves from an explicit lack of concern with a Jewish homeland—seeing the role of the Jewish people as a "light to the nations" instead of as a nation itself—to affirmation of the state for which Political Zionists were laying the groundwork. This turn of face does not reject the earlier position but considers growing persecution and concern about the rise of the Nazis while the establishment of a Jewish homeland can be fitted into Reform thought and mission.

Thus, experience is a decisive factor in a major shift for Reform thought while in Orthodox thought experience cuts both ways. Orthodox Judaism is "split down the middle by Political Zionism." On one side, it is squarely rejected due to inconsistency between the biblical descriptions of the messianic state and observed reality, as well as the charge that Zionists are "forcing the hand of God" through their efforts. Scripture and tradition are held up to experience. Still other Orthodox leaders opt for accommodation and acceptance largely on the basis of their experience on the ground of the settlements and the impressive accomplishments of settlers. Rather than a forcing of God's hand, God is working through Zionist efforts and providing an opportunity to inspire deeper devotion to Torah. Again, a shift comes about as a function of experience and pragmatic concerns.

Christian Zionism

Christian responses to Zionism (or their own expressions of Zionism) are long lived and diverse; yet, they map neatly onto the same typology of rejection-accommodation-acceptance. Restorationists in 17th century England read the biblical prophesies of Jewish return to the Land literally and see their own role as facilitating that return through political or even military means. The later Dispensationalist offshoot of British Restorationism begins from a similar starting-point of holding a literal return to the Land as part of God's plan. However, Dispensationalism add a new, imaginative hermeneutical twist. Darby and others who come after him make the purely subjective move of imposing an external framework—like a jigsaw puzzle—into which eschatological statements and motifs across the canon should be fitted together without regard for historical or literary context. The result is an elaborate picture against which the events of history are interpreted. Experience is, once again, key but here its use is not pragmatic but rather a matter of historical discernment. Scripture must correspond to the "signs of the times." Of course, each time the literalist approach and predictions fail, the lines must be redrawn and the picture revised. Like Orthodox Jewish traditions that accept the aims of Jewish statehood, Christian

Zionism—especially of the contemporary American variety—has no qualms about "forcing God's hand."

Regardless of where one stands on the merits or points of concern in these Christian responses, they are significant shifts from the supersessionist, allegorical narrative that endured for the first 1,500 years of Christian history. Even that long-lived interpretation places historical experience at the center of its interpretive choices. The Jewish repatriation of the Land is a non-issue in the early church since—according to the supersessionist allegory—the destruction of the Temple is a concrete sign that the Jews have been rejected by God and the Church has replaced them as the spiritual heirs of God's promises, which are fulfilled spiritually in Christ.

Mainline Protestant Responses

Although the allegorical spiritualizing solution that held up for centuries no longer finds much support today, there are options beyond the literalism of Restorationism. Prof. Alexander suggests that the trajectory of these responses depends on whether one recognizes a special, ongoing role for the Jewish people in God's unfolding plan. If not, as a supersessionist would maintain, then the State of Israel is a purely political reality and should be understood in secular, political terms. If God still holds a special place in God's heart for the Jews—and this is hard to deny in light of Romans 9–11—then we must discern the nature of this chosenness, how it relates to the State of Israel, and how this affects one's response. Once again, these are questions of the nature of the biblical text and how one approaches it. Once again, experience is determinative.

Typical of Mainline Protestant approaches to these questions is the assumption of modern, historical-critical scholarship that highlights the multivocal character of the canon and the multiplicity of contexts—both historical and literary—in which texts must be read. The resulting response is one that "sets the call of the biblical prophets and indeed the Torah itself for social justice over against the promises of restoration." The promises cannot be divorced from the requirements of justice. Furthermore, justice and concern for the oppressed are aspects of the life, teaching, and work of Jesus emphasized by mainline churches in the West.

Prof. Alexander holds up the work of Naim Ateek as an "authentic" example that "grows out of the Palestinian experience of Jewish restoration." Ateek's emphasis on justice is critical to maintaining the authority and unity of Scripture. It allows him to hold onto the Hebrew Scriptures that other Christians are all too ready to quote to justify the displacement and brutalization of his people. Drawing on the resources of Liberation Theologies, Ateek places experience at the center of his hermeneutics.

Palestinian testimonies display the distance between lived experience—what is—and the biblical demands of justice—what ought to be.

Summary and Questions for Discussion

From this hurried and necessarily broad survey, we see that Jewish and Christian responses to Political Zionism follow similar patterns. What is more, they demonstrate that Political Zionism and the State of Israel pose a problem for the Church that is best understood as hermeneutical in nature and experience is a decisive factor in each case. How then are we to respond—especially we who have no direct experience of the Land or the conflict located there? It is tempting to dismiss the issues as merely political, not theological, and too far from home. However, the role of experience—and especially Ateek's use of experience—exposes to us that the problem is not only hermeneutical but also ethical.

The late American jurist Robert Cover averred that "legal interpretation takes place in a field of pain and death."[1] That is, when judges interpret the text of law and render a decision, they "occasion the imposition of violence . . . somebody loses his freedom, his property, his children, even his life."[2] For this and other reasons, Cover insists that legal interpretation is not a mere subfield of the humanities alongside, say, literary criticism.[3] I submit that experience dictates a similar truth concerning biblical interpretation. When I teach introductory courses, I hope to impart to students that our biblical interpretations have real-world consequences. In the present case, interpretations of biblical texts concerning God's promise and future restoration of the Land are carried out "in a field of pain and death." The Land is a site of bloody conflict, with pain and death on all sides. Is such violence carried out with our blessing? In the name of God, no less?

As we proceed in our reflection, we ought to ask the basic hermeneutical questions raised in Prof. Alexander's paper: What is the nature of biblical statements about the Land? How should we read them? What is the role of experience in our reflection? I would add to these a question that touches the ethical dimension of biblical interpretation: if we somehow bring into focus the full range of experience—to include all impacted by the restoration of the Land, Israelis and Palestinians—how might the effects, the fruits, of various interpretations help us judge between them?

---

1. Robert Cover, "Violence and the Word," in Minow, Martha, Michael Ryan, and Austin Sarat (eds.) *Narrative, Violence, and the Law: The Essays of Robert Cover* (Ann Arbor: University of Michigan Press, 1995) 203.

2. Cover, "Violence and the Word," 203

3. Robert Cover, "The Bonds of Constitutional Interpretation: On the Word, the Deed, and the Role," *Georgia Law Review* 20:4 (Summer 1986) 815–17.

In conclusion, I propose two suggestions for such a reflection.[4] First, as Christians, let us recall the measure established by Christ: "love of God and neighbor" (Matt 22:37–40; Mark 12:29–31; Luke 10:27; Gal 5:14). Can any interpretation that promotes, justifies, or excuses violence ever meet that standard? Second, as interpretive conflicts arise, let us always return to the biblical text in which we encounter the Word of God. While experience is certainly determinative in the interpretive process, the text of Scripture is the constant—the control—in our journey together. The Bible in its final form comes to us from particular contexts, in particular forms and language that set limits on the potential meaning of texts.[5] Against these we must always check our readings.

---

4. I wish to thank Dr. Joel Willitts, whose comments and questions brought out the need to articulate these concluding thoughts, however briefly.

5. I am informed here by the work of Dr. Brian K. Blount, especially Brian Blount, *Cultural Interpretation: Reorienting New Testament Criticism* (Minneapolis: Fortress, 1995).

ANOTHER LOOK AT "EARLY" IDEOLOGIES OF THE LAND IN THE HEBREW BIBLE IN LIGHT OF RECENT STUDY

K. Lawson Younger, Jr.

Introduction

With a topic like "The Bible and the Land," where does one start? One might think immediately of the present-day environment and questions about what the Bible says. Current uses of the Bible, especially the Hebrew Bible, in modern political discussions could be listed and critiqued. Yet, what is the basis for the critiques? It seems ultimately an understanding of the various biblical texts that address the issue of the "Land" must be where one starts. However, this raises its own set of problems and issues since there are many different passages that must be addressed, each with their own array of interpretive challenges. These passages are, in one important sense, textual artifacts from very different times and cultures (the Hebrew Bible was not written in a monolithic culture); and therefore, they evince the different ideologies of their writers.

This essay will investigate some of the different "early" ideologies of the land. First, it will examine the fundamental issue of what exactly was "the land of Canaan," since it is the basis for the different constructions of ideology of the land as encountered in the rest of the Hebrew Bible. Second, utilizing this examination as a foundation, this essay will explore the different ideologies of the land in the book of Joshua.

I have deliberately put "early" in quotes. Biblical scholars have ascribed the various texts of the Hebrew Bible to different sources with different, debated dates. However, one must be careful, because while a passage may date later, it may nevertheless convey data from a much earlier period. Historical accuracy is not a result of a chronological ratio. An example of this, I believe, can be seen in the biblical use of the ideology of "the land of Canaan" (see below).

As regards "ideology," I am working with the following neutral definition: "Ideology is a 'schematic image of social order,' 'a pattern of beliefs and concepts (both factual and normative) which purport to explain complex social phenomena' in which there may be simplification by means of symbolic figurative language, code shifting and/or overloading."[1] Ideologies "embrace a cluster of images and symbols that reflect levels of meaning rather than a distortion of reality."[2]

Ideology can and often is expressed by highly rhetorical communication (especially seen in the use of hyperbole). Unfortunately, one doesn't have to go very far to encounter this (current politicians supply us with plenty of examples of hyperbole!). Of course, ancient and modern myths communicate their respective ideologies. But so too do everyday documents (e.g., letters, economic texts, etc.); and of course, historical narratives. Thus, the level of rhetoric may vary, but they all are communicative acts that relay underlying ideological structures. It all goes to how we humans see our world; or want to see it.

It cannot be assumed that our current ideologies of land will coincide "by some lucky anachronism"[3] with the biblical or ancient Near Eastern ideologies of land as preserved in their ancient texts. For one thing, none of their ideologies were secular. Instead, they were utterly interconnected with the divine, whether in ancient Egypt, Assyria, or Israel.[4] Biblical ideologies were complex patterns of ideas and ideals which, although expressed in the texts, were not always systematically integrated.[5]

One of the important ways that ideologies work is through the use of ethnicons, both for expressions of self-identification, and very importantly, for the identification of the "other." In the Hebrew language, ethnicons (gentilics or *nisbes*) are formulated three ways[6]: (1) commonly the endings -*î*/*îm* attached to X; (2) most often with the use of *bn*/*bny* + X; or (3) rarely *'yš*/*'nšy* + X. These formulations are used on all entity levels where X equals: family, clan, tribe, polity.[7]

Another important ideological notion is "border." Nili Wazana has noted, as others have as well, the significant distinction between "border" and "frontier."[8] Some

---

1. K. Lawson Younger, Jr., *Ancient Conquest Accounts: A Study of Ancient Near Eastern and Biblical History Writing*, JSOTSup 98 (Sheffield: Sheffield University Press, 1990) 51. This definition is based on the work of Clifford Geertz, "Ideology as a Cultural System," in *Ideology and Discontent*, edited by David E. Apter (New York: Free Press, 1964) 47–76. See also Norman C. Habel, *The Land is Mine. Six Land Biblical Ideologies*, OBT (Minneapolis, MN: Augsburg Fortress, 1995) 16.

2. Habel, *The Land is Mine*, 13.

3. Thomas A. Middlebrook, "The Place of Narrative Space Theory in Biblical Exegesis: A Case Study from 1 Samuel 23:14—26:25" (Ph.D. Dissertation. Trinity Evangelical Divinity School, Trinity International University, 2018) 48.

4. Ronald A. Simkins, *Creator and Creation: Nature in the Worldview of Ancient Israel* (Peabody, MA: Hendrickson, 1994) 90–91.

5. Edward Shils, "Ideology: The Concept and Function of Ideology," in *International Encyclopedia of Social Sciences*, edited by David Sills (New York: Macmillan, 1968) 7:66–75.

6. The slash indicates the singular/plural forms.

7. See the discussion in K. Lawson Younger, Jr., *A Political History of the Arameans: From Their Origins to the End of Their Polities*, ABS 13 (Atlanta: SBL Press, 2016) 43–48.

8. For Wazana, the difference between the two is a matter of width. See Nila Wazana, *All the*

of the distinction is inherent in the geography (or more precisely the topography): rivers (precise) vs. mountains (lacking precision); or agricultural fields (precise) vs. pasturelands/steppe/desert (lacking precision). The different ideologies develop and are impacted by these physical features. However, they are conveyed, not by graphic symbols on a pictorial map, but as boundary lists, "by narratives that evoke place by consecutive enumeration of limits."[9]

Wazana has also observed that "spatial merisms" can contain more than two members. Thus "the prepositions 'from' (*mn*) and 'to' (*ʿd*) and the conjunction 'and' (*w*) are combined, although without necessarily creating a complete extremities formula . . . It is therefore unnecessary to emend the text whenever an extremities formula is deficient or lacking . . ."[10] Joshua 1:4 is an example.[11]

This means that multiple objects of the preposition, in both syndetic and asyndetic forms, occur in border descriptions. The use of the conjunction with the preposition for the *terminus ad quem* (*ʿd*) also occurs in such descriptions. Such a construction is commonly found in the Semitic languages.[12] The point is one must pay attention to the multiple derivation points or the multiple *termini ad quem* in an ancient text in order to understand what the text is saying.

The Land of Canaan

The "land of Canaan" is a fundamental ideological issue in the biblical texts. In order to understand the different ideologies encountered (especially in the book of Joshua) it is essential to establish the actual extent of the land of Canaan, the land of Promise.

The term "Canaan" is found in much earlier texts than the Hebrew Bible. Therefore, the biblical texts that give information about that land's parameters are rooted in the reality of the 2nd millennium BC. Knowing this information allows the reader

---

Boundaries of the Land. The Promised Land in Biblical Thought in Light of the Ancient Near East, translated by Liat Qeren (Winona Lake, IN: Eisenbrauns, 2013) 14–15. She states: "A border is a line that separates and divides specific geographical expanses. Its width is fixed and can reach several meters, usually clearly and prominently indicated on the ground . . . A frontier comprises territory that is undefined in political terms, the breadth of which may reach several kilometers." Specificity is another way of understanding the difference: a border is more specific; a frontier is more general. Originally a frontier was an area lying beyond a polity's jurisdiction and its usufruct but into which it might expand. Andrea Mura, "National Finitude and the Paranoid Style of the One," *Contemporary Political Theory* 15.1 (2016) 58–79. Border (*finis*) and frontier (*limes*).

9. Rachel S. Havrelock, "The Two Maps of Israel's Land," *JBL* 126 (2007) 649–67, esp. 649.

10. Wazana, *All the Boundaries of the Land*, 65–66.

11. See esp. Wazana, *All the Boundaries of the Land*, 66n24.

12. For an example, see K. Lawson Younger, Jr., "Tiglath-pileser I and the Initial Conflict with the Arameans," in *Wandering Arameans. Arameans Outside Syria: Textual and Archaeological Perspectives*, edited by A. Berlejung, A. M. Maeir, and A. Schüle, Leipziger Altorientalische Studien 5 (Wiesbaden: Harrassowitz, 2017) 193–226, esp. 208–9.

of Joshua to discern more efficiently and accurately what the different ideologies are doing. Consequently, in this section, I will first discuss briefly the meaning and significance of "the land of Canaan" outside of the Bible, and then its usage in the Bible.

Outside of the Bible, Canaan was a geo-political entity that had people of many different ethnicities living in it, due to the many immigrations throughout the centuries into the region. Throughout history, the southern Levant was a melting pot of different peoples, with multiple immigrations coming from multiple directions.[13]

One can see this, for example, in the inscription of Idrimi (see below) where there are immigrants from various north Syrian polities (whose ethnic compositions were Semitic [in this case, Amurrite] or Hurrian). Thus, it is not just how the term "Canaan" is used; it is also how the term "Canaanite" functions in the different texts.

Although there is no ancient Near Eastern document that describes the precise borders of Canaan, there are cuneiform and Egyptian sources that attest to this entity and indicate its basic parameters. These sources give ample evidence for the use of the terms "Canaan" and "Canaanite."[14]

Cuneiform Sources

The earliest textual attestation of the ethnicon "Canaanites" dates from a Middle Bronze Age cuneiform letter from the site of ancient Mari (dating to ca. 1775–1750 BC). The text was sent by Mutu-bisir to Shamshi-Addu I in connection with the former's sending of 20,000 troops to aid Ishhi-Addu of Qatna in suppressing a rebellion comprised of brigands and Canaanites (*Kinaḫnum*).[15] Nadav Na'aman concludes: "It

---

13. The biblical texts also describe the various ethnicities in the land through lists and narrative descriptions: e.g., "The Amalekites live in the land of the Negeb; the Hittites, the Jebusites, and the Amorites live in the hill country; and the Canaanites live by the sea, and along the Jordan" (Num 13:29).

14. Lemche argued that the term "Canaan" in the ancient Near Eastern texts of the second millennium BC was imprecise and ambiguous because it could designate anything from a large area including all the Levant and southeastern Anatolia to a small area in Lower Galilee. See Niels P. Lemche, *The Canaanites and their Land: The Tradition of the Canaanites*, JSOTSup 110 (Sheffield: JSOT Press, 1991) 33–39. However, this has not been accepted by scholars since the evidence leads to a different conclusion. See Nadav Na'aman, "The Canaanites and Their Land: A Rejoinder," *UF* 26 (1994) 397–418, esp. 397–8; Nadav Na'aman, "Four Notes on the Size of Late Bronze Age Canaan," *BASOR* 313 (1999) 31–37; Anson F. Rainey, "Who is a Canaanite? A Review of the Textual Evidence," *BASOR* 304 (1996) 1–15; Richard S. Hess, "Occurrences of 'Canaan' in Late Bronze Age Archives of the West Semitic World," in *Past Links: Studies in the Languages and Cultures of the Ancient Near East*, edited by Sholomo Izreel, Itamar Singer, and Ran Zadok, Israel Oriental Studies 18 (Winona Lake, IN: Eisenbrauns, 1998) 365–72.

15. LÚ.*ke-na-aḫ-núm*.MEŠ. See Georges Dossin, "Une mention de Cananéens dans une letter de Mari," *Syria* 50 (1973) 277–82. Anson F. Rainey, "Toponymic Problems (cont.) *Rāḫiṣum* = *Rôǵiṣu*?, Canaan and Canaanites," *Tel Aviv* 6 (1979) 158–62; D. Charpin, "Mari entre l'est et l'ouest: politique, culture, religion," *Akkadica* 78 (1992) 1–10, esp. 3–4; Na'aman, "The Canaanites and Their Land," 398; J.-M. Durand, *Documents épistolaires du palais de Mari*, 3 vols. (Paris: Les Éditions du Cerf,

is thus evident that in the mid-18th century BCE people called 'Canaanites' lived south of the kingdom of Qatna, i.e., in the same area where they are located in the Late Bronze Age."[16]

The first occurrence of the "land of Canaan" (written: *ma-at ki-in-a-nim*^{ki})[17] is in the inscription of Idrimi of Alalaḫ (twice, lines 18 and 19). The inscription dates to around 1470–1440 BC.[18] There has been debate about whether this text is historical or fictional.[19] For me, the arguments for it being fictional are not convincing. It is better described as an Old Syrian inscribed *Grabdenkmal* (funerary monument)[20] that utilizes in its text numerous rhetorical devices and motifs.[21]

According to the text, Idrimi was the youngest son of Ilī-ilimma (DINGIR-*i-lim-ma*) the king of Ḫalab (Aleppo). A coup, perhaps encouraged by the king of Mitanni, overthrew Idrimi's father and he had to flee to the hometown of his mother, Emar on the Euphrates. Feeling stifled there, Idrimi left Emar, traveling south into the steppe where he spent a night with the Sutū pastoralists. The next day, he began his journey to "the land of Canaan" (*ma-at ki-in-a-nim*^{ki}) and settled there in the town of Ammiya (^{iri}*am-mi-ia*^{ki}),[22] which the inscription states was specifically in "the

---

1997–2000) 1:456; and Jesper Eidem, *The Royal Archives from Tell Leilan. Old Babylonian Letters and Treaties from the Lower Town Palace East*, PIHANS 117 (Leiden: Nederlands Instituut voor het Nabije Oosten, 2011) 20n29. There are other texts from Mari that mention "Canaanites."

16. Na'aman, "The Canaanites and Their Land," 398.

17. For the text, see "electronic Idrimi": http://oracc.museum.upenn.edu/aemw/alalakh/idrimi/corpus/.

18. The Idrimi statue comes from the archaeological level of Alalaḫ IV. Idrimi claims to have ruled Alalaḫ for 30 years (Idrimi, line 102). The date is based on synchronisms with the Egyptian king, Thutmose III (1479–1425 BCE; sole rule: 1457–1425 BCE) and the Mittanian king, Parattarna/Barattarna I (ca. 1470–1450 BCE) in connection with Idrimi (vassal king of Parattarna/Barattarna I).

19. For the identification as fictional autobiography, see Tremper Longman III, *Fictional Akkadian Autobiography: A Generic and Comparative Study* (Winona Lake, IN: Eisenbrauns, 1991) 62–66. I am following Lambert's discussion of this issue. See W. G. Lambert, "Exiles and Deportees: A Third Category," in *Nomades et sédentaires dans le Proche-Orient ancien: Compte rendu de la XLVIe Rencontre assyriologique internationale, Paris, 10–13 juillet 2000*, edited by C. Nicolle, Amurru 3 (Paris: Éditions Recherche sur les civilisations, 2004) 213–16, esp. 214n2). It seems that Idrimi fits into the category of a *kaltum*. See the discussion of Adam Miglio, *Tribe and State: The Dynamics of International Politics and the Reign of Zimri-Lim*, Gorgias Studies in the Ancient Near East 8 (Piscataway, NJ: Gorgias, 2014) 131–33; Adam Miglio, "A Comparative Political History: Israel, Geshur and the "Amurrite Age," *JSOT* 38 (2014) 441–44.

20. See Dominik Bonatz, *Das syrohethitische Grabdenkmal: Untersuchungen zur Entstehung einer neuen Bildgattung in der Eisenzeit im nordsyrischsüdostanatolischen Raum* (Mainz: von Zabern, 2000) 49, 65–144.

21. But even if it is fictional, the world that the text is describing is a real one, i.e. the places that it names are real places.

22. This town is mentioned in a number of Amarna tablets. See Anson F. Rainey, *The El-Amarna Correspondence. A New Edition of the Cuneiform Letters from the Site of El-Amarna based on Collations of all Extant Tablets*, vol. 1 edited by William M. Schniedewind, vol. 2 edited by Zipora Cochavi-Rainey, HdO 110 (Leiden; Boston: Brill, 2015) EA 74:25 (URU.*Am-mi-ia*) (454–57; 1416–17); 95:45

land of Canaan" (lines 19b–20a) (see Map 1 below). This town is to be identified with ʿAmyūn in the mountains east of Byblos, near the coast in modern northern Lebanon.[23] In the town, there were other immigrants from Ḫalab (Aleppo) as well as from other north Syrian polities in the vicinity of Ḫalab. These people made him their leader. Eventually, Idrimi returned by sea and became king of Alalaḫ, also becoming a vassal king to Parattarna/Barattarna I, king of Mitanni.

Clearly, the readers of the Idrimi inscription would have known what the descriptor "the land of Canaan" meant when Idrimi's scribe (a man named Šarruwa) used it. Obviously, the descriptor was not invented the year the inscription was written, but must have had significance going back to a time before the Mari letter cited above. Idrimi fled to a point beyond the control of the king of Mitanni. It appears that the town of Ammiya was, in fact, beyond that border (see Map 1). Naʾaman states: "The fact that the author of this profoundly literary inscription chose to emphasize that Ammiya was located 'in the land of Canaan' may well indicate that he regarded the town as the northernmost Canaanite centre along the coast."[24]

There are many other cuneiform documents from Alalaḫ,[25] Ugarit,[26] Amarna,[27] Ḫattuša,[28] Assur and Emar that mention "Canaan." I will only comment on four of these (since these shed light on important different matters).

(ʿURUʾ.ʿAm-mi-iaʾ) (534–37); 99:2 ([UR]U.Am-mi-ia) (546–47; 1443); 139:14 (KUR.Am-mi-ia) (712–15); and 140:11 (KUR.Am-mi-ya) (716–17).

23. Rainey, "Who is a Canaanite?" 4; Anson F. Rainey in Anson Rainey and R. Steven Notley, *The Sacred Bridge: Carta's Atlas of the Biblical World* (Jerusalem: Carta, 2006) 62; Lemche, *The Canaanites and their Land*, 41. Earlier, E. P. Dhorme, "Les pays bibliques au temps d'El-Amarna: D'après la nouvelle publication des lettres," *RB* 5 (1908) 500–519, esp. 509, who identified Ammiya with Efneh, about 8 miles down the coast from Tripoli [followed by Alan Millard, "Canaanites," in *Peoples of Old Testament Times*, edited by Donald J. Wiseman. (Oxford: Clarendon, 1973) 29–52, esp. 49 n14, about 16 miles north of Byblos, see map on 31]. J. A. Belmonte Marín, *Die Orts und Gewässernamen der Texte aus Syrien im 2. Jt. v. Chr*, RGTC 12.2, BTAVO B/7 (Wiesbaden: Reichert, 2001) 20 gives the following: Modern ʿAmyūn (34° 16′ / 35° 48′) 15 km south and inland from Tripoli; see R. Dussaud, *Topographie historique de la Syrie antique et médiévale*, BAH 4 (Paris: Librairie Orientaliste Paul Geuthner, 1927) 117 n1 (apparently the first to suggest ʿAmyūn).

24. Naʾaman, "The Canaanites and Their Land," 399.

25. AT 48; AT 154; AT 181; and AT 188. For discussion, see Naʾaman, "The Canaanites and Their Land," 399; Rainey, "Who is a Canaanite?" 3–4; Hess, "Occurrences of 'Canaan' in Late Bronze Age Archives," 366–67.

26. RS 20.182; RS 11.840 = KTU 4.96. For discussion, see Naʾaman, "The Canaanites and Their Land," 403; Rainey, "Who is a Canaanite?" 4; Hess, "Occurrences of 'Canaan' in Late Bronze Age Archives," 367.

27. EA 8; EA 9; EA 30; EA 109; EA 110; EA 131; EA 137; EA 148; EA 151; EA 162; EA 367. For discussion, see Naʾaman, "The Canaanites and Their Land," 399–403; Rainey, "Who is a Canaanite?" 6–11; Hess, "Occurrences of 'Canaan' in Late Bronze Age Archives," 368–70. Canaan is written as Kinaḫ(ḫ)u in the Amarna tablets (the writing with ḫ in this case is indicative of the *ayin*).

28. *KBo* XXVIII: 1; *KUB* III 37 + *KBo* I 17; *KUB* III 57; *KBo* I 15 + 19. Naʾaman, "The Canaanites and Their Land," 404–5;

First, in a text from Alalaḫ (AT 181) a man named Šarniya is identified as a "Canaanite" (DUMU KUR.*ki-en-a-ni*ᵏⁱ) while another person "Azira" is identified as a citizen of "the city of Ammiya." In this case, Azira must have been a person living in the city of Ammiya (as Idrimi did) but was of a different ethnicity (i.e., non-Canaanite, perhaps an Amurrite like Idrimi).[29] The fact is that in a few occurrences, "Canaanite" is used in a narrow, strict ethnic sense of a particular indigenous group who spoke the Canaanite language. In some contexts, the term seems to refer to the aboriginal inhabitants of the southern Levant with roots in the Chalcolithic and Early Bronze periods.[30]

Second, in an Amarna letter (EA 36) the king of Alashiya (Cyprus) wrote to the king of Egypt about a shipment of copper from there to Egypt in return for a shipment of grain from "the province of Canaan" (⸢*pi*⸣-*ḫa-ti ša ki-na-ḫi*).[31] This text demonstrates that there was an actual Egyptian province with the name "Canaan."

Third, in another Amarna letter (EA 8),[32] Burnaburiash, king of Babylonia, complains to the Egyptian pharaoh, Akhenaten, that his merchants "were detained in Canaan for business matters, then they were robbed and finally killed "in Ḫinnatūna of the land of Canaan" by the rulers of Acco and Shamḫūna. Burnaburiash states:

> [The land of C]anaan is your land, and [its] kings [are your servants]. [I]n your land, I have been despoiled. Bring [them] to account; make compensation for the money that they took away, and as for the men who [ki]lled my servants, kill them, and avenge their blood. But if you do not kill these men, they will do it again; either my caravan or your own envoys they will kill, and the envoy between us will be cut off (i.e. no messengers will get through) (lines 25–33).

Na'aman rightly observes that "The Pharaoh is the lord of the land of Canaan and is responsible for everything that happens within its confines."[33] The kings of Canaan are his vassals and answer to him. It is his responsibility to deal justly with evildoers. "Thus, 'Canaan' is used to refer to a particular territory under the dominion of the

---

29. Oded Tammuz, "Canaan—A Land Without Limits," *UF* 33 (2001) 501–43, esp. 506 seems to miss this point.

30. See the discussions of Keith N. Schoville, "Canaanites and Amorites," in *Peoples of the Old Testament World*, edited by Alfred J. Hoerth, Gerald L. Mattingly, and Edwin M. Yamauchi (Grand Rapids: Baker, 1994) 157–82, esp. 162–64. See Killebrew's discussion of the culture, though she does not use "Canaanite" with ethnic connotations: Ann E. Killebrew, *Biblical Peoples and Ethnicity. An Archaeological Study of Egyptians, Canaanites, Philistines, and Early Israel, 1300–1100 BCE*, ABS 9 (Atlanta, GA: Society of Biblical Literature, 2005) 96–148. I agree that most uses are not ethnic, but a few are.

31. Rainey, *The El-Amarna Correspondence: A New Edition*, 344–47, 1381; Rainey, "Who is a Canaanite?" 7–8; *CAD* P 365, s.v. *pīḫātu*. Some scholars have questioned whether *pīḫātu* "province" was used in this period. There are *kudurru*s that use the term with this meaning.

32. Rainey, *The El-Amarna Correspondence: A New Edition*, 88–91.

33. Na'aman, "The Canaanites and Their Land," 399–400.

Egyptian Pharaoh."[34] What is intriguing is that the Hebrew Bible presents Yahweh as the sovereign over the whole earth, in particular "the land of Canaan,"[35] who, in turn, is judging the inhabitants of his dominion. It seems that the biblical writers have seized on the concept expressed in this letter, casting Yahweh in the role of carrying out justice in the land, whereas the Pharaoh (supposedly also a deity) could not.

Fourth, a ritual text from the city of Emar mentions "the storm-god of Canaan."[36] This demonstrates that a major deity could be specially associated with and ascribed jurisdiction over this geo-political entity. This deity is distinguished from the storm-god (of Aleppo) in the ritual, and interestingly, receives the largest animal sacrifice in the text (one ox and six sheep). Here too, the biblical texts seem to play off of the notion of "the deity of the land" in a polemical fashion. In other words, the storm-god is not the god of the land, Yahweh is.

Egyptian Sources

There were native Egyptian terms for the Levant.[37] The term Retjenu (*rtnw*) was used as a descriptor of all the Levant.[38] Gardiner understood the Egyptian designation "Djahy" (*Ḏ3hy*) to mean Palestine as far as the Lebanon. But Vandersleyen argued that Djahy had a wider meaning (including Palestine, Syria and northern Mesopotamia). Nevertheless, there are occurrences of Djahy and also the term, Ḫurru (*Ḫ3rw*) that are used to describe only Canaan.[39] The Egyptians often referred to the inhabitants of the region as ʿAamu (*ʿ3mw*) "Asiatics," without making a distinction between the different ethnicities in that region.[40]

In Egyptian sources, "Canaan" or "Canaanites" are mentioned in sixteen texts dating from the 18th–22nd dynasties.[41] The ethnicon ("Canaanites") occurs first in

34. Ibid. 400.

35. The Lord is seen as the universal king who controls all lands, of which Canaan is one (Gen 17:8; Exod 6:4; Lev 14:34a; 25:38; Deut 4:39; 10:14; 17).

36. Emar 446: 107–8 reads: ᵈIM *ša ki-na-i*. See Daniel E. Fleming, "'The Storm God of Canaan' at Emar," *UF* 26 (1994) 127–30; Daniel E. Fleming, "Six Months of Ritual Supervision by the Diviner," *COS* 1: 436–39 (Text 1.124); Daniel E. Fleming, *Time at Emar: The Cultic Calendar and the Rituals from the Diviner's Archive*, MC 11 (Winona Lake, IN: Eisenbrauns, 2000) 142–73, 268–80.

37. The Egyptians used terms like *t3š* "border" and *drw* "limits" to describe frontiers and boundaries. See José M. Galán, *Victory and Border: Terminology Related to Egyptian Imperialism in the XVIIIth Dynasty*, Hildesheimer Ägyptologische Beiträge 40 (Hildesheim: Gerstenberg Verlag, 1995) 102–35, esp. 133–35.

38. CDME 154; Gardiner, *AEO* 1:142–49. See also C. Vandersleyen, *Les Guerres d'Amosis* (Brussels, 1971) 90–100; Lichtheim, *AEL* 2:38, n3.

39. CDME 319, s.v. *Ḏ3hy*; *AEO* I 142–45; CDME 184, s.v. *Ḫ3rw*; *AEO* I 180.

40. Donald B. Redford, *Egypt, Canaan, and Israel in Ancient Times*. Princeton: Princeton University Press, 1992) 100–101.

41. Manfred Görg, "Der Name 'Kanaan' in Ägyptischer Wiedergabe," *BN* 18 (1982) 26–27. He

the inscriptions of Amenhotep II (1427–1401 BC),[42] where it is referring to elite people from Canaan. In a number of texts, "Canaan" is used in connection with Gaza. The reason for this seems to be the fact that Gaza was one of the most important cities in Canaan; in fact, the first one encountered when traveling out of Egypt into the Levant. Hence, Gaza was sometimes designated "the Canaan" (*p3kn'n*). In Papyrus Anastasi I (27:1) the senior scribe patronizingly says to the young scribe: "I have told you of the farthest lands of the land of Canaan, but you do not answer me, good or bad; you do not report to me."[43] Such a statement indicates that the land of Canaan was a significant geo-political entity with other lands contained within it. This is entirely accurate since Canaan was comprised of numerous city-states with "kings/kinglets." This usage coincides with what Ann Killebrew has described as a social boundary, stating: "One can identify, archaeologically speaking, a second-millennium material culture in this region that shares many features in common and forms a 'social boundary.'"

One text that has not been utilized in this discussion is "The First Hittite Marriage Inscription." During the thirty-fourth year of his lengthy reign, Ramesses II (1279–1213) celebrated a sort of "Jubilee" (*Hb-sd*) and married a daughter of the Hittite king.[44] This marriage was memorialized in a monumental inscription placed on temple walls throughout Egypt during Ramesses' reign. Without going into the details of the inscription, the narrative comes to the point where an Egyptian official informs Pharaoh of his bride's travels:

> Then one came to inform His Majesty (i.e. Ramesses II) saying: "Look the Great Ruler of Ḫatti [34] has given his eldest daughter carrying much tribute, with everything they are covering this which is from [. . .]—the Ruler of Ḫatti together with the officials—[The excess] of the land of Ḫatti is with them! They have passed many remote mountains and difficult roads and they have reached the borders of His Majesty. [35] Let the troops and officials set out to receive them, O King of Upper and Lower Egypt, Usermaatre Setepenre, son of Re, Ramesses II, beloved of Amun, given life."[45]

The text then records that the Pharaoh dispatched his army and officials to escort the bride from the border safely through Canaan to Egypt (to the amazement of the all the

---

includes in his count one Ptolemaic inscription. In contrast, Aḥituv lists 14 occurrences. See Shmuel Aḥituv, *Canaanite Toponyms in Ancient Egyptian Documents* (Jerusalem: Magnes, 1984) 83–84.

42. Urk. IV., 1300–1309; Elmar Edel, "Die Stelen Amenophis' II. aus Karnak und Memphis," *ZDPV* 69 (1953): 98–175; *COS* 2: 19–23, esp. 21 (lines 15b–17a); *ANET* 246.

43. Papyrus Anastasi I (27.1). Translation: James P. Allen, *COS* 3: 9–14, esp. 14.

44. Maat-Ḥor-Neferu-Re, the eldest daughter of Ḫattušili III.

45. *KRI* II, 247:10–248:9. Translation: Oliver A. Hersey, "The Marriage at Mount Sinai: Reading Exodus in the Context of Ancient Near Eastern Diplomatic Marriage." (Ph.D. Dissertation. Trinity Evangelical Divinity School, Trinity International University, 2019) 175–76.

inhabitants of the land of Canaan).⁴⁶ This border would have been at the point where the land of Amurru ended and where the land of Canaan began, or very near to it.

In fact, Ḫattušili was informed by Ramesses II of the itinerary concerning the northern Levantine cities where the envoy should stop. Ramesses had already written to his governor, Suta, in the town of Ramesses-Meramum (ancient Kumidi) in Upe, to make arrangements for the impending arrival of his Hittite bride.⁴⁷ The city of Lab'u (later Lebo-Hamath) on the border with Amurru was a likely place for the meeting of the parties. It later was a border town between the polities of Damascus and Hamath.

In Papyrus Anastasi IIIA 5–6 and IV 16:4, there is mention of "Canaanite slaves from Ḫurru." In this text, the term "Canaanite" seems to be used to describe the ethnicity of the slaves from the area of Ḫurru (i.e., Palestine).⁴⁸ This is another usage of "Canaanite" in a narrow, strict ethnic sense of a particular indigenous group who spoke the Canaanite language.

Canaan and Ḫurru also appear together, along with six other entities in the famous Merenptah stela. The first two entities are traditional national enemies of Egypt, while the other four Ashkelon, Gezer, Yanoam and Israel are located in Canaan/Ḫurru.⁴⁹ The text reads:

> All the rulers are prostrate saying: "Shalom!"
>
> Not one dare raise his head among the Nine Bows:
>
> plundered is Tjehenu (Libya),
>
> Hatti is pacified.
>
> carried off is Canaan with every evil.
>
> brought away is Ashkelon,
>
> seized is Gezer,
>
> Yanoam is made nonexistent;
>
> Israel is wasted, his seed is not.
>
> Hurru is become a widow for Egypt.

46. *KRI* II, 248:7–249:3.

47. Benedict G. Davies, *Egyptian Historical Inscriptions from the Nineteenth Dynasty*, Documenta Mundi. Aegyptiaca 2 (Jonsered, Sweden: Paul Åströms Förlag, 1997) 150; Elmar Edel, *Die ägyptisch-hethitische Korrespondenz aus Boghazköi in babylonischer und hethitischer Sprache*, 2 vols. (Opladen: Rheinisch-Westfälische Akademie, 1994) 2:228 See specifically *KUB* 3.37; 57; and *KBo* 1.17.

48. Otherwise, this statement would be redundant.

49. The determinative for Israel is not a haphazard designation. It means that the Egyptians did not regard Israel as a city-state with fixed borders like e.g., Gezer. In this phrase, Israel is understood to be a collective, a distinct people, not named after any particular territory or city. In Egyptian, the names of countries, cities, and provinces are feminine. But the masculine pronoun is used with Israel which possibly indicates an identity with an eponymous ancestor. See Younger, *Ancient Conquest Accounts*, 324, n19).

> All lands in their entirety are (now) at peace,
> and everyone who roamed has been subdued.

In sum, the following can be noted. There was a geo-political entity "Canaan," which had a real actual border between it and the lands to its north. Although there is no Egyptian or cuneiform document delineating that precise border, it can be reconstructed with a high degree of accuracy, because certain towns are described as being in Canaan while others are outside of it. Of course, the biblical texts also provide data.

Biblical Texts

In the Hebrew Bible, the terms "Canaanite" and "Amorite" are used in three ways: (1) A narrow, strict ethnic sense of a particular indigenous group. In some contexts, the term "Canaanite" seems to refer to the aboriginal inhabitants of the southern Levant with roots in the Chalcolithic and Early Bronze periods. The term "Amorite," in this instance, seems to be a reference to the Amurrite ethnic groups that spoke the Amurrite language. (2) A limited synecdoche of the part for the whole. Thus, Canaanite can designate "plain dweller" and can be used in a merism with Amorite "hill-dweller" to represent all the inhabitants of the land. Likewise, Canaanite can designate "city dweller" and can be used in a merism with Perizzite "rural person" to mean all the inhabitants of the land. See Table 1.

Table 1: Uses of Canaanite, Amorite and Perizzite as limited synecdoches

In Joshua	*In Judges 1*
Canaanite = "plain/city dweller"	Canaanite = "city dweller"
Amorite = "hill-dweller"	Perizzite = "rural person," "dweller of an unwalled city"[50]

(3) A broad synecdoche of the part for the whole: each term can be used to describe "all Cisjordanian inhabitants." This usage is probably based on the fact that these two groups appear to be the most dominate population groups in the geo-political entity. The first and third usages are found in the cuneiform and Egyptian texts (see above). The second seems to be a unique usage of the Hebrew Bible.

Furthermore, the Hebrew Bible has two concepts of "Canaan": (1) the bulk of the occurrences of the term describe "Canaan, the full extent" (i.e., the early geo-political entity, the Egyptian province); and (2) a few instances describe "Canaan, the limited extent," i.e., just Phoenicia (a later developed usage). In the first instance, the biblical writers have appropriated "the land of Canaan" as seen in the ancient

---

50. For a similar merism, see Gen 13:7b.

texts, i.e. the Egyptian province, as the Promised Land.[51] In the second instance, certain later biblical writers present a territorially more limited Canaan that appears to correspond to the Phoenician coast whose inhabitants are the Canaanites, or perhaps for accurately, their descendants.[52]

The Egyptian Province of Canaan = the Promised Land

There are several biblical texts that delineate the borders of Canaan: Num 13:21; 34:2–12; Josh 13:2–6; Ezek 47:13–23; 48:1. The first three passages are clearly connected to "the land of Canaan." This is clearly stated in all three texts, twice in Num 34. The borders are presented "as those already associated with Canaan with or without the presence of Israel."[53] The last two texts (in Ezekiel) are apparently drawing on the same source material as the first three.[54] Yet, the rhetoric and purposes are quite different.[55] While Ezekiel grounds his rhetoric about the future in the past, that rhetoric transcends all past and future physical realities to the present-day.[56] These two passages are part of a wider passage (Ezekiel 47:13–48:35) where the prophet envisages a return from exile and a new division of the land, where space and access to the temple are of critical importance.[57] So, while the outer borders for the land are more or less the same,[58] the inner space is radically different. There is a different placement with all twelve tribes west of the Jordan;[59] the north–south order of the tribes is quite different; and yet, they all have the same size of allotment per tribe! See Map 2 below.

51. Nadav Na'aman, *Borders and Districts in Biblical Historiography: Seven Studies in Biblical Geographic Lists*, JBS 4 (Jerusalem: Simor, 1986) 39–73.

52. Roland de Vaux, "Le pays de Canaan," *JAOS* 88 (1968) 23–30, esp. 30; Na'aman, "The Canaanites and Their Land," 397.

53. Havrelock, "The Two Maps of Israel's Land," 651.

54. de Vaux, "Le pays de Canaan," 30.

55. Steven S. Tuell, *The Law of the Temple in Ezekiel 40–48*, HSM 49 (Atlanta: Scholars Press, 1992) 155–56 has suggested that the difference between the passages in Numbers and those in Ezekiel is one of perspective: Numbers envisions the land from an Egyptian perspective, while Ezekiel sees it from an Assyrian or Persian perspective. However, while the former perspective is accurate, the second may be questioned (i.e., did Assyria or Persia really ever envision *these borders* for their holdings in the Levant? I doubt that they did).

56. This is in a sense "territorial rhetoric." See Thomas Renz, *The Rhetorical Function of the Book of Ezekiel* (Leiden; Boston: Brill, 2002) 123; Kalinda R. Stevenson, *Vision of Transformation: The Territorial Rhetoric of Ezekiel 40–48*, SBLDS 154 (Atlanta: Scholars Press, 1996) 143, 149–51.

57. Stevenson, *Vision of Transformation*, 151.

58. However, they have different starting points: Num 34 starts with the southern border; the Ezekiel passages with the northern border (Rainey, "Who is a Canaanite?" 11).

59. The territory of Transjordan, which was occupied by the two and a half tribes for most of Israel's history, is not included in the vision of the renewed land. Their territories are now included in Cisjordan.

Nevertheless, even though the phrase "land of Canaan" is not used in these passages in Ezekiel, a comparison of these key passages is very informative. The most important boundaries for our purposes are the northern and eastern ones (see Tables 2 and 3 below).

Numbers 13 and 34 are typically ascribed by scholars to the Priestly document (P).[60] This would make these late texts.[61] However, it is important to remember that older material can be used in a later composition. Thus, a Late Bronze Age or early Iron I ideology of land might be used for literary reasons in an Iron II composition because it actually reflects the way an Iron I person would have understood things and reinforces the ideology of the Iron II composition.[62] Second, later material can be used to describe an earlier context where the later material fills in the correct data contained in the earlier context (e.g. some of the town lists of Judah may date from a later time period, but they fill in the data for the earlier period). Thus, they are functionally anachronistic for the later readers, yet contain a general accuracy of description for the earlier context.

Finally, it is important to realize that the Hebrew Bible often uses a second toponymic descriptor to define further a single descriptor. This can be seen in the common addition of the term "Aram" to a number of different toponyms (apparently in order to create clarity for the texts' readers of a later period): Aram Naharaim, Aram-Zobah, Aram-Damascus, etc. This is seen in one instance in the border toponyms encountered here: Lebo + Hamath = Lebo-Hamath (see below). This particular example is the reason why Mazar,[63] having suggested that the border described in Numbers 34 reflected the political status after the Egyptian-Hittite treaty between Ramesses II and Ḫattušili III, recognized that the text conformed this to the Iron I–II context when Hamath was the capital of a Luwian-Aramean polity.[64] Thus, the Late Bronze Age Labôʾ is called Lebo-Hamath in an Iron II context.

---

60. The phrase "land of Canaan" is supposedly a characteristic phrase of P. See Leslie C. Allen, *Ezekiel 20–48*, WBC 29 (Dallas, TX: Word Books, 1990) 280. This seems rather odd, since "Canaan" is a significantly ancient name for the region that surely was used long before P. Furthermore, the land of Canaan is envisioned as the larger, earlier Canaan, not the later smaller version of Canaan (Phoenicia) (see all the examples above). I must confess bewilderment at such "traditional, higher critical" statements.

61. Rainey states: "However, this does not mean that it is an invention of the Exilic or even of the late Monarchic period." See Rainey, "Who is a Canaanite?" 11.

62. For example, the Middle Assyrian empire's borders at the Euphrates were restored by the early Neo-Assyrian kings who use rhetoric to this effect.

63. Benjamin Mazar (Maisler) "Lebo-Hamath and the Northern Border of Canaan," in *The Early Biblical Period: Historical Studies*, translated by Ruth and Elisheva Rigbi, edited by Shmuel Aḥituv and Baruch A. Levine (Jerusalem: Israel Exploration Society, 1986) 189–202.

64. For that polity's history, see Younger, *A Political History of the Arameans*, 425–99.

There have been two scholarly views for the location of the northern border: (1) a small view, i.e., the northern border began at the Mediterranean coastline somewhere in the vicinity of a line that ran from Tyre to Dan and extended in an easterly direction to a point north of the Sea of Galilee[65] (see Map 1, represented by the wide solid line); and (2) a large view, i.e., the northern border began at the Mediterranean coastline somewhere north of Byblos, and ran east to modern Lebwe, Ṣadad, and Qayatein, before turning south (Map 1, dashed line).[66] This latter view is correct. The former does not give any firm site identifications.[67] In the case of some of its adherents, the authenticity of the border description in Num 34 is questioned.[68]

The passage from Joshua 13:1–7 is significant to the comparison and analysis because it is commonly accepted by scholars that "the land that remains" is describing the gap between the "land of Canaan" and "the borders of the twelve tribes,"[69] and that the land of Canaan is larger than the twelve tribes system.[70] The biblical description of "the land that remains" stands in marked contrast to the small view mentioned above, which sees Canaan as the land south of Dan and north of the wadi of Egypt (see further remarks in the Assessments of the Tables 2 and 3 below).

---

65. Martin Noth, *Numbers: A Commentary*, trans. J. D. Martin (Philadelphia: Westminster, 1968) 250–51; Robert North, "Phoenicia-Canaan Frontier LᵉBÔ of Hama," *Mélanges de l'université Saint-Joseph* 46 (1970) 71–103; Peter C. Craigie, *Ezekiel*, The Daily Study Bible (Philadelphia: Westminster Press, 1983) 183; Allen, *Ezekiel 20–48*, 280. For Noth (249–50) the view depended on (1) the supposition that Num 34:7–11 was a "description of the frontier of the tribe of Dan from the 'system of the tribal frontiers'" (250) and (2) the conviction that none of the toponyms mentioned in the description of the northern boundary in verses 7–11 "can be fixed with any certainty" (249). It seems that the first supposition blurred his ability to assess the second. Noth (98) argued that "*Lᵉbô' Ḥamat* means 'the Ḥama corridor'" (that is the Beqa' valley in his thesis) and that "the *point* where this corridor coincides with the known northern frontier of Israel" is "along the Tyre-Dan line." He states: "We tend therefore to think of Lebô' at Dan-Banyas itself, and thus rejoin the essential position of both Noth and Robinson." In order to hold this position, he must reject the relevance of all the extrabiblical textual evidence (a point that he admits [see 99])!

66. Benjamin Mazar (Maisler) "Canaan and the Canaanites," *BASOR* 102 (1946) 7–12; Mazar, "Lebo-Hamath and the Northern Border of Canaan," 189–202; Yohanan Aharoni, *The Land of the Bible: A Historical Geography*, 2nd ed. (Philadelphia: Westminster, 1979) 50; Na'aman, *Borders and Districts in Biblical Historiography*, 42; Na'aman, "The Canaanites and Their Land," 410; Rainey, "Who is a Canaanite?" 6.

67. In fact, Noth argued that not one single site in Num 34:7–11 can be identified with any assurance. However, in my opinion, this can only be maintained by denying all of the extrabiblical textual data.

68. Noth, *Numbers*, 248–50.

69. Na'aman, *Borders and Districts in Biblical Historiography*, 39–73; Richard S. Hess, *Joshua. An Introduction and Commentary*, TOTC (Leicester: InterVarsity, 1996) 45.

70. Na'aman, "The Canaanites and Their Land," 410–11.

K. Lawson Younger, Jr.   "Early" Ideologies of the Land in the Hebrew Bible

Table 2: Northern Border Descriptions

"Land of Canaan"			Future "Land of Israel"		
Numbers 13:21 (P)	Numbers 34:7–9 (P)	Joshua 13:1–7 (13:2–6 = pre-Dtr; 13:1, 7 = Dtr²; P)	Ezekiel 47:13–16 (H)	Ezekiel 47:17 (H)	Ezekiel 48:1–2 (H)
⁽¹⁾ Yahweh said to Moses: ⁽²⁾ Send men to spy out **the land of Canaan**, which I am giving to the Israelites; from each of their ancestral tribes you shall send a man, every one a leader among them."	⁽¹⁾ Yahweh spoke to Moses, saying: ⁽²⁾ Command the Israelites, and say to them: When you enter **the land of Canaan**, this is the land which shall fall to you for an inherited/ entitled estate —the land of Canaan, by its borders: …	⁽⁴⁾ all **the land of the Canaanite** (i.e. Canaan),	⁽¹³⁾ Thus says Lord Yahweh: This is the border, (by) which you shall apportion as an inherited estate **the land for the twelve tribes of Israel**. Joseph shall have two portions. ⁽¹⁴⁾ You shall divide it equally, (that) which I swore to give it to your ancestors, and this land shall fall to you as your inheritance.		
	⁽⁷⁾ This shall be (*hyh*) your **northern border** (*gbwl*):		⁽¹⁵⁾ This shall be the border of the land: On the **north side**,	⁽¹⁷⁾ So, the border will be	⁽¹⁾ These are the names of the tribes: Beginning at the **northern edge/ border**,
	from **the Great Sea**		from **the Great Sea**	from **the Sea**	
	you shall delineate (*t'h*) for yourself **Mount Hor** (*hôr*);				
		and from **'Arah**, which belongs to the **Sidonians**, to **Aphek(a)** and (to) the border/territory of the **Amorite** (= Amurru); ⁽⁵⁾ and the land of the **Gebalite (Byblos)** and all **the Lebanon**, to the east,			
			(to) **the way of Ḥetlōn** (Ḥeitela?)		on **the way of Ḥetlōn** (Ḥeitela?),
. up to **Reḥob**,					
Lebo-Hamath.	⁽⁸⁾ from Mount Hor you shall delineate (*t'h*) **Lebo-Hamath**,	from **Baal-gad** below **Mount Hermon** to **Lebo-Hamath**,	(to) **Lebo(-Hamath)**,*		(to) **Lebo-Hamath**,
	and the limit (*tôṣ'ōt*) of the border (*gbwl*) shall be (*hyh*) at **Zedad** (Ṣedād);		and (to) **Zedad** (Ṣedād) ⁽¹⁶⁾ **Hamath***		

53

			(to) **Berothah**,		
	(9) then the border (*gbwl*) shall go forth (*yṣ'*) to **Ziphron** (Ziprōn),		(to) **Sibraim**, which (lies) between the border of **Damascus** and the border of **Hamath**,		
	and its limit/termination (*tôṣ' ōtāy*) shall be (*hyh*) at **Hazar-enan** (*ḥaṣar-'ēynān*);		(to) **Hazer-hatticon** (error for: **Hazer-enon**),** which is on the border of **Hauran**.**	to **Hazar-enon**, which is north of the border of **Damascus**, and the border of **Hamath** to the north.	(to) **Hazar-enon** which is on the border of **Damascus**, with **Hamath** to the north,
	this shall be (*hyh*) for you **the northern border**.			This shall be the **north side**.	
		(6) all the inhabitants of the hill country from **the Lebanon** (range) to **Misrephoth-maim**—all **Sidonians**.			and extending from the east side to the west, **Dan**, one portion.

* The MT of Ezek 47:15–16 (*lᵉbô ṣᵉdâ ḥămāt*) is corrupt and should read: *lᵉbô ḥămāt ṣᵉdâ*.
** BHS: OG: *aulē tou Saunan*. 1 *ḥăṣērâ 'ēnō(w)n*, cf. 17; 48:1; Num 34:9

In the second row, the different traditional sources have been listed in parentheses (P = Priestly Source; H = the Holiness Code). I personally have a high level of skepticism about these sources, but I have listed them so that the table bears all the information necessary for analysis.

Table 3: Eastern Border Descriptions

"Land of Canaan"	Future "Land of Israel"
Numbers 34:10–12 (P)	Ezekiel 47:18 (H)
(10) You shall delineate (*t'h*) for yourselves the **eastern border** (*gbl*)	(18) On the **east side**,
from **Hazar-enan** (*ḥaṣar-'ēynān*) to **Shepham** (*šᵉpām*); (11) and the border (*gbwl*) shall go down (*yrd*)	
from **Shepham** to **the Riblah/Arbela** (Heb. *Hāriblāh* / Gk. *Arbēla*) on the east side of **Ain/the spring**; and the border shall go down (*yrd*),	from between **Hauran** and from between **Damascus**;
and reach (*māḥāh*) the eastern slope (*ketep*) of the **sea of Kinneret** (*kinnēret*);	
(12) and the border shall go down (*yrd*) to **the Jordan**,	from between **Gilead** and from between **the land of Israel**—**the Jordan**;
and its limit/termination (*tôṣ' ōtāy*) shall be (*hyh*) at **the Dead Sea (Salt Sea)**.	from the territory of **the eastern sea** and as far as **Tamar**.
	This shall be the **east side**.

Assessment of Table 2

Aharoni rightly remarked: "The keys to establishing the northern border are Lebo-Hamath and Zedad."[71] A number of scholars over the years have believed that Lebo-Hamath is not the name of a city, but instead is simply a phrase *lbwʾ ḥmt* meaning "the entrance to Hamath" (Hamath on the Orontes river).[72] This view takes the first term *lbwʾ* to be an infinitive of the verb *bwʾ* + the preposition *l* with an adverbial sense "entering, coming, i.e., the way leading to Hamath."[73] Gray stated:

> ... the use of מִן [*mn*] (e.g. 1 Kgs 8:65; Amos 6:14) or עַד [*ʿd*] (Josh 13:6) ... before the whole phrase, shows that the phrase as a whole had become virtually equal to a term for a place or district. Originally ל [*l*] may have had a local sense *at*, or *towards*.[74]

Some scholars that understand *lbwʾ ḥmt* in this way identify the reference with Marj-ʿAyûn[75] or Dan-Banias[76] (this is the small view described above). Aharoni asserted that the expression *mlbwʾ ḥmt* in Amos 6:14 argues against this view;[77] but if Gray's point is granted, this is not on target.[78] However, there are two major problems with this understanding of *lbwʾ*: (1) there is no parallel to such a construction with the meaning anything like "corridor" and with the great distance involved as North proposed (see footnote 65 above); and (2) most importantly, there is no external evidence from the ancient Near Eastern sources to support it. The association of *lbwʾ* with Hamath makes Marj-ʿAyûn extremely doubtful. Being so far away from Hamath (ca. 215 km) there is no way that this site can be understood to have any connection to Hamath. The same criticism applies to North's theory that Lebo-Hamath

---

71. Aharoni, *The Land of the Bible*, 72.

72. RSV; Félix M. Abel, *Géographie de la Palestine*, 2 vols. (Paris: Gabalda, 1933–38) 1: 300–301.

73. For such an interpretation, see the targums: *lmty ḥmt* [Targum Onqelos]; *mmʿlnʾ dḥnt* [Targum Jonathan]; Old Greek of Num 13:21: *eōs Raab eisporeuomenōn Ephaath*, "as people enter Hemath"; Num 34:8: *eisporeuomenōn eis Emath*, "as they enter into Hemath."

74. George Buchanan Gray, *A Critical and Exegetical Commentary on Numbers*, ICC (Edinburgh: T. & T. Clark, 1903) 140.

75. Marj-ʿAyyoun (33°21ʹ30ʺN 35°35ʹ20ʺE; Gird position 135/158; just north of modern Metulla, Israel). Scholars like van Kasteren and Legendre situated Lebo-Hamath at Marj-ʿAyûn. J. van Kasteren, "La frontière septentrionale de la Terre promise," *RB* 4 (1895) 23–36, esp. 29; A. Legendre, "Émath [+ Entrée dʾ]," in *Dictionnaire de la Bible* (Paris: Letouzey, 1899) Columns 2: 1715–20. See also Abel, *Géographie de la Palestine*, 1: 301.

76. See North, "Phoenicia-Canaan Frontier LᵉBÔ of Hama," 99.

77. Aharoni, *The Land of the Bible*, 65.

78. However, the syntax is *preposition* (usually *ʿd*) + the *infinitive construct with a 2ms suffix + city name* (see Judg 6:4; 11:33; 1 Kgs 18:46). See *HALOT*, 113, s.v. qal, 2. b).

is this "Ḥama Corridor"⁷⁹ (not a known geographic term in Biblical Hebrew) with its starting point in the area of Dan-Banias (250 km away from Hamath).⁸⁰

Therefore, it is best to understand *lbwʾ* as a toponym (with a localization at modern Lebwe in the Beqaʿ Valley, 25 km northeast of Baalbek, 30 km south of Ḥama).⁸¹ This was an important city on the southern border of the land of Hamath (thus the combination: city name + land name).⁸² This city is attested in Egyptian inscriptions and cuneiform sources.⁸³ Labaʾu appears in Thutmose III's List (no. 10: *r-b-n* = *la-bā-na*; no. 82: *la-bú-ʾu/la-bú-ʾú*)⁸⁴ and the Amarna texts: EA 53:35, 57; EA 54:27, 32 (URU.*la-bá-na*).⁸⁵ Lebo-Hamath occurs eleven times in the Old Testament.⁸⁶ It is mentioned in Neo-Assyrian sources.⁸⁷ Tiglath-pileser III listed it immediately after a summation of the cities of Hamath.⁸⁸ Thus, it appears in his list as belonging at that time to Damascus,⁸⁹ though obviously it was a border town between the two polities.

---

79. North, "Phoenicia-Canaan Frontier LᵉBÔ of Hama," 99.

80. Hutchens follows North ("Phoenicia-Canaan Frontier LᵉBÔ of Hama") and Lemche (*The Canaanites and Their Land*) and attempts to add a cult interpretation. See Kenneth D. Hutchens, "Defining the Boundaries: A Cultic Interpretation of Numbers 34:1–12 and Ezekiel 47:13–48:1, 28," in *History and Interpretation: Essays in Honour of John H. Hayes*, edited by M. Patrick Graham, William P. Brown, and Jeffrey K. Kuan (Sheffield: JSOT Press, 1993) 215–30. This fails, in part, because he does not really look closely at the cuneiform evidence and too easily follows these scholars' arguments without consulting scholars like Naʾaman, *Borders and Districts in Biblical Historiography*.

81. Parpola and Porter rate the identification as certain. See Simo Parpola and Michael Porter, *The Helsinki Atlas of the Near East in the Neo-Assyrian Period* (Helsinki: The Casco Bay Assyriological Institute and the Neo-Assyrian Text Corpus Project, 2001) 12. For discussion of the evidence, see Wolfgang Röllig, "Labaʾum," *RlA* 7 (1980–83) 410.

82. Interestingly, the Old Greek appears to understand it this way in a few instances (see Judg 3:3 *lbwʾ ḥmt* = *eōs Lobōēmath*).

83. Some scholars (Noth, *Numbers*, 250; North, "Phoenicia-Canaan Frontier LᵉBÔ of Hama") have argued that Lebwe was too far south of Hamath (130 km) to be under its control. However, since the kingdom of Hamath stretched this far to the north (Hatarikka, modern Tell Afis) there is no difficulty.

84. Rainey, *The Sacred Bridge*, 72–73. Also, in Amenhotep II (Urk. IV, 1304:5) and Ramesses II (Qadesh Inscription). Possibly earlier in the Execration Texts (no. 31) written *lú-u-b-ya*, see G. Posener, *Princes et pays d'Asie et de Nubie. Textes hiératiques sur des figurines d'envoûtement du moyen empire* (Brussels: Fondation égyptologique reine Élisabeth, 1940) 80.

85. See Younger, *A Political History of the Arameans*, 444; Gunnar Lehmann, *Bibliographie der archäologischen Fundstellen und Surveys in Syrien und Libanon*, Orient-Archäologie 9 (Rahden/Westf.: Leidorf, 2002) 316.

86. Written: *lbʾ ḥmt/lbwʾ ḥmt*. See Num 13:21; 34:8; Josh 13:5; Judg 3:3; 1 Kgs 8:65; 2 Kgs 14:25; 1 Chr 13:5; 2 Chr 7:8; Ezek 47:20; 48:1; and Amos 6:14.

87. A. M. Bagg, *Die Levante*, Part 1 of *Die Orts und Gewässernamen der neuassyrischen Zeit*, RGTC 7.1, BTAVO B/7 (Wiesbaden: Reichert, 2007) 151.

88. RINAP 1: 108–10, Text 43, ii.25.

89. Hayim Tadmor, *The Inscriptions of Tiglath-Pileser III King of Assyria* (Jerusalem: Israel Academy of Sciences and Humanities, 1994) 149.

Zedad (*Ṣedad*) can be identified with the modern town of Ṣadad, east of the Anti-Lebanon (56 km / 35 mi east of Lebwe). In this case, the ancient name is preserved in the modern name and the location matches the textual description (i.e., it is east of Lebo-Hamath).[90] Thus, with these two identifications, there can be little doubt that the border was in this zone.

The exact location on the coastline where the border began is more difficult. Mount Hor (written twice as *hōr hāhār*) is clearly "a sacred peak like the Mount Hor in the Negeb."[91] There are three different suggested identifications for Mount Hor: (1) Jebel ʿAkkar (7,270 ft / 2,216 m) east of Tripoli (2) Jebel Makmel (10,128 ft / 3,087 m) a little south of Jebel ʿAkkar; and (3) Ras Shaqqah (1,597 ft / 487 m) a summit not too far north of Byblos.

Rainey, who favors Ras Shaqqah, argues against the first two identifications because "these ridges are far from the coast."[92] However, the wording of Num 34:7b ("from the Great Sea you shall delineate (*tʾh*) for yourself Mount Hor") does not necessitate a location right by the sea, because verse 8a ("from Mount Hor you shall delineate (*tʾh*) Lebo-Hamath") using the same verb and syntax, does not necessitate Lebo-Hamath being located right beside Mount Hor (to which, with any of the suggested identifications, it is not near).

In Ezekiel 47:15 and 48:1, Mount Hor is not mentioned. Instead, one encounters: "(the) way of Hethlon" (*hadderek ḥetlōn*). Some scholars have suggested that Hethlon should be identified with Ḥeitela,[93] 23 miles northeast of Tripolis (2.5 mi / 4 km south of Nahr el-Kabir). This town is only 12 mi / 20 km north of Mount ʿAkkar (more or less at the foot of this mountain). Thus, Ezekiel's "the way of Hethlon" might be a reference to the "Eleutheros road," an important route along the Nahr el-Kabir used by the Egyptian army of Ramesses II, among many others.

Joshua 13:4 indicates that the region called "the land that remains" included the territory of Byblos and that it extended "to Aphek(ah) to the Amorite border," i.e. the kingdom of Amurru in northern Lebanon. It states:

> all the land of the Canaanite (i.e. Canaan),
>
> and from ʿArah,[94] which belongs to the Sidonians,

---

90. Karl Elliger, "Die Nordgrenze des Reiches Davids," *PJ* 32 (1936) 34–73.

91. Aharoni, *The Land of the Bible*, 73. This Mount Hor, however, should be differentiated from the toponym with the same name where Aaron died (Num 20:22–29).

92. Rainey, *The Sacred Bridge*, 35. So too Aharoni, *The Land of the Bible*, 71, map 4. It was the hallowed *Theouprosopon* located between Byblos and Tripolis.

93. Dussaud, *Topographie historique de la Syrie antique*, 17, 47; Abel, *Géographie de la Palestine*, 1:302–3; Naʾaman, *Borders and Districts in Biblical Historiography*, 54; "The Canaanites and Their Land," 410; Barry J. Beitzel, *The Moody Atlas of the Bible* (Chicago: Moody Publishers, 2009) 26.

94. Hess, *Joshua*, 231, n1 states: "This interpretation (*mēʿārâ*) best explains developments to the

to Aphek(ah) (*'pqh*),

to the territory/border (*gbwl*) of the Amorite (i.e. Amurru).

This could be understood as meaning (1) "to Aphek(ah) (that is) to the border of Amurru" (i.e., two termini that are virtually the same) or as (2) "to Aphek(ah) (and on) to the border of Amurru" (i.e., two termini that are on the same directional line). If the former, then Aphek(ah) would be on the border with Amurru; if the latter, then Aphek(ah) is a terminus, but the final terminus is the border with Amurru. Beitzel[95] argues that the border likely followed a natural, ancient boundary like the Nahr el-Kabir, which runs through the Homs/Akkar Gap, emptying into the Mediterranean Sea just south of Tell Kāzil (ancient Ṣumur).[96] This natural boundary is the border between modern Syria and Lebanon and was "approximate to an established boundary during several periods in antiquity."[97] Na'aman has long advocated that the border passed along the Nahr el-Kabir.[98]

Both Rainey[99] and Aharoni[100] understood the border to run from Mt. Hor (Ras Shaqqah) to Ammiya (modern ʿAmyūn, east of Byblos) to Apheka to Lebo-Hamath (Lebwe). This is approximately 55 km south of the Nahr el-Kabir (see Map 1). However, the line from Aphek(ah) to Lebo-Hamath does not have a good pass through the Lebanon range. The better passes are either north to modern Hermel or south to Baalbek.

On the other hand, if Mount Hor is identified with Mount ʿAkkar and Hethlon with Ḥeitela, the two toponyms would be approximate to one another. The natural boundary would run the border along the Nahr el-Kabir and then curve around the Lebanon range at Mount ʿAkkar and run along the edge of the range to the area of Lebo-Hamath (Lebwe).

Some scholars equate Berothah (*bērôtāh*) with Berotay (*bērōtay*, 2 Sam 8:8).[101] It is often identified with Bereitan, 12 km south of Baalbek. However, this location is impossible in the context of the northern border (Baalbek is south of Lebwe; so,

---

MT's 'cave' (*meʿārâ*) and to the LXX's 'from Gaza' (*mēʿazzâ*)." See D. Barthélemy, *Josué, Juges, Ruth, Samuel, Rois, Chroniques, Esdras, Néhémie, Esther*, vol. 1 of *Critique textuelle de l'Ancien Testament*, OBO 50.1 (Fribourg: Universitätsverlag; Göttingen: Vandenhoeck & Ruprecht, 1982) 27–28; Na'aman, *Borders and Districts in Biblical Historiography*, 52 n23."

95. Beitzel, *The Moody Atlas of the Bible*, 26.
96. The "Zemarites" (*Ṣumur*) of the Bible (Gen 10:18).
97. Beitzel, *The Moody Atlas of the Bible*, 26.
98. Na'aman, *Borders and Districts in Biblical Historiography*, 54; "The Canaanites and Their Land," 410. See earlier Guy Kestemont, "Le Nahr el-Kebir et le pays d'Amurru," *Berytus* 20 (1971) 47–55.
99. Rainey, "Who is a Canaanite?" 2, fig. 1.
100. Aharoni, *The Land of the Bible*, 71, map 4.
101. Aharoni, *The Land of the Bible*, 73.

this would be considerably south of Lebwe, i.e., Lebo-Hamath). It has also been identified with the northern Transjordan site of Bereiten, which is out of the question due to its place in the list. Therefore, it seems that Berothah must have been a place on the border between Damascus and Hamath, in between Zedad (*Ṣedād*) and Ziphron/Sibraim.

The toponym Ziphron (*Ziprōn*) in Num 34:9 is only mentioned in this passage and is unidentified.[102] Ezekiel 47:16 has the toponym Sibraim,[103] which may be the same place: *zprn* compared with *sbrym/n*.[104] Aharoni suggested identifying it with the desert oasis of Ḥawwarin.[105]

A number of scholars have identified Hazar-Enan with the desert oasis of Qayatein (60 miles east of Lebo of Hamath, and about seventy miles northeast of Damascus).[106]

Misrephoth-maim is commonly identified with Khirbet el-Musheirifeh (just north of Rosh ha-Niqra).[107] However, this is problematic since excavations demonstrate no remains from the Late Bronze Age or early Iron Age.[108] Aharoni suggested possibly that Mishrephoth-maim is the Litani River (whose name is not mentioned in the Bible).[109] Na'aman rightly notes that the issue is the direction of the geographic descriptors: an east-west orientation or a north-south orientation; and that the best interpretation is a north-south one.[110] Thus, he concludes that "Misrephoth-maim must be located somewhere on the Litani river, on the (missing) northern border of Naphtali's inheritance." He tentatively suggests that the place might be identified with modern Serifah, approximately two km south of the river, 17 km west of Tyre.

Assessment of Table 3

The repetition of Hazar-enan in Numbers 34:10 clearly indicates that the border of the future renewed land of Israel would turn south on this point. However, "The eastern border until it reaches the eastern slopes of the sea of Galilee (the shoulder

---

102. Baruch A. Levine, *Numbers 21–36. A New Translation with Introduction and Commentary*, AB 4a (New York: Doubleday, 2000) 535.

103. Sibraim is taken by some scholars to mean Sepharvaim in Syria (2 Kgs 17:24, 31; 18:34; 19:13).

104. The change from *z* (alveolar, voiced sibilant) to *s* (alveolar, voiceless sibilant) is entirely possible. The interchange of *p/b* is widely attested. The Old Greek, however, reads *Dephrōna*, which would indicate *ḏ* (an interdental, voiced spirant).

105. Aharoni, *The Land of the Bible*, 73.

106. Aharoni, *The Land of the Bible*, 73.

107. Robert G. Boling, *Joshua*, AB 6 (Garden City, NY: Doubleday, 1982) 308.

108. Aharoni, *The Land of the Bible*, 238.

109. Aharoni, *The Land of the Bible*, 238; 281, n. 146.

110. Na'aman, *Borders and Districts in Biblical Historiography*, 48–50.

of the sea of Chinnerth) is quite problematic."¹¹¹ The next three places listed in Num 34:10–11 (Shepham, the Riblah/Arbela [Heb. *hāriblāh* / Gk. *Arbēla*], and Ain) cannot be located.

The second toponym should not be identified with the important historical site, Riblah on the Orontes River in the territory of Hamath.¹¹² In the first place, that toponym is always written Riblāh without the definite article.¹¹³ Here, in Ezekiel it is written with the article *hā-riblāh*. Second, and, more important to the point, is that toponym is completely out of the way and cannot serve as a descriptor of the eastern border. The famous site of Riblah is some distance north of Lebo-Hamath (ca. 60 km) and northwest of Zedad (ca. 55 km). Although it is possible that the text is corrupt at this point, it is more likely that this is a different toponym. Some manuscripts of the Samaritan Pentateuch in Numbers read *h'rblh*, and the Old Greek has *Arbēla*.¹¹⁴ Therefore, this must be a place on the desert fringe south of Hazer-enan (Qayatein).

Yigal Levin has recently suggested that the appearance of Riblah in the list in Num 34 indicates that the passage must date to the time of Josiah and Pharaoh Necho II due to the role that city plays historically in that period.¹¹⁵ But beside the

111. Gordon J. Wenham, *Numbers. An Introduction and Commentary*, TOTC 5 (Leicester and Downers Grove, IL: InterVarsity, 1981) 232.

112. Levine, *Numbers*, 535; Aharoni, *The Land of the Bible*, 73; HALOT, 1179–80, s.v. רִבְלָה. This important toponym is mentioned in 2 Kgs 23:33–34; 25:21; Jer 39:5; 52:9, 27. Perhaps corresponding to Eg. *šá-b-tu-na*. See Wolfgang Helck, *Die Beziehungen Ägyptens und Vorderasiens zur Ägäis bis ins 7. Jh. v. Chr.* 2nd edition, Erträge der Forschung 120 (Darmstadt: Wissenschaftliche Buchgesellschaft, 1979) 200.

113. Gray, *Numbers*, 461; HALOT, 1179–80.

114. Could this be understood as *hr bl'/h* (Mount Bēla)?

115. Levin states, "The only known period in which Riblah achieved any kind of prominence was during the brief period from 609 to 586 BCE, as the northern administrative center of the first Egyptian and then Babylonian controlled Levant, under Necho II and Nebuchadrezzar." See Yigal Levin, "Numbers 34:2–12, The Boundaries of the Land of Canaan, and the Empire of Necho," *JANESCU* 30 (2006) 55–76; Yigal Levin, "The Three Biblical Maps of Israel: Small, Medium, and Large," (2019) http://thetorah.com/three-biblical-maps-of-israel-small-medium-and-large/.

But Levin's statement regarding Riblah is not accurate. In a Neo-Assyrian letter from the time of Tiglath-pileser III, Riblah is mentioned as an important place tied to Hamath (Eni-el, king of Hamath, 738–732[?] is mentioned in the letter). The city must have been in existence for some time prior to its mention by Tiglath-pileser's chief eunuch. Moreover, there is no necessity for Riblah to be an administrative center. None of the other sites mentioned in the description in Num 34 is an administrative center during the Egyptian or Babylonian periods, or any other periods for that matter.

Levin also argues that the presence of Kadesh in the list also added evidence for this date because Kadesh-barnea is not known from either literary sources or from archaeological evidence in the Late Bronze or the Early Iron Ages, and therefore its inclusion in the boundary description cannot date from those periods. However, this is an unreasonable demand. Qadesh was an ancient campsite used by nomadic groups for millennia. I see no reason why a place of this sort needs to have a permanent dwelling occupation in order to be a known entity for a border description. There are many nomadic campsites with names that play into the geography of the ancient Near East. It was a well-known oasis campsite that at a later time had a fortification (Iron II-Persian period). But it was not necessary for such a place to have a fortification in order to have a name and be known. It lies in a natural boundary

K. Lawson Younger, Jr.   "Early" Ideologies of the Land in the Hebrew Bible

fact that this is a very narrow time window (609–605 BC) this city is not the toponym in view in Num 34.

The text of Ezekiel describes the future eastern border running between Hauran and Damascus. This line is impossible to delineate accurately without the firm identification of some of these listed toponyms. The border is described as reaching the eastern side (*ketep* "shoulder") of the Sea of Galilee (Kinneret) possibly running along the Yarmuk River. From this point, it runs southward along the Jordan River "between Gilead and the land of Israel"[116] to the Dead Sea. As has been noted by all scholars, the territories of the tribes of Reuben, Gad and Manasseh (the Transjordan) are not included in this future "land of Israel."[117] While one should be cautious about drawing conclusions about the land of Canaan based on the passage in Ezekiel, there is no evidence that the land of "Canaan" ever included the Transjordan region. Moreover, this is clearly asserted by the text of Num 34. That the Jordan is the border is also seen in Num 13:29 where the spies report on the land: "The Amalekites are dwelling in the land of the Negev; the Hittites, the Jebusites, and the Amorites are dwelling in the hill country; and the Canaanites are dwelling by the sea, and along the Jordan." Levin notes: "what is important to us here is that the sea-coast and the Jordan seem to serve as the outer limits of the Land, while the Negeb and the hills serve as its interior."[118]

It is clear that Num 34 is "a real geographical concept that originally goes back to the Late Bronze Age and probably earlier; it is not the invention of some Judaean scribe, regardless of the date of the passage."[119]

---

slot.

116. It is sometimes stated that Ezekiel used the Assyrian-Babylonian provinces of his day, describing the border in two separate sections: between Hauran and Damascus; and between Gilead and Israel (i.e. Samarina). However, Gilead was not a province.

117. Na'aman ("The Canaanites and Their Land," 411) states: "As for the location of the tribe of Dan on Canaan's northern border (Ezek 48:1) it was observed long ago that the disposition of the tribes in Ezek 48:1–8 is entirely different from that of the system of the twelve tribes. See the maps in Walter Zimmerli, *Ezekiel. A Commentary on the Book of the Prophet Ezekiel*, 2 vols. Hermeneia (Philadelphia: Fortress Press, 1983) 2: 537;

Zecharia Kallai, "The Reality of the Land and the Bible," in *Das Land Israel in biblischer Zeit: Jerusalem-Symposium 1981 der Hebräischen Universität und der Georg-August-Universität*, edited by G. Strecker (Göttingen: Vandenhoeck & Ruprecht, 1983) 76–90, esp. 77. The tribes in Ezekiel's vision are arranged in a schematic north-south row in the area west of the Jordan, and the tribe of Dan is the northernmost in this schematic tribal 'map.' Lemche's claim (*The Canaanites and Their Land*, 81) that "the Danite tribal territory hardly ever included the whole of southern Syria" is historically correct but is irrelevant in reference to Ezek 48:1.

118. Yigal Levin, "The Jordan River in Biblical Geography: From Boundary to Allegory," *Aram* 29 (2017) 221–34, esp. 224.

119. Rainey, "Who is a Canaanite?" 12. He points out two additional factors: (1) All the towns listed in the anti-Egyptian coalition against Thutmose III who were defeated at the battle of Megiddo derive from south of the Num 34 northern border description, except for Qidsu (Qadesh) whose

61

Canaan = Phoenicia

A later development brought about a shift from the original provincial territory to a more limited area, so that "Canaan" became equated with the region termed in classical contexts as Phoenicia. This was the result of the restricting of the "Canaanite" inhabitants to those parts of Canaan that had not been subjugated, i.e., Phoenicia.[120] This is most clearly seen in Isaiah 23:11. Through a neologism, "Canaan" and "Canaanite" became a synonym for "merchant" or "trader" because trade, particularly maritime trade, was the economic engine of the Phoenician coast (Isa 23:8; Hos 12:8 [Eng. 7]; Zeph 1:11; Zech 11:7 [OG: *Chanaanitin*], 11 [OG: *Chananaioi*. Either from this or as a separate development, "Sidonian" functioned as a descriptor of "Canaanite" (Deut 3:9; Judg 18:7; 1 Kgs 11:5, 33; 2 Kgs 23:13).

Conclusion

In sum, the evidence is very extensive and informative yielding the following points. (1) It provides the earliest attestation of "Canaanites" (ca. 1775 BC)—contemporaneous with the biblical patriarchal period; (2) it demonstrates that there was an actual Egyptian province of Canaan with clear borders; (3) it indicates what cities were in Canaan and what areas were not in it: Palestine and Lebanon were part of Canaan; central Syria, north of Lebo-Hamath (including cities like Ugarit and Alalaḫ) was not in Canaan.[121] (4) it shows that the Pharaoh was considered "the lord of the land of Canaan" who was responsible for everything that happens within its confines; and (5) it gives evidence that there was a "storm-god of Canaan," to whom jurisdiction over this land could be ascribed. However, in contrast, the biblical writers ascribe rule and jurisdiction to Yahweh, not Pharaoh or the storm-god.

---

prince led the coalition. (2) There is a clear distinction in dialects between the southern and northern Levant regions as seen in the Amarna tablets. The southern region contains West Semitized jargon absent in the northern texts which are in the Hurro-Akkadian dialect of northern Syria. He concludes: "It can hardly be coincidental that this dialectical situation conforms to the division of the Levant into northern and southern areas as divided by the border in Num 34:7–11" (Rainey, "Who is a Canaanite?" 11–12). That the southern part is designated as Canaan by biblical tradition conforms to the cuneiform evidence (see Rainey, "Who is a Canaanite?" 1–11).

120. de Vaux, "Le pays de Canaan," 30; Na'aman, "The Canaanites and Their Land," 399.

121. Hess states: "Like the scribes of Alalakh and Ugarit, the writers of the Bible perceive the identity of their own people to be distinct from that of the Canaanites (Genesis 24:3, 37; 28:1, 6, 8). However, unlike Alalakh and Ugarit, the land of Canaan was identical to that given by Israel's God to his people (Genesis 10:15–19; 33:18; Numbers 13:17–29; 32: 33:5; 35:10, 14; Deuteronomy 1:7; 11:30; 32:49; Judges 14:1)." Hess, "Occurrences of 'Canaan' in Late Bronze Age Archives," 370. See also Na'aman, "Four Notes," 36.

The Land Ideologies of the Book of Joshua

It is well-known that the issue of land and territory dominate the book of Joshua.[122] It contains 358 place names out of the total of 746 toponyms mentioned in the Hebrew Bible. Of these, 198 occur only in Joshua.[123] Much of this material is contained in border descriptions and town lists. Scholars have tended to interpret all the land issues in Joshua along a couple of different lines.

First, many scholars attempt to understand the border descriptions and town lists in terms of an actual real historical context. Thus, when do these texts date historically to a reality on the ground? In this approach, the scholar's work becomes essentially discerning what is the most compelling actual historical contexts out of which these texts would have been produced (e.g., the period of the Davidic kingdom, the period of Josiah, the exile, etc.).

Second, some scholars feel that if the texts do not reflect a reality that can be firmly attributed to a particular historical time, then they must be simply and only idealistic, imaginary visions of ancient scribes.[124] However, things are a bit more complicated than this.

I have suggested that one of the impositional structures in the book of Joshua is "ideology."[125] There are numerous ideologies of the land in the Hebrew Bible. Norman Habel highlighted six of these.[126] This is by no means all of the different ideological views of land in the Old Testament. Not all of Habel's ideologies occur in the book of Joshua; yet there are others that he did not develop. The book of Joshua utilizes at least seven different "land" ideologies (whether anchored in concrete reality or purely idealistic or a mixture). Often, readers of the book of Joshua skip over some of these and concentrate on one particular ideological view. However, these "mental maps" conceptualize the land, producing tensions within the narration for any careful reader. In my opinion, they set the stage for irony. These different views are not mutually exclusive. The first two are tied, more or less, to reality; the second two are not tied to any ancient reality, but are idealistic. The fifth view is a theocratic

---

122. Douglas A. Knight, "Joshua 22 and the Ideology of Space," in *"Imagining" Biblical Worlds: Studies in Spatial, Social and Historical Constructs in Honor of James W. Flanagan*, edited by D. M. Gunn and P. M. McNutt, JSOTSup 359 (Sheffield: Sheffield Academic Press, 2002) 51–63, esp. 59.

123. Shmuel Aḥituv, *Joshua: Introduction and Commentary*, Mikra Leyisra'el, in Hebrew (Jerusalem: Magnes, 1995) 218–324.

124. Thus, for example, it is common to see Num 34:1–12 and Ezek 47:13–48:35 as reflections of the same historical context. Yet, within the literary contexts of each, they are functioning quite differently.

125. K. Lawson Younger, Jr., "Joshua," in *Eerdmans Commentary on the Bible*, edited by J. D. G. Dunn and J. W. Rogerson (Grand Rapids: Eerdmans, 2003) 174–89, esp. 174–75.

126. Habel, *The Land is Mine*, 17–133.

ideology that understands the land as a conditional grant based on a treaty.[127] Here, there is a reality, but that reality could change. The sixth view is a tribal ancestral ideology, an ideology of the *naḥᵃlāh*. The seventh is encountered in the conquest narratives, namely an "imperialistic ideology." An eighth ideology will also be touched on. It does not occur in the book of Joshua; but needs to be mentioned.

The "land of Canaan" is the starting point, grounded in historical reality. Prior to Israel's conquest, it is depicted in the biblical texts as a conglomeration or hodgepodge of royal lands ("these kings and their lands" [Josh 12:1]) which, in fact, is quite the reality of Canaan of the envisioned period that was, nevertheless, a delimited geo-political entity (i.e., "the king of Egypt's land" with these kings being his servants/vassals).

However, the real owner of the land according to the Scriptures, because he is the Creator of heaven and earth, is Yahweh. Thus, these monarchs were ruling the city-polities in Yahweh's land. Due to their wickedness, it is he who defeats and dispossesses these kings and their populations. Yahweh fights for Israel as the divine warrior.

There is also, of course, a "tribal" ideology in the book of Joshua. In the first instance, the intended audience of the book is expected to know ancient Israelite—for that matter, Semitic—tribal structures. This is true in the role of Joshua, the stories of Rahab, Achan, and Caleb, in the allotments, etc. Thus, the different tribal structural levels and leadership positions are mentioned again and again throughout the book, which pass right by most modern readers. This is the basis for the sixth ideology of the land outlined below.

In what follows, I will introduce each separate ideology and make some comments on each. These will be sketched out in broad strokes. A full discussion of each one is beyond the limitations here.

1. The ideology of land, that predominates the book of Joshua, sees the true land of inheritance as the land west of the Jordan (Cisjordan, i.e., the land of "Canaan") (cf. Deut 12:10). This view is based on the reality of the geo-political entity "Canaan."[128] It considers the Jordan river as the land's eastern border. It is certainly this image that lies behind the belief that crossing the Jordan was a step of outstanding

---

127. Habel, *The Land is Mine*, 36–53.

128. Weinfeld asserts that envisioning "the Land" as Cisjordan (i.e., Canaan) is a pre-Deuteronomic view. See Moshe Weinfeld, "The Extent of the Promised Land—The Status of Transjordan," in *Das Land Israel in biblischer Zeit: Jerusalem–Symposium 1981 der Hebräischen Universität und der Georg-August-Universität*, edited by G. Strecker (Göttingen: Vandenhoeck & Ruprecht, 1983) 59–75; Moshe Weinfeld, *The Promise of the Land. The Inheritance of the Land of Canaan by the Israelites*, The Taubman Lectures in Jewish Studies 3 (Berkeley: University of California Press, 1993) 35–40.

significance—it takes a miracle to cross the river at flood stage (Josh 3–4).[129] This view also creates ironic tensions in Josh 22:10-34. Moreover, it is tied to the third view (below). This view of the land understands it as a gift of the national and personal deity, Yahweh, to his people.

Thus, the tribal allotments of Joshua 14–19 are a vision of this ideology. This is also true of Judges 1. Josh 14–19 envisions the borders of the allotments as they "should be" with implicit indications that reality was different (e.g. Josh 16:10). Judges 1 makes this quite explicit. This text assumes that there are definable allotment borders that can be used to *assess* the success or failure of the individual tribes in possessing their allotments (*yrš* "drive out/possession" and *yšb* "dwell/occupy").[130] Without this assumption, there can be no assessment and that whole passage flops.

2. A contrasting ideology is that of the land belonging to all twelve tribes (both west and east of the Jordan) comprising the land.[131] They are seen as completely "filling up" the land (Josh 13–19; cf. Deut 4:45-49). In this view, the two and a half Transjordanian tribes are an integral and vital part of "all Israel," which includes the land that Moses allotted (Num 32; Josh 13:8-32). Deuteronomy 4:45-49 sums up the possession of the Transjordan:

> (45) These are the decrees and the statutes and ordinances that Moses spoke to the Israelites when they had come out of Egypt, (46) beyond the Jordan in the valley opposite Beth-peor, in the land of King Sihon of the Amorites, who reigned at Heshbon, whom Moses and the Israelites defeated when they came out of Egypt. (47) They occupied his land and the land of King Og of Bashan, the two kings of the Amorites who were on the eastern side of the Jordan. (48) from Aroer, which is on the edge of the Wadi Arnon, as far as Mount Sirion (that is, Hermon) (49) together with all the Arabah on the east side of the Jordan as far as the Sea of the Arabah, under the slopes of Pisgah.

Deuteronomy 34:1-3 is another passage that expresses Ideology 2.

> (1) Then Moses went up from the steppes of Moab to Mount
> Nebo, the top of Pisgah, which is opposite Jericho, and Yahweh showed
> him the whole land:
>
> **Gilead as far as Dan,**
> (2) all Naphtali,

---

129. Richard D. Nelson, *Joshua. A Commentary*, OTL (Louisville: Westminster John Knox, 1997) 2.

130. See K. Lawson Younger, Jr., "The Configuring of Judicial Preliminaries: Judges 1:1–2:5 and its Dependence on the Book of Joshua," *JSOT* 68 (1995) 75-92 (esp. the diagrams at the end of the article).

131. Nelson (*Joshua*, 2) describes this view as "the dominant map." However, in terms of its occurrences in the book of Joshua, it is second behind the view of the land as the Egyptian province, Canaan.

the land of Ephraim and Manasseh,

all the land of Judah as far as the Western Sea,

(3) the Negev,

and the Plain—that is, the valley of Jericho, the city of palm trees—

as far as Zoar.

(4) Yahweh said to him, "This is the land of which I swore to Abraham, to Isaac, and to Jacob, saying, 'I will give it to your descendants'; I have let you see it with your eyes, but you shall not cross over there."

In addition, it is clear that the envisioned systems of "Levitical Cities" (Josh 21:1–42; Num 35:1–8) and "Cities of Refuge" (Josh 20:1–9; Num 35:9–34) included the Transjordanian tribes. These systems are expressions of this ideology. Thus, the Transjordanian tribes are an essential part of the confederated tribal polity of Israel.[132]

Moreover, it is interesting that there are texts that picture the Jordan river, not as a boundary, but as an integral part of the land, with Israel in fact settled on both sides. Some of these texts are concentrated in the Elijah and Elisha stories.[133]

In Ideology 1, the land of the allotments to the two and a half Transjordanian tribes do not count. However, like the first ideology, this Transjordanian territory is also envisioned as a gift from Yahweh, though a separate one from the land of Canaan (Num 32; Josh 13:8–32). Thus, altogether, this mental image sees the entire territory as one. This ideology has connections with the fourth ideology below which envisions the land as larger than "the land of Canaan."

It is quite apparent that tensions arise between Ideologies 1 and 2. How should Israel envision itself? Are those tribes in Cisjordan "real" Israel because they are in the land of Canaan, or is "real" Israel, not only the Cisjordanian tribes, but also the Transjordanian tribes?[134] Joshua 22:19a is quite informative about this tension between the two ideologies:

> But now, if the land of your seizure/possession (*'ḥzt*) is unclean (*ṭm'*) cross over (*'br*) into the land of the possession of Yahweh (*'rṣ 'ḥzt yhwh*) where the "tabernacle" (*mškn*) of Yahweh now "tabernacles (*škn*)," and take (*'ḥz*) for yourselves a possession among us; but against Yahweh do not rebel (*mrd*) or against us do not rebel (*mrd*) by building for yourselves an altar other than the altar of Yahweh our God.

---

132. Levin, "The Jordan River in Biblical Geography," 225. He states: "So while the two and a half tribes' territory is 'outside' the Land, 'across the Jordan,' they themselves are to remain very much a part of the nation of Israel."

133. See Levin, "The Jordan River in Biblical Geography," 231.

134. See David Jobling, "The Jordan a Border: Transjordan in Israel's Ideological Geography," in *The Sense of Biblical Narrative II: Structural Analyses in the Hebrew Bible*, JSOTSup 39 (Sheffield: JSOT Press, 1986) 88–134.

The wording creates a stark contrast between "the land of your possession" (which is *ṭmʾ* "unclean") and the "land of Yahweh's possession" (where the sacred "tabernacle" is!!!).[135] Clearly, the Transjordanians do not live in "the land of Yahweh's possession" in the minds of the Cisjordanians. It is also worth noting the Cisjordanians' wording in Josh 22:16: "Thus says the whole congregation of Yahweh …" By their very wording, "the whole congregation of Yahweh" (*kl ʿdt yhwh*) does not include the Transjordanians! In Josh 22:18, their use of another phrase, "the whole community of Israel" (*kl ʿdt yśrʾl*) to describe the Cisjordanians is further evidence of the ideological perspective that, in ways, does not count Transjordanians as "real Israelites." However, the writer of this passage uses this tension to create irony, for on this occasion, the Transjordanians are faithful to Yahweh and it is the Cisjordanians who have misjudged the spiritual disposition of their fellow Israelites! They have, in fact, revealed their own weakness in thinking that they alone are in the land of Yahweh's possession (*ʾrṣ ʾḥzt yhwh*) since Yahweh, as Creator, has gifted the Transjordan to Israel too.

Throughout the biblical texts, particularly in Deuteronomy and Joshua, the phrase *ʿēber hayyardēn* "across/beyond the Jordan" is used from two different perspectives: mostly speaking of Transjordan, but sometimes of Cisjordan (e.g. Josh 5:1; 9:1; 12:7 [contrast 12:1]; Deut 3:20). It is manifest that the Jordan was a boundary marker. It was the determination point for "outside the Land" and "inside the Land" in a certain way of thinking. When the Israelites crossed the Jordan (Josh 3–4) they were no longer "outside the Land," they are "in the Promised Land."[136]

That historically there were tensions between Cisjordanian and Transjordanian tribal groups is attested in the famous tribal war between Ephraim and the Gileadites led by Jephthah (Judg 12:1–6). However, the situation was more complicated.[137] There were connections between Jabesh-Gilead and Benjamin (Judg 21:8–14; 1 Sam 11:1–11). There were complicated connections between the clan of Machir and its sub-clans on both sides of the Jordan, which is beyond the scope of this essay. The point is: ideology 2 sees the tribes of Cisjordan and Transjordan as one, that is "Israel."

3. The third land ideology found in Joshua views the land claimed but unconquered, "the land that remains," i.e. the territories of the Philistines and Canaanites (13:2–6). It is based on Ideology 1, the reality of the geo-political entity of Canaan's borders. This ideology recognizes the limits of Israelite territory in Cisjordan and

---

135. Labeling the land as "unclean" (*ṭmʾ*) implies a position of being "outside of the camp" in the Wilderness terminology. The implication is that the Transjordanians live in the place of those who are ritually disqualified from the community, like lepers.

136. It is not possible to develop here the observation of Polzin that there are two perspectives in the narration of Josh 3–4 that psychologically tie to inside and outside the land. See Robert Polzin, *Moses and the Deuteronomist. A Literary Study of the Deuteronomistic History. Part One: Deuteronomy, Joshua, Judges* (New York: Seabury, 1980) 91–113. See also Younger, "Joshua," 176–77.

137. The understanding of the words of the Ephraimites in Judg 12:4 is debated.

corresponds to the remainder of the Egyptian province of Canaan when combined with the first view above, yielding the equation:

Borders of Canaan = Borders of Tribal Allotments + Land Remaining
(ANE textual data)   (Josh 15–19)   (Josh 13)

Thus, Ideology 1 has reality limits. While there was the ancient reality of the borders of the land of Canaan, there was a tension created by the reality of what was actually possessed of that entity's territorial extent. There were areas that simply had not been possessed. Thus, a tension persisted between what should have been and what was. Since there is a clear implication that the areas unpossessed should yet be taken, this ideology has an expansionist feel to it. Therefore, in this respect, it has attitudinal connections with the fourth ideology. There are also links here to land ideology 8 (below).

4. A fourth ideology is an expansionistic, utopian "Euphratic Israel," which claims the distant Euphrates River as the northern boundary for Israel's ultimate inheritance (Josh 1:4; Gen 15:18; Deut 1:7; 11:24).[138] Joshua 1:3–5 reads:

> (3) Every place that the sole of your foot will tread upon I have given to you, as I promised to Moses.
>
> (4) From the wilderness and this Lebanon
>
> as far as the great river, the river Euphrates,
>
> [all the land of the Hittites][139]
>
> to the Great Sea in the west shall be your territory.
>
> (5) No one shall be able to stand against you all the days of your life. As I was with Moses, so I will be with you; I will not fail you or forsake you.

Genesis 15:18–21 states:

> (18) On that day, Yahweh made a covenant with Abram, saying, "To your seed/descendants I give this land,
>
> —from (*mn*) the river of Egypt
>
> to (*'d*) the great river, the river Euphrates—
>
> (19) (the land of) the Kenites, and the Kenizzites, and the Kadmonites, (20) and the Hittites, and the Perizzites, and the Rephaim, (21) and the Amorites, and the Canaanites, and the Girgashites, and the Jebusites."

---

138. Nelson, *Joshua*, 2. Two other passages should be mentioned as attestations of this ideological vision: (1) Exod 23:31: "I will set your border from the Sea of Reeds to the Sea of the Philistines and from the wilderness to the river ..." The Old Greek of this verse has "to the great river Euphrates"; (2) 1 Kgs 5:4: "For he had control over all the region west of the River (i.e. the Euphrates) from Tiphsah to Gaza, over all the kings west of the River (Euphrates); and he had peace on all sides."

139. This is likely a later gloss since it is not found in the Old Greek.

From these passages, one can clearly see the expression of this view of the land. Interestingly, in the second passage, there are ten ethnicons listed in verses 19–21. The number ten plays a very significant structuring role in the book of Genesis. The first three in this list were generally located in the Transjordan. The identities of these ethnicons reflect a period later than the time of Abram/Abraham—namely, the period around 1200 BCE. Hence, they are functionally anachronistic.

Deuteronomy 1:7–8 also expresses this Euphratic vision:

> Turn and journey, and enter the hill country of the Amorites and to all of its neighboring regions,
>
> in the Arabah, in the hill country, in the Shephelah, in the Negev, and
>
> in the seacoast
>
> —the land of the Canaanites and the Lebanon—
>
> as far as the great river, the river Euphrates.
>
> (8) See, I have set the land before you; go in and take possession of the land that I swore to your ancestors, to Abraham, to Isaac, and to Jacob, to give to them and to their descendants after them."

Finally, Deuteronomy 11:22–25 combines the Euphratic (Ideology 3) and theocratic (Ideology 5) elements in a seamless fashion under the commandments (of the Torah).

> (22) If you will really keep this entire commandment which I am commanding you to do it —to love Yahweh, your God, by walking in all his ways, and by holding fast to him, (23) then Yahweh will drive out all these nations from before you, and you will dispossess nations larger and mightier than you. (24) Every place wherein the sole of your foot treads shall be yours:
>
> from the wilderness and the Lebanon,
>
> and from the River, the river Euphrates,
>
> and to the Western Sea shall be your territory.
>
> (25) No one will be able to stand against you; Yahweh, your God, will put the fear and dread of you on all the land wherever you tread, as he promised you.

These last two notions (Ideology 3 and Ideology 4) instill the book of Joshua with the flavor of unredeemed promise, and again set the stage for irony. The text develops two understandings of Israel's unfulfilled idealistic expectations. First, "the incomplete conquest is judged to be the result of Israel's disobedience or military inability" (Josh 15:63; 16:10; 17:12–13; 19:47).[140] This is the basis for future threats to Israel's expulsion from the land (Josh 7:12; 23:12–13). Second, these expansionistic

---

140. Nelson, *Joshua*, 2.

land ideologies function as hopeful "prophecies" of future land blessings to Israel (Josh 13:6b; 17:18; 23:5).[141]

5. A theocratic ideology understands the land as a conditional grant of a treaty.[142] This ideology has its grounding in the explicitly expressed treaty in the book of Deuteronomy. The portrayal of Yahweh "promoted in Deuteronomy is that of a universal monarch who controls vast domains, of which Canaan happens to be one" (Deut 4:39; 10:14; 17).[143] This king of the universe chooses a group of slaves in Egypt to be the nation through whom he will demonstrate his rule to the peoples of the earth (Deut 7:6; 10:14–15). Thus, with respect to the land, Habel rightly observes:

> Within the ideological framework of YHWH's claim to absolute dominion, the land of Canaan is relentlessly promoted as a gift or grant. In theological terms, this concept is usually interpreted as an expression of unequivocal divine grace. In social and political terms, however, the continuous reminder that the Israelites who invaded the land have not earned the land is designed to create a sense of total indebtedness and dependency on YHWH as the universal ruler and land-giver. Canaan is YHWH's land grant to Israel.[144]

Deuteronomy makes it clear that it is Yahweh, the universal monarch, who is giving this land to Abraham, Isaac, and Jacob and to their descendants (Deut 6:10, 18; 7:13; 8:1; 10:22; 11:9). Israel must accept this land grant by driving out and dispossessing (*yāraš*) the land's current inhabitants (Deut. 7:1, 2, 20, 22, 24; 4:38; 9:1, 3, 4; 11:23). Actually, the Lord is the one who accomplishes this (Deut 9:3). "The Israelites cannot claim that they have any right to the land by virtue of their mighty exploits or their righteous ways. On the contrary, they receive the land by default; the wickedness of the original inhabitants demanded their expulsion (9:4–7)."[145] Israel must settle (*yāšab*) in the land (Deut. 11:31; 12:10; 17:14; 26:1; 30:20) and find rest (*nwḥ*) from its enemies (Deut 3:20; 12:9, 10; 25:19). God is the one who grants this rest in the land of Canaan, that is the land grant.

---

141. Ibid. Havrelock ("The Two Maps of Israel's Land," 660) argues that "the Euphrates map" conceives of ancient Israel in Babylonian imperialistic terms, imagining "Israel mirroring Babylonia, with vast stretches of terrain defined by a mighty river that originated with creation (Gen 2:14)." It reflects "the political climate during the Neo-Babylonian period" and "can be explained as a technique introduced by Deuteronomic (Dtr₁) scribes and reproduced in later versions by their successors" (664). Biblical writers took the Babylonian notion of Eber Nari or Transeuphrates and "reformulated it from their own perspective" (665). This explanation seems doubtful. It seems to me that the Euphrates was such a well-known border, even in the Egyptian empire period, that a homegrown Israelite expansionistic ideology is a more likely explanation.

142. Habel, *The Land is Mine*, 36–53.
143. Habel, *The Land is Mine*, 37.
144. Habel, *The Land is Mine*, 39.
145. Habel, *The Land is Mine*, 40.

However, this land grant treaty only gives Israel conditional title to the land of Canaan. "Israel's retention of the allotted territory of Canaan is conditional on keeping the stipulations of the landowner as articulated in the new polity for the land."[146] Israel's possession is based on its keeping of the stipulations of the treaty: no making of idols (4:15–31); no worship of other gods (6:4–5,[147] 14; 7:4; 8:19; 11:16); etc. Disobedience to the Law (the stipulations of the treaty) can ultimately have dire consequences. Yahweh can drive out and dispossess (*yāraš*) Israel, just like he did with the Canaanites (Deut. 4:26, 38; 8:20; 28:63). This can be summed up:

> A divine promise to Israel's ancestors, a divine demonstration of conquering might, and a divine gift of the good land—all confirm Israel's entitlement to the land. This right, however, is conditional. Israel must obey the laws of the proposed polity for the land or face losing the land ... The Israelites have no natural right to the land, only a promise of tenure if they are a faithful vassal people. Canaan is territory under treaty; the land grant is conditional.[148]

In this theocratic ideology, the land grant functions in three different ways in this ideology. First, it reinforces "Israel's indebtedness to Yahweh." Second, it serves as the explicit "charter of Israel's rightful entitlement to the land." Third, it serves "to justify the dispossession of the original inhabitants of the land and negate their rights."[149] Therefore, it is clear that Yahweh is the actual, real owner of the land. It is Yahweh who decides to allot his land to the tribes (Josh 13–19) as a conditional inheritance.[150]

6. The sixth ideology encountered in the book of Joshua is a tribal ancestral ideology. The land is envisioned as "a cluster" of lots, each being a *naḥᵃlāh*, the ancestral

---

146. Habel, *The Land is Mine*, 44.

147. The exclusivity of worship is already implicit in Deut 4:39: "So know (sing.) today and take to heart that Yahweh, he is God in heaven above and on the earth beneath; there is no other."

148. Habel, *The Land is Mine*, 50.

149. Ibid.

150. Weinfeld argued that both the Abrahamic and Davidic covenants were, in fact, ancient Near Eastern royal land grants, which were unconditional by their nature. See Weinfeld, "The Extent of the Promised Land," 59–75; *The Promise of the Land*, 40–42. However, Knoppers has demonstrated through a close study of the historical and literary setting of royal grants that most are actually conditional. See Gary N. Knoppers, "Ancient Near Eastern Royal Grants and the Davidic Covenant: A Parallel?" *JAOS* 116.4 (1996) 670–97. https://doi.org/10.2307/605439. Importantly, he observes: "There may be unconditional language used within the context of a contract, grant, or treaty. Again, the application of such absolute language does not imply that the arrangement is completely one-sided. The very acceptance by one party of a solemn pledge from another party normally entails a degree of involvement in the life of the recipient, his family, or his realm by the other party. Continuing or future loyalty can be assumed or stipulated, even though the basic promise may be unaffected by (dis)loyalty. Hence, even in the most one-sided arrangements (e.g., Ulmi-Tešup; 2 Samuel 7, Psalm 89) there may be an element of reciprocity. The clearly bilateral dimension of such special relationships is but one more illustration of the complexity of covenant within ancient Israel and the ancient Near East" (696).

family estate.¹⁵¹ In this ideology, the divine granting (*ntn*)¹⁵² of the land means the seizure of the royal lands of the various Canaanite polities and their division (*ḥlq*) and redistribution into plots with recognizable borders assigned to the ancestral clans (*mšpḥh*). Thus, on one level, the entire land of Canaan can be identified as a *naḥᵃlāh* "inherited estate" granted by the Lord to the Israelites (e.g. Deut. 4:21; 12:9). This granting of a *naḥᵃlāh* is an entitlement to the property. Joshua 11:23 puts it this way:

> So, Joshua took all the land, just as Yahweh had said to Moses. And Joshua gave (*ntn*) it as an estate (*nḥlh*) to Israel according to their tribal allotments. Then the land had quiet from war.

The allotment is designated a *gōral* (Josh 15:1; 16:1; 17:1; 18:11; 19:1; etc.). This lexeme refers both to the "casting of lots" by which the allotment was divinely determined, and to the allotment or estate itself. Each tribe, clan and ancestral family household received its own *naḥᵃlāh* from the former royal lands. The *gōral* of the individual ancestral families of each tribe is clearly identified as its divine "entitlement," its *naḥᵃlāh* (Josh 14:2).¹⁵³ These entitlements were granted in both Transjordan and Cisjordan (Josh 13–19). Because these are issued by divine lot (i.e. divine decree) there is a sacral justification for the land ownership. In Joshua 18:8–10, the allotment to the seven tribes is grounded in document, "a sacred text of title deeds."¹⁵⁴

Although these allotments were legally recognized, there were two aspects that made them conditional: (1) initiative, based on faith, was required for the initial possession of the *naḥᵃlāh*; and (2) loyalty to the covenant and obedience to the Law was required for the long term possession of the *naḥᵃlāh*.¹⁵⁵ The stories of Caleb, Othniel and Achsah (Josh 14; 15:13–19) illustrate the former. Caleb, in particular, stands out as a paradigm of one taking the initiative to gain his *naḥᵃlāh*. Ironically, this non-Israelite (Kenizzite),¹⁵⁶ who is blessed (*brk*) by Joshua, and who obtains his entitlement as promised by Moses, serves as both an example and an indictment for the other Israelites.¹⁵⁷ In the case of the latter, (2) above, the warning of Joshua to the

---

151. Habel, *The Land is Mine*, 57.

152. For discussions of the legal connotation of *ntn*, see Harry M. Orlinsky, "The Biblical Concept of the Land of Israel: Cornerstone of the Covenant between God and Israel," in *The Land of Israel: Jewish Perspectives*, ed. L. A. Hoffman (South Bend, IN: University of Notre Dame Press, 1986) 27–64; Raymond Westbrook, *Property and Family in Biblical Law* (Sheffield: Sheffield Academic Press, 1991) 85–88.

153. Habel (*The Land is Mine*, 33–35) argues in an extended excursus that *naḥᵃlāh* carries the connotation of "entitlement."

154. Habel, *The Land is Mine*, 58.

155. In this regard, the Phoenician Cebelires Daği Inscription is an interesting text with its land grant (*grl*) and dispossession connected to the *šph*. See COS 3: 137–39.

156. Ironically, one of the people groups listed in Gen 15:18–21.

157. "The message of Caleb's example seems to be that if a committed non-Israelite can claim his

people (Josh 24:19–20) is an illustration. The Lord does not tolerate the worship of other deities. In his land, he demands utter loyalty to him from his people. Failure can result in exile (Josh 23:13).

7. There is an additional ideology utilized in the book of Joshua, especially in the conquest narratives. This is an "imperialistic ideology."[158] Areas of similarity of this ideology with its ancient Near Eastern counterpart can be seen in numerous ways: in a similar view of the enemy, in the calculated terror, in the high use of hyperbole, in a jural aspect, and in the use of stereotyped syntagms to transmit the high-redundance message of the ideology.

8. The Limited land. "From Dan to Beersheba."[159] The reality reflected in the statements about failures in the tribal allotments reflect this conceptional notion. It also reflects the situation at some point after the migration of the tribe of Dan (to Laish, Judg 18). This reflects the later settlement reality and thus is interestingly not found in the book of Joshua. It is encountered in Judges 20:1:

> Then all the Israelites came out, and the congregation assembled in one body from Dan to Beer-sheba, and (i.e. including) the land of Gilead, before Yahweh at Mizpah.

Conclusion

While one can, in ways, isolate these different ideologies within the text of Joshua, it would be a mistake to see them as mutually exclusive and utterly contradictory. Another one of the impositional structures in the book is the role of the Law (the Torah). There is a great stress on full obedience to the Torah, with dire warnings throughout of the consequences of disobedience. It is the Torah that is able to integrate these different ideologies. But this does not require a systematic integration within the book itself.

In my thinking, the author of the book of Joshua is, in many instances, drawing on these different ideologies in order to serve his literary goals in the construction of irony. These structures of irony, in turn, build the theological message of the book that is intended for God's people.

Obviously, this far-from-perfect analysis of the ideologies encountered in the text of Joshua does not have the final say. The remainder of the Hebrew Bible, and for

---

heritage as an inalienable entitlement promised by Moses, surely the ancestral families of Israel could do the same" (Habel, *The Land is Mine*, 64).

158. Younger, *Ancient Conquest Accounts*, 232–37; 253–60.
159. Levin's middle size ("The Three Biblical Maps of Israel").

Christians the New Testament, adds significant additional ideologies regarding "the Land," and develops the idea of "rest."

Map 1: Canaan – Northern and Eastern Borders

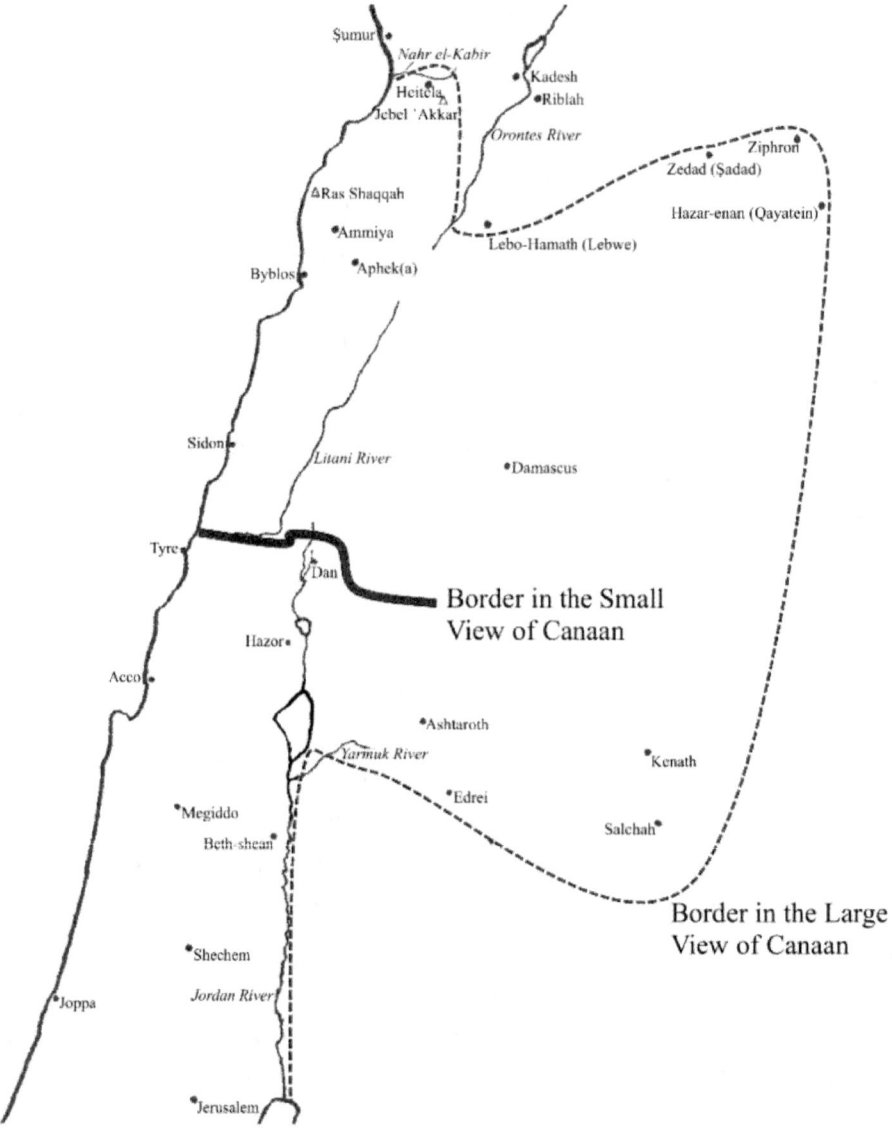

MAP 2: EZEKIEL'S VISION

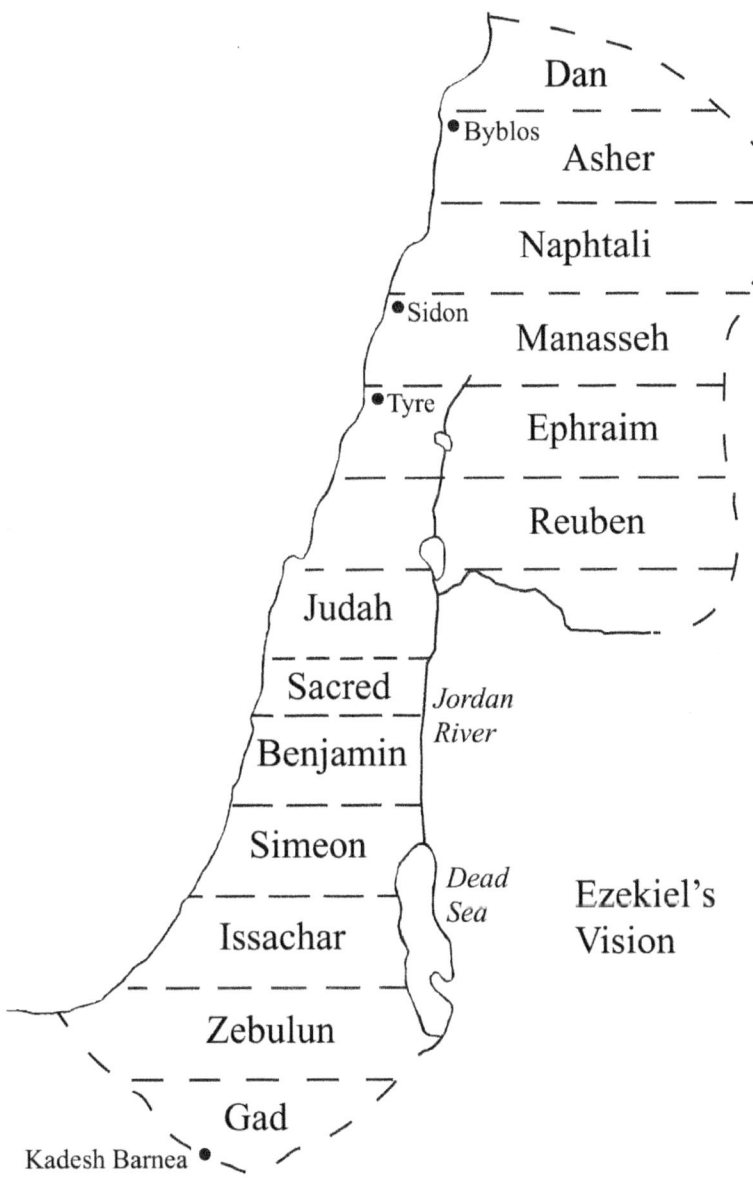

RESPONSE TO YOUNGER

J. Nathan Clayton

Having studied in the past with Lawson Younger at Trinity Evangelical Divinity School as both a masters and a doctoral student, it is a joy for me to have the opportunity to respond to his paper on the land ideologies of the Hebrew Bible, especially as they are developed in the biblical book of Joshua. I will present my response in three steps: (1) I will give a brief summary of what I perceive to be some key highlights from Younger's paper, (2) I will emphasize a couple of areas that I found particularly helpful, and (3) I will conclude with a few questions for further reflection.

First, I will present some key points that stand out to me in this essay. Younger proposes to investigate the ideologies of the land mainly found in the book of Joshua. From the outset in his introduction, he provides what he calls a "neutral" definition of ideology: "a schematic image of social order, a pattern of beliefs and concepts both factual and normative, which purport to explain complex social phenomena in which there may be simplification by means of symbolic figurative language, code shifting and/or overloading." In the ancient Near East, such ideologies were invariably connected to the *divine*, often communicated by means of ethnicons (the names of tribes, ethnic groups, peoples etc.). When it comes to *land* ideologies specifically, nuances may be found between the notions of "border" (more clearly defined) and "frontier" (less clearly defined). Younger concludes his introduction by arguing that hence there is a need to "pay attention to the multiple derivation points or the multiple *termini ad quem* in ancient texts in order to understand what the text is saying." Younger then develops his detailed exploration of land ideologies in two major movements: first, he focuses on the terms "Canaan" and "Canaanites" in historical and geographical contexts, and second, he argues that seven distinct land ideologies exist in the canonical form of the book of Joshua.

In the first major section, "The Land of Canaan," Younger notes that the defining of the land of Canaan is a "fundamental ideological issue in the biblical texts" and he then proceeds to investigate the identity of the land of Canaan from a selection of second millennium BCE texts: cuneiform sources, Egyptian sources, and, related biblical texts. For example, the earliest mention of the ethnicon "Canaanites" comes from one of the Mari letters in the 18th century BCE and the earliest mention of the phrase "the land of Canaan" comes from the inscription of Idrimi of Alalakh from the 15th century BCE. Both of these early written sources help support the notion that "Canaan/Canaanites" were a known reality at least by the early 2nd millennium BCE. Other cuneiform sources reveal that the term "Canaanite" could be used either in a more narrow ethnic sense, or in a broader geographical sense denoting general aboriginal inhabitants of the southern Levant. Egyptian sources from the New Kingdom period, roughly parallel to the late Bronze Age and early Iron Age I in the Levant, also show awareness of the land of Canaan as a significant geo-political entity.[1] The reader may note that on a maximalist perspective of Old Testament history, the transition from the late Bronze Age to Iron Age I in the Levant relates broadly to the biblical periods of the early generations of Israelite life in the land.[2]

In the biblical texts, Younger notes how "Canaanite/Amorite" and "Canaan" are used in varying ways. He then engages in a careful and detailed geographical study of key biblical texts related to the borders of Canaan (especially the northern and eastern borders) in Numbers, Joshua and Ezekiel, to conclude that (1) Canaan can be affirmed as the geo-political entity's name for the Egyptian province in Asia in the late Bronze Age, (2) the promised land in Scripture can be *equated* to this basic geographical understanding of the land of Canaan (with more northern areas such as Alalakh and Ugarit understood to be beyond both "Canaan" and the "promised land)," and that (3) at the same time, the biblical Israelites understood their *ethnic* identity to be *distinct* from that of the Canaanites.

The second major section of Younger's essay, "The Land Ideologies of the Book of Joshua," builds on his established notion of the land of Canaan in the late second millennium BCE to advance seven distinct ideologies emanating from the biblical text of Joshua. Younger understands these ideologies to be part of the literary artistry of the book. They are "mental maps" that conceptualize the land in varying ways, to produce intended tensions for the reader, as a means of communicating *irony* overall. For Younger, the first two ideologies, the first of which includes within the land only the Cisjordan area, while the second includes both the Cisjordan and the

---

1. A concise introduction to the historical periods of the ancient Near East operating in the background of Younger's paper may be found in William W. Hallo and William Kelly Simpson, *The Ancient Near East: A History* (2nd edition; Belmont, CA: Wadsworth/Thomson, 1997), 67–117. For a constructive study of the Old Testament historical periods broadly under consideration, see Iain Provan, V. Phillips Long, and Tremper Longman III, *A Biblical History of Israel* (2nd edition; Louisville, KY: Westminster/John Knox, 2015), especially chapters 6 and 7.

2. For an influential maximalist perspective on Old Testament historiography, see K. A. Kitchen, *On The Reliability of the Old Testament* (Grand Rapids, MI: Eerdmans, 2003). For an influential minimalist perspective, see Philip R. Davies, *In Search of "Ancient Israel"* (JSOTSup 148; Sheffield: Sheffield Academic, 1992).

Transjordan areas, are rooted more or less in reality. The third ideology "of the land claimed but unconquered," and the fourth ideology "of the utopian Euphratic Israel" are *idealistic*. The fifth "theocratic" ideology is rooted in reality but is also subject to change. The "tribal ancestral" ideology and the "imperialistic" ideology represent the sixth and seventh ideologies.

Second, I will now emphasize a few areas from the paper that I found particularly helpful. Generally speaking, Younger's paper offers a convincing and detailed analysis and achieves it goal: exploring the land ideologies of the book of Joshua from its broader ancient Near Eastern context, especially in the second millennium BCE. Further, I appreciate the regular distinctions made between the basic textual *data* (be it biblical or extra-biblical) and the various scholarly *theories* related to that data. Younger is willing to let the actual textual data speak first, though he is also willing to admit when the basic data is limited or silent on a given issue.

That is, Younger has highlighted some of the benefits of allowing the contextual method to make a contribution to our interpretation of the biblical text. For example, in discussing an Amarna letter, Younger shows how, in that extra-biblical source, the Egyptian Pharaoh Akhenaten is assumed to be the "lord" at that point in time of the physical land of Canaan—so, his rule was operative over a land beyond the territory of Egypt. The point is that this extra-biblical evidence helps give some clarity to the contrasting *biblical* statement of Yahweh being the Lord of Canaan, and, thus, highlights something of the biblical, Yahweh-centered polemic against the supposed divinity of the Pharaoh.[3]

Further, when it comes to the book of Joshua itself, I think Younger provides helpful clues for a nuanced literary understanding of some of the more difficult issues in this Old Testament book: such as the reality of the Israelites conquering the Canaanites in "their" land, or such as the surface tensions apparent between the expansive claims of the land conquered on the one hand and the actual on-the-ground reality on the other hand.

Younger argues that these various land ideologies remain purposefully unresolved in the final canonical shape of the text of Joshua. In my view, this is a reminder that, at least in the Western tradition, we gravitate towards the *systematization* of ideas and concepts. If we expect such a systematized approach in a book like Joshua, then we are probably forcing this biblical text into a conceptual mold that is foreign to itself. *Not* smoothing over literary and theological tensions probably

---

3. For an in-depth study of the contextual method in Old Testament studies, the reader may find the following work to be helpful: John H. Walton, *Ancient Near Eastern Thought and the Old Testament: Introducing the Conceptual World of the Hebrew Bible* (2nd edition; Grand Rapids, MI: Baker, 2018).

remains a challenge for contemporary interpreters—at least, perhaps, for the biblical interpreter in the West.

Third, and in conclusion, I will put forth a few questions. When it comes to the rhetorical structure of the actual paper, I remain slightly unclear as to the exact relationship between the first major section on Canaan/Canaanites and the second major section on the seven land ideologies of Joshua. For example, must we agree specifically with professor Younger's geographical conclusions on Canaan in his first major section, *fully* to grasp the significance of the land ideologies in his second major section? This relates to the overall thesis, which, perhaps, could be a bit more clearly stated—especially in regards to the relationship between these two major sections.

Also, when it comes to the ideologies of land in Joshua, my basic question is: are we to assume that each one carries as much rhetorical and interpretive weight as the other? I know Younger addresses this briefly, but it might help his readers if he could (1) further develop his views on the *interrelationship* of these ideologies, and (2) explore a bit more how one is intended to engage with these ideologies as a current interpreter.

This leads me to my final, and more general, question: how may a Christian interpreter—a Christian teacher and preacher, for instance—faithfully interpret and communicate these land ideologies for the church? Or put another way, in what sense are these ideologies ultimately God's written communication for His people? Two elements stand out to me as fruitful for further reflection in this vein. First, the contrast between the first land ideology (of the Cisjordan only and its connection to the *tabernacle*) and second land ideology (of the Cisjordan *and* the Transjordan, and the concurrent notion of the Transjordan being somehow *beyond* the land of Yahweh's possession) represent one such avenue for further exploration. Second, the manner in which the Torah frame of the book of Joshua ultimately governs these various perceptions of land also calls for further theological reflection.

All in all, I found this to be an engaging paper, especially as it raises key issues related to our ability as biblical interpreters, teachers, and preachers more precisely to interpret this multifaceted theme of the land in Joshua.

READING THE GOSPEL OF JOHN IN THE PALESTINIAN CONTEXT[1]

Yohanna Katanacho

Introduction: Hermeneutics and Christological Identity

All of us read the Gospel of John from a particular perspective. Let us imagine that this perspective is a mental lens that we use in order to look at the text. For example, when we look at our hands, we see specific things such as our skin or perhaps some dirt, but, with a microscope, we see things that were invisible to the naked eye. In fact, the more lenses we use, the more perspectives we encounter. If we use yellow lenses or red lenses, what we see looks different because we see different colors. If we use a magnifying glass or a glass that reduces size, then the size of the text is not the same. Put differently, certain perspectives exaggerate particular features while others minimize specific traits.

People have been studying the Gospel of John for almost two thousand years. It is not my goal to address the numerous publications in the twentieth century, let alone throughout history.[2] But we must ask ourselves some important questions: What is the lens that we use when we look at the text? What are the factors that shape our mental lenses? Do we have a Christian or a Muslim or a Jewish lens when we look at the text? Is our lens Catholic, Baptist, Coptic, Presbyterian, Lutheran, Pentecostal, or Greek Orthodox? Obviously, the lenses about which I am talking are part of our mindset and are the factors that shape the way in which we look at

---

1. This article is comprised of material drawn from Yohanna Katanacho, *Reading the Gospel of John through Palestinian Eyes* (Carlisle: Langham Preaching Resources, 2020). Used with permission. The sections of the book drawn upon are chapters 1 and 2, and also the introduction and conclusion.

2. For details about recent research on the Gospel of John, please see the following: Frank Pack, "The Gospel of John in the Twentieth Century," *ResQ* 7 (1963) 173-85; Harold Songer, "The Gospel of John in Recent Research," *RevExp* 62 (1965) 417-28; Robert Kysar, "The Gospel of John in Current Research," *RelSRev* 9 (1983) 314-23; Mark Stibbe, *The Gospel of John as Literature: An Anthology of Twentieth Century Perspectives* (Leiden: Brill, 1993); Stanley Porter and Ron Fay, *The Gospel of John in Modern Interpretations* (Grand Rapids: Kregel, 2018). See also Joel Elowsky, ed., *Commentary on the Gospel of John: Theodore of Mopsuestia* (Downer's Grove, IL: InterVarsity, 2010), and Joel Elowsky, ed., *Commentary on John: Cyril of Alexandria*, 2 vols. (Downer's Grove, IL: InterVarsity, 2013, 2015).

things. In short, our perspectives are shaped by our social, political, educational, and religious locations.

It is unwise, therefore, to claim that our interpretations have no assumptions. They are not neutral or unbiased. Some in Israel/Palestine claim that their interpretation is "biblical." They usually use an Arabic equivalent (*Ktaby*) that literally means "scriptural." Such people argue that theirs is the correct or divine interpretation of the Bible, the interpretation that every believer would discover if he or she sincerely searched for it. This approach ignores the role of the interpreter and his or her biases. Consequently, the so-called "scriptural" interpretation might become an abusive tool in the hands of some dominant churches, some leaders, or those of a particular school of thought.

Usually, this approach ignores different translations of the Bible, different manuscript traditions, the history of interpretation, diverse interpretations, hermeneutical developments, social sciences, and archaeology. The interpreter replaces God in claiming absolute truth and affirms: "Thus says the Lord." Therefore, whoever disagrees with his or her scriptural interpretation opposes God. I do not mind using the Arabic expression "scriptural" (*Ktaby*) as long as we confess that our interpretations are open to criticism and correction.[3] Wise interpreters do not ignore the history of scholarship of a particular book or text. On the contrary, we, being sinful, must humble ourselves and adorn ourselves with the virtues of the kingdom of God as we seek divine truth. To say that our interpretations are 100 percent accurate, without allowing for possible faults in our perceptions, is problematic. It is arrogant and not compatible with a theology of humility. On the other hand, it is wise to affirm that our backgrounds and sociopolitical and cultural locations influence the way we think; even better, in fact, to state that our assumptions shape the way we perceive. With this affirmation we become humble and better listeners as we travel along the path of interpretation in search of the truth.

In short, the same text could have several interpretations: Zionist, Catholic or Protestant. Some interpretive lenses draw us closer to divine truth while others drive us farther afield. But God is the judge who fully discerns what is true from what is false. Only God, the ultimate standard, is 100 percent true. As for human beings, time plays an important role in guiding us as we seek to distinguish right from wrong and differentiate between eternal and ephemeral wisdom. Time helps us to test our perspectives and discover whether they bring forth a blessing or a curse. Furthermore, Christ is the interpretive compass that guides us to a better

---

3. The Arabic word *Kitab* usually means a book. The related word *Ktaby* ("scriptural") in many Christian circles denotes not only what is in the Holy Bible but also what is normative. All Arabic transliteration generated by "Arabic to Latin Converter," MyLanguages.Org, 2019, http://mylanguages.org/arabic_romanization.php.

understanding of Scripture. The universal church throughout the ages is a wise guide for all those who search for truth.

From the aforementioned interpretive perspective, and from a mindset that resists pride and does not look down on other points of view, I would like to present a Palestinian Israeli Christian reading of the Gospel of John. At the same time, I acknowledge that there are several Palestinian Christian views and that I do not represent all of them.[4] However, it is fair to say that most contemporary Palestinian Christian perspectives, if not all, have been shaped by similar sociopolitical and religious events, for we live in the context of occupation, discrimination, denominationalism, religious extremism, Judaization, Islamization, wars, hatred, and a tribal patriarchal society. For Palestinian Christians, our questions have been born and grown to what they are in this context. We have specific sociopolitical questions that have shaped the way in which we study the word of God and the kind of answers we seek. This is true for me as well.

I read the Scriptures, including the Gospel of John, as a Palestinian who holds Israeli citizenship. I do not claim that my Palestinian reading or culture is superior or sinless (God alone is sinless). Yet, beginning with my identity as I have described it, I approach a text seeking the will of God and desiring to obey it. I read the Scriptures through a Palestinian cultural lens, and I read them as a Christian who lives within a Jewish majority, a fact that distinguishes my reading from other Arab Christians in other parts of the world.[5] It is also important to assert that my Palestinian identity is not a sin but a blessing and a bridge that needs to be sanctified in Christ. It enhances other readings and leads to the enrichment of the diverse perspective of the universal multicultural church. My reading challenges those that overlook the centrality of Christ and abuse the text in order to spread a view that empowers the oppressor rather than the oppressed. It challenges ethnocentric and nationalist perspectives and interpretations that are not interested in empowering every repentant person regardless of his or her cultural background.

Among the mindsets that I encounter in my context, some Messianic Jews believe that Jewish culture is indispensable for a proper understanding of the Gospel of John. Though the perspectives of Messianic Jews are diverse, and some accept the dominant ecclesiastical interpretations of the ages, most feel uncomfortable with Hellenistic culture and its language, which dominated church history.[6] Conse-

---

4. For a survey of some of Palestinian perspectives, see Yohanna Katanacho, "Palestinian Protestant Theological Responses to a World Marked by Violence," *Missiology: An International Review* 36 (2008) 289-305.

5. I read the Arabic text and also consult the Greek text, as well as other languages, in order to verify my interpretations.

6. Further details about Messianic Jews can be found in Richard Harvey, *Mapping Messianic Jewish*

quently, it is not uncommon to hear Messianic Jews challenging — or even refusing the use of — expressions like "Christ," "church," or "Trinity." They usually affirm the doctrinal realities behind these expressions, but they feel uncomfortable using "Hellenistic" expressions. Such proponents highlight the importance of Jewish culture and claim it as a foundation for understanding the text (an approach that presents serious problems in seeking shared doctrinal commitments).[7]

But these claims are not accurate when speaking of Jewish culture in the singular, as there exists in fact a spectrum of Jewish cultures and perspectives. For example, there is the Judaism of the Pharisees, the Essenes, and the Sadducees, as well as other forms of Judaism in the first century, to say nothing of many diverse embodiments of Judaism throughout the ages. Furthermore, each of these is perceived in different ways by its adherents and its opponents. In addition, it is not accurate to equate Judaism with the Old Testament. Rabbinic Judaism, for example, is not centralized around the priesthood, temple, and sacrifices. Also, some do not distinguish between the Jewishness of Jesus and the Jewishness of the members of the modern state of Israel. Thus, they turn the Jewishness of the Messiah into an identity that pushes away Palestinians and Arabs. His Jewishness, then, becomes a dividing wall that discriminates between his Jewish and his Gentile followers. This approach fails to understand the theological meaning of Jewishness because it overlooks the fact that the Jewishness of Jesus is sinless, with no addition of selfishness, bigotry, or even ethnic exclusivism. Such an approach ignores the uniqueness of the Jewishness of Jesus that alone embodies the dreams of the Old Testament, calling all nations to worship the one true God. It paves the way for a new age; the prophets of the Old Testament hoped for a day in which the law would be internalized in the hearts of all peoples. Their dreams reached beyond ethnic Jewishness to eschatological covenantal Jewishness, namely, the hope and transformative worldview associated with the coming of the kingdom of God. In the latter, not only is the law internalized but also those who were considered strangers are able to become equal members in the family of God.

In addition to Messianic Jews, another Jewish group reads the Gospel of John in Israel, but they feel uncomfortable with its claims. For example, Adele Reinhartz is concerned because the Jesus of the Gospel of John describes first-century Jews as an unbelieving satanic seed (John 8:44) as well as being blind, sinners, and unable to understand their own Scriptures.[8] No wonder that some Israeli Jews are not inter-

Theology (Milton Keynes: Paternoster, 2009) 96–139.

7. See, for example, Eli Lizorkin-Eyzenberg, *The Jewish Gospel of John* (Tel Aviv: Lizorkin-Eyzenberg, 2015).

8. Adele Reinhartz, "A Nice Jewish Girl Reads the Gospel of John," *Semeia* (1997), 179. See also Adele Reinhartz, *Befriending the Beloved Disciple: A Jewish Reading of the Gospel of John* (New York:

ested in Jesus at all. In fact, some call him *yēšû* which has a different meaning from *yēšûaʿ*. *Yēšû* is a disputed expression. Some argue that it is a Hebrew acronym for a sentence that reads, "May God obliterate his name and memory!"⁹ Jews in Israel use *yēšû* even in public spaces, including TV broadcasting, newspapers, and museums.

On the other hand, some Palestinians affirm that there is a sociocultural, geopolitical, and psychological continuum between the different oppressed peoples who have inhabited Palestine throughout the ages.¹⁰ From this perspective, this unique connection includes modern Palestinians and makes Jesus a Palestinian. It is important to note that the term "Palestinian," used before 1948, included Jews who lived in Palestine, and Jesus was part of the same geography, culture, and geopolitical and psychological realities as other residents of Palestine. Palestinians continue the argument, saying that the identity and works of Jesus represent and embody the hopes of the Palestinian people more than other nations.

In addition, many Muslims see Jesus as a Muslim and a Palestinian prophet. They add that the Gospel of John includes prophecies about the coming of Muhammad, arguing that the referent of the Greek word *paraklētos* is Muhammad, not the Holy Spirit.¹¹ Furthermore, some Palestinian Christians affirm that Jesus Christ is the Son of God who was born in the Palestinian town of Bethlehem, while Palestinian liberation theologians claim that the Palestinian Jesus is facing Herod again. This time, his encounter is through the struggle of his church with the Israeli occupation.¹² In other words, we have made Jesus part of the problem instead of seeing him as part of the solution; we have overstated our arguments as we affirmed the Jewish or Palestinian identity of Jesus. No doubt, the identity of Jesus, his deeds, and

---

Continuum, 2001).

9. The Hebrew text is ימח שמו וזכרו. It is transliterated as *yimmaḥ šĕmô wĕzikrô*. The literal translation is "Let his name and his memory be obliterated." See Kai Kjaer-Hansen, "An Introduction to the Names Yehoshua/Joshua, Yeshua, Jesus and Yeshu." JewsforJesus.org (1992); available from https://jewsforjesus.org/answers/an-introduction-to-the-names-yehoshua/joshua-yeshua-jesus-and-yeshu/

10. Mitri Raheb, "Toward a Hermeneutics of Liberation: A Palestinian Christian Perspective," in *The Biblical Text in the Context of Occupation: Towards a New Hermeneutic of Liberation*, ed. Mitri Raheb (Bethlehem: Diyar, 2012) 11–27; Mitri Raheb, *Faith in the Face of Empire: The Bible through Palestinian Eyes* (Maryknoll, NY: Orbis Books, 2014).

11. The common translation of paraklētos is "comforter." For further discussion, see the following Arabic books: Ahmed El Sakka, (السقا), بيركليت [*Berkelet*] (Cairo: Mktbh Almtyʿey, 1972), 24–68; Farouk Abdel Salam (عبد السلام), محمد في إنجيل يوحنا [*Muhammad in the Gospel of John*] (Cairo: Mrkz Alslam Ltjhyz Alfny, 2006), 69–99; Muhammad Zahran (زهران), إنجيل يوحنا في الميزان [*The Gospel of John in Scales*] (Alzqazyq: Dar Alarqm, 1991); Amir Yakan (يكن), محمد رسول الله [*Muhammad is the Messenger of God*] (Damascus: Mktbh Alasd, 1999).

12. Rafiq Khoury (خوري), من أجل حدود مفتوحة بين الزمن والأبدية: نحو لاهوت متجسد [*For an Open Border between Time and Eternity: Towards Incarnational Theology*] (Bethlehem: Mrkz Allqaʾ, 2014), 455. See also Naim Ateek, *A Palestinian Christian Cry for Reconciliation* (Maryknoll, NY: Orbis Books, 2008); Mitri Raheb, *I Am a Palestinian Christian* (Minneapolis: Fortress, 1995); Katanacho, "Palestinian Protestant Theological Responses to a World Marked by Violence."

his teachings are important to all of us. The better we understand these things, the more we understand God's plan for humanity. By presenting Jesus from a Palestinian Israeli evangelical perspective, it is my hope that this perspective will help us to discover our Lord Jesus Christ and to find our identity in him instead of conforming him to our identity. Furthermore, I hope that my study will contribute to a better understanding of the Gospel of John within the global church and also empower Palestinian contextual theologians as they reflect on Jesus Christ.

It is fitting, now, to explain my statement that we Palestinians and Messianic Jews have made Jesus part of the struggle instead of making him part of the solution. Many of our leaders have tried to make Jesus a "Jew" or a "Palestinian" in order to make political or ideological gains. Consequently, we have not paid enough attention to the identity of Jesus as declared by the ecumenical councils, especially at Chalcedon in 451.[13] The council known by that name declared that Jesus is fully God and fully human. He is 100 percent God and 100 percent human. The Father and the Son have the same divine essence. What is more, Jesus Christ has the same human essence as the rest of humanity. The fully eternal one, God the Son, was born of the Father before all ages. The fully human one, God incarnate, was born of the Virgin Mary, the mother of God.[14] He has two natures without mixture or transformation or division or separation. Each nature preserves all of its characteristics in one person that cannot be divided into two persons. This is the Chalcedonian Christ who represents all of humanity regardless of ethnic background.[15]

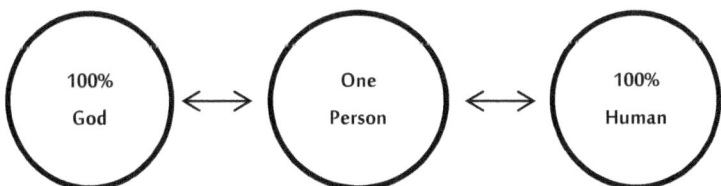

As an aside, it is true that Oriental Orthodox Christians (Copts, Syrian Orthodox, Ethiopian, Armenian Orthodox, and others) did not accept the Chalcedonian Creed. They do believe that Jesus Christ is fully God and fully human, and that he is one person, but they refuse to accept the phrase "two natures." They argue that it is not accurate to call them Monophysites, a term that is related to a heresy that

---

13. John Lorimer (لوريمر), تاريخ الكنيسة [*Church History: Part Three*] (Cairo: Dar Althqafh, 1988) 228–29.

14. For further information about the role and place of the Virgin Mary, especially the meaning of *Theotokos*, see Yohanna Katanacho and Dina Katanacho (كتناشو و كتناشو), أطلقوني [*Free Me*] (Jerusalem: Knysh Alathad Almsyhy, 2002) 43–53.

15. Mark Nestlehutt, "Chalcedonian Christology: Modern Criticism and Contemporary Ecumenism," *JES* 35 (1998), 175–96; James Moulder, "Is a Chalcedonian Christology Coherent?" *Modern Theology* 2 (1986) 285–307; Frances Young, "The Council of Chalcedon 1550 Years Later," *Touchstone* 19 (2001) 5–14.

accepted the divinity of Christ but rejected his humanity. They prefer the expression Miaphysites, meaning that the one nature of Christ is fully human and fully God without mixture, change, division, or separation.

It seems that Chalcedonian and non-Chalcedonian Christians agree in principle, even though they disagree about terminology.[16] Yet many, regardless of their denomination, are far from the Chalcedonian Christ. Ignoring the fact that Christ is fully human, and that his humanity represents people of all nations, including both Palestinians and Jews, they instead present an exclusive Christ. Thus, the Chalcedonian definition of Jesus is indispensable for a better understanding of the identity of Jesus Christ.

Nevertheless, the Chalcedonian definition does not address the relationship between the inclusive humanity of Jesus and his particular ethnicity. It does not address how Jesus can be a peacemaker, not only between humanity and God, but also between Jews and non-Jewish nations. In other words, Chalcedon does not clarify the meaning of the Jewishness of Jesus.

Therefore, I believe that we need to consider the identity of Jesus in new ways. Without doubt, the Gospel of John can enrich our understanding of valuable traditions related to the person of Jesus Christ, his life, and deeds. In light of the above, I suggest reading the Fourth Gospel in light of the following concerns: How can the Jewish Jesus, who was born in Palestine, and who is fully human, be our peacemaker and liberator? How can he represent both Palestinians and Jews as the humble servant who suffered, died, and rose from the dead? How can the Gospel of John reveal the full humanity of Christ in the context of the Palestinian-Israeli conflict and in an age in which humanity is distorted? The Gospel of John provides a promising theological space for such reflections.[17]

Put differently, those who understand the identity of Jesus in exclusive, national, and ethnic ways are advocating a political depiction of Jesus that is contrary to the inclusive Christ promoted in the Gospel of John. John challenges exclusive Pharisaic Judaism by rereading its major components in light of the inclusive Christ. I am not interested in reconstructing Pharisaic Judaism from an historical point of view, but in following its Johannine representation.[18] John is responding to a form of exclu-

---

16. In 1984, the former Syrian Orthodox patriarch, Mar Ignatius Zakka I Iwas, issued a common declaration with Pope John Paul II. See "Common Declaration of Pope John Paul II and Hh Mar Ignatius Zakka I Iwas," Centre Pro Unione, Franciscan Friars of the Atonement, 23 June 1984, http://www.prounione.urbe.it/dia-int/oo-rc_syrindia/doc/i_oo-rc_syrindia_1984.html.

17. Yohanna Katanacho, "Reading the Gospel of John through Palestinian Eyes," in *Jesus without Borders: Christology in Global Context*, edited by Gene Green, Stephen Pardue, and K. K. Yeo (Carlisle: Langham Global Library, 2014) 103–22.

18. For further information about Pharisaic Judaism, see Jacob Neusner, *From Politics to Piety: The*

sive Judaism which I shall call Pharisaic Judaism. My interest is in John's response and the way he rereads his perceptions in light of the coming of Christ. Indeed, John examines the relationship of Jesus to Jacob (4:12), to Moses (6:12; 9:28), and to Abraham (8:53). He examines how Jesus and his followers relate to the traditions of cleansing (2:1–11), holy space (2:18–22; 4:20–24), and holy time. He explains that Jesus works on the Sabbath (5:16; 9:16). He also examines the relationship of Jesus with the holy calendar, especially as it relates to Moses (6:1—8:29). He understands the holy Abrahamic community (8:30–59), and the holy land (10:1–21), in light of the coming of Christ. Thus, John presents a new world order that starts with the "enhumanization" of the second person of the Trinity and is fully established with his death and resurrection. Enhumanization entails both enfleshment and ensoulment. It is etymologically a better rendering than incarnation, that is, enfleshment. Jesus became fully human, or following in the footsteps of the Nicene Creed, enhumanized.[19] In the folds of this new world order, we discover the importance of the centrality of the inclusive Christ.

In this article I will focus on describing the nature of the new world order established by the inclusive Christ and on a single episode, the sign at the wedding of Cana (2:1–11) that expresses the new order in narrative form. However, it is helpful first to see how the reality of the "new beginning" brought by Christ shapes the literary structure of the overall narrative of John's Gospel. The different aspects for John of this new beginning are holy space, holy time, holy history, holy community, holy land, and a new perception of the meaning of life. These components are not only important in the Gospel of John but are also important for a theological reflection today. It is also helpful to reflect on the meaning of the Old Testament from the perspective of John, and it is also empowering in the battle against ethnocentric exclusive theologies. The Gospel of John introduces christological Jewishness that is centered on the inclusive identity and works of Jesus Christ. The following table represents the structure of John's narration of the radical new beginning initiated through Christ:

Emergence of Pharisaic Judaism (Eugene, OR: Wipf & Stock, 2003).

19. Alan Richardson and John Bowden, eds., *Westminster Dictionary of Christian Theology* (Louisville: Westminster John Knox, 1983) 169.

John	The Theme in a Christocentric World
1	The Enhumanization and the New World Order
2:1–11	The Water of Cleansing in the Wedding of Cana
2–4	Holy Space
5	The Sabbath
6–8	Mosaic Holy History
8	Relationship with Abraham
9	The Struggle between the Followers of Jesus and Those Who Follow Moses and Reject Jesus
10	Holy Land
11–12	Life in Light of the Death and Resurrection of Jesus

The book of signs (chs. 1–12) so-named because of the prominence of Jesus' miracles in this part of the Gospel, and their significance in pointing to his true identity, starts with the enhumanization and ends with the death/resurrection of Christ. It consists of seven signs: transforming water into wine (2:1–11), healing the royal official's son in Capernaum (4:46–54), healing the paralytic at Bethesda (5:1–15), feeding the five thousand (6:1–14), Jesus walking on the water (6:16–24), healing the man blind from birth (9:1–7), and raising Lazarus (11:1–45). John informs us that these signs were written so that people may believe that Jesus is the Messiah, the Son of God, and that by believing they may have life in his name (20:31).

Similarly, the book of the hour (chs. 13–21) starts with servant leadership (ch. 13) which is associated with the enhumanization and ends with Jesus's death/resurrection (chs. 18–21). The hour refers to the crucifixion of Christ, his death, and resurrection, which cannot take place until the time appointed in God's purposes has arrived. In the book of the hour, we encounter the following identities of the followers of the Christ:

Chapter	Main Identity Encountered
13	The People of Love
14, 16	The People of the Spirit
15–16	The Persecuted People
15	The People of the Vine
17	The People of Unity
18–19	The People of the Cross
20–21	The People of Resurrection

The Nature of the New Beginning

After outlining the way in which the reality of the new beginning helps to structure John's overall narrative, it is time to unpack John's presentation of the nature of the new world order that dawned with the messianic age when Christ was born.[20] This new world order, rooted in the Old Testament, fulfills the dreams of the Old Testament prophets. It is the age they hoped for — the Davidic or messianic age in which the divine promises will be fulfilled, exile will end, and human beings will experience joy, freedom, and divine covenantal grace (Ezek 34:23; 37:24). It is the divine season when God's glory will be revealed and seen by all (Isa 40:5). It is the fullness of time in which the people walking in darkness will see a great light (Isa 9:2). It is the age in which the God of heaven will set up a kingdom that will never be destroyed (Dan 2:44).

From a Christian perspective, this is the messianic age that dawned when Christ came, the kingdom that Christ embodied and preached. John invites us to reflect on this issue from the perspective of the God who became human, from a Christocentric point of view. His insistence on the centrality of Christ raises questions related to understanding the Old Testament and the role of biblical Israel. Such reflections are important, especially in light of theological discussions concerned with the relationship of the messianic age to the state of Israel or with seeing the state of Israel as the fulfillment of certain Old Testament prophecies. These discussions are crucial in Israel/Palestine.[21]

Our investigation of John's perception of the messianic age looks first at his introduction in chapter 1. Scholars agree that both Genesis in the Septuagint and the Gospel of John have similar beginnings.[22] Both books open with the phrase: "In the beginning." Genesis 1:1 says, "In the beginning God created the heavens and the earth," while John 1:1 says, "In the beginning was the Word." Genesis 1 describes the role of God's spoken word in creating the world and everything in it and also discusses the themes of life and light. The same themes appear in the Gospel of John. However, life and light are related to the word of God who became human.

---

20. For further information about the hopes of the Old Testament for a messianic age, see Anthony Hoekema, *The Bible and the Future* (Grand Rapids: Eerdmans, 1994).

21. I have addressed this issue in Yohanna Katanacho, *The Land of Christ: A Palestinian Cry* (Eugene, OR: Pickwick, 2013).

22. George Beasley-Murray, *John*, WBC 36 (Dallas: Word, 2002) 10; John Suggit, "Jesus the Gardner: The Atonement in the Fourth Gospel as Re-creation," *Neot* 33.1 (1999) 161–68; H.D.M. Spence-Jones, *The Pulpit Commentary: St John* (New York: Funk & Wagnalls, 2004); Peder Borgen, "The Logos Was the True Light: Contributions to the Interpretation of the Prologue of John," *NovT* 14 (1972) 115–30; N. T. Wright, *John for Everyone: Part 1: Chapters 1–10* (Louisville: Westminster John Knox, 2012).

Theology is thus associated with anthropology and cosmology. John is providing christological cosmology and is structuring the whole world around Christ, who is fully human and fully God.[23]

Some interpreters argue that the similarity between the two biblical books includes John's structuring of his discourse in seven days. In Genesis, God created the world in six days and rested on the seventh day. In the Gospel of John, the Jews of Jerusalem ask John the Baptist about his identity on the first day (1:19–28); then, we encounter the expression "on the next day" several times (1:29, 35–42, 43). It is possible to suggest that each time the expression "on the next day" occurs it refers to another day. Thus, we have four days total. If the wedding at Cana is on the third day (2:1) from the fourth day, it is then on the seventh day (four plus three).[24] More similarities to the book of Genesis can be seen in the account of the wedding at Cana, as will be further explored later.

Regardless of our understanding of the days mentioned in John, we cannot ignore the emphasis on the new age or era that John is advancing. The Gospel declares that God became human; he entered our world through the womb of the Blessed Virgin. I prefer the use of the word "human" instead of the word "flesh," as the former highlights the reality that Jesus became fully human, not only that he received a human body.

Put differently, the invisible God became visible (1:18). The Holy One who could not be touched became one of us (1:14). The God of the whole universe became a citizen of an insignificant town, thus demonstrating his humility. He became human in the womb of a virgin living in Nazareth, a town that had less than 480 people.[25] Nazareth is the place where God became human and Bethlehem is the place where he was born.

Stated differently still, the second person of the Trinity became human. We touched him, we saw him, we heard him, and we saw his glory. Because of the incarnated God, we have seen the Father (14:9) and the Spirit (1:32–33). The Holy Spirit appeared and rested on Jesus. The Son of God became human and dwelt amongst us; the Spirit of God came down at his baptism, and the heavens opened up; the angels of God ascended and descended (1:51). This angelic scene expresses a new era, a divine moment that will last forever in Christ. We also read the words of Jesus, "Behold an Israelite without deceit" (1:47). The ascending and descending angels together with the expression "Israel" echo the story of Jacob in which we encounter

23. Kathleen Rushton, "The Cosmology of John 1:1–14 and its Implications for Ethical Action in this Ecological Age," *Colloq* 45 (2013) 137–53.

24. Don A. Carson, *The Gospel according to John* (Grand Rapids: Eerdmans, 1991) 168; Stephen Kim, "The Relationship of John 1:19–51 to the Book of Signs in John 2–12," *BSac* 165 (2008) 323–37.

25. James Strange, "Nazareth," *ABD* 4:1050.

ascending and descending angels as well as a man called Israel (Gen 28:10–22). It is helpful to explore the details of this story.

Jacob desired to steal the blessing that belonged to his brother. Therefore, he went to Isaac, their blind father, and impersonated Esau in order to receive his older brother's blessing. His father was indeed deceived. When Esau heard what had happened, he was full of rage and decided to kill his brother. Jacob ran away as far as possible to escape. When he got tired, he slept in a place that he later named Bethel, the house of God. At Bethel, he dreamed. In his dream he saw angels ascending and descending upon a ladder and the Lord standing at the top of the ladder. The dream was connected to the Abrahamic promise, which included the Abrahamic blessing, the land, and divine care. In that dream, Jacob heard God saying:

> I am the Lord, the God of Abraham your father and the God of Isaac; the land on which you lie I will give to you and to your descendants; and your descendants shall be like the dust of the earth, and you shall spread abroad to the west and to the east and to the north and to the south; and by you and your descendants shall all the families of the earth bless themselves. Behold, I am with you and will keep you wherever you go, and will bring you back to this land; for I will not leave you until I have done that of which I have spoken to you. (Gen 28:13–15)

When Jacob woke up, he called the place the "house of God" and the "gate of heaven."

This story is important if we are to understand the discourse between Jesus and Nathanael. The similarities between the two stories are compelling. In the account of Jacob and Esau, we see that Jacob is known to be deceitful. When Isaac explained to Esau what his younger brother had done, he said, "Your brother came deceitfully and took your blessing." Esau said, "Isn't he rightly named Jacob? This is the second time he has taken advantage of me: He took my birthright, and now he's taken my blessing!" (Gen 27:35–36). The birthright belongs to the firstborn son as he is the one who is responsible to lead the family, or the tribe, after the death of his father, and he receives two portions of the inheritance instead of one. Furthermore, the firstborn was the priest of the family who stood before God representing his family and who represented God before his family.[26] Jacob deceitfully took the birthright of Esau, and so his name is now connected to deceit. Nevertheless, by his grace, God lavished God's blessings on Jacob.

Jesus brings this story to the first century and relates it to himself. Jesus, rather than Bethel, is now the house of God. Nathanael represents Israel (Jacob) but, unlike Jacob, he is without deceit. Instead of referring to the fulfillment of the Abrahamic

---

26. Anne Davis, "Israel's Inheritance: Birthright of the First Born," *Chafer Seminary Journal* 13 (2008) 79.

promise through Jacob, Jesus is declared as king of Israel. Put differently, the king of Israel has come and shall establish the kingdom of God on earth. In some manuscripts John 1 ends with the words "from now" or "hereafter," pointing to the dawn of a new age.[27]

A new era is dawning, one in which the heavens are connected to the earth through the God who became human. The secrets of the Father are now revealed by the Son. Jesus explains the Father in a perfect way. John states, "No one has ever seen God; the only Son, who is in the bosom of the Father, he has made him known" (1:18). The expression "made him known" means to have elaborated and explained accurately. John unpacks the way Jesus reveals the Father via seven signs in the book of signs (chs. 1–12).[28]

It is important to distinguish between a miracle, a wonder, acts of power, and a sign:

1. A miracle refers to the supernatural. It cannot be explained by scientific or natural laws.
2. A wonder creates a response in which we marvel.
3. Acts of power require investments of power beyond human capacity.
4. Finally, a sign is a thing that points to something else.

The signs in John refer to the dawning of the Davidic age, the identity of Jesus, and belief in him (20:31). In Christ, the promises of the Old Testament are fulfilled. He is the king of Israel. To unpack this new beginning that starts in Jesus, we shall now discuss the first sign in the Gospel of John, the wedding at Cana.

The Sign of the Wedding of Cana

The wedding at Cana addresses the new beginning, describing in narrative form the first dramatic manifestation of the messianic age in the ministry of Jesus. It is indeed interesting to reflect on this wedding in light of the similarities between the Gospel of John and the book of Genesis. The latter book describes the relationship of the first couple, Adam and Eve, while John presents a wedding in Cana, the first in a series of signs. John's rendering is similar to Genesis in that he presents God's work with humanity as beginning with a couple. John's account of a wedding paves the way for the introduction of the dawn of a new age, a messianic age. First-century

---

27. For further details, see the footnote of verse 51 in Nestle-Aland, *Novum Testamentum Graece*, 28th rev. ed. (Stuttgart: Deutsche Bibelgesellschaft) 296.

28. C. H. Dodd, *The Interpretation of the Fourth Gospel* (Cambridge: Cambridge University Press, 1953) x.

Jewish weddings were replete with symbolism that pointed to God's relationship with Israel. Thus, it is significant that the first sign in the Gospel of John was a wedding, and, more specifically, that the wedding occurred on the third day (2:1).

There are several ways to understand the phrase "on the third day." First, we can focus on its linguistic and historical meanings. In Jewish culture, the third day is Tuesday. Jews call Sunday *yôm ri'šôn*, which means the first day; Monday is *yôm šēnî*, the second day; Tuesday is *yôm šĕlîšî*, the third day, etc. Usually, Jews in the first century married in the middle of the week because they wanted to avoid violating the laws of the Sabbath. Law keepers insisted on having enough time to prepare for weddings without profaning the Sabbath, while it was also considered wise to avoid the Sabbath in case the court needed to be convened (if, for instance, the groom claimed his bride was not a virgin).[29]

In concord with getting married in the middle of the week, some Jews believed that the third day is the best day to marry, as the use of the word "good" in Genesis occurs only once on the first, fourth, and fifth days, does not occur at all on the second day, but is used twice on the third and sixth days (Gen 1:1–31).

Second, we can reflect on the phrase "on the third day" from a literary point of view. If we count this as the third day after the four days mentioned in chapter 1, perhaps John is presenting seven days. On the first day, John the Baptist declares that he is not the Messiah but a voice that precedes the coming of the Lord (1:19). On the second day (1:29), we witness the baptism of Jesus and the appearance of the Spirit of God. On that day, John the Baptist declares that Jesus is the Lamb of God who takes away the sin of the world and baptizes with the Holy Spirit. On the third day (1:35), Andrew and Simon find the Messiah. On the fourth day (1:43), Philip and Nathanael follow the Son of God (also referred to as the king of Israel and the Son of Man). Looking at the chronology of the days in John 1, it is possible to suggest that the expression "on the third day" at the beginning of John 2 is used in relation to the days mentioned in chapter 1. From this perspective, the third day at the beginning of John 2 is connected to the fourth day in John 1—that is, it is the seventh day. John 1 ends with a scene in which Jesus engages Nathanael from Cana (see 21:2) promising him that he would see greater divine acts (1:50). John 2 is a fulfillment of that promise and takes place in the town of Cana, Nathanael's hometown. If the sign happened on the third day from the fourth day, we add four and three which equals seven. This suggestion might have theological significance in light of the similarities between the beginnings of the Gospel of John and the book of Genesis.

---

29. See b. Ketub. 2a ("Ketubot 2a:1–11," *The William Davidson Talmud*, Sefaria, https://www.sefaria.org/Ketubot.2a.1-11?lang=bi).

Third, John wrote his gospel decades after the resurrection of Christ. During the time he wrote, the connection between the expression "on the third day" and the resurrection of Christ was widespread. Let us consider biblical examples that preceded the Gospel of John. The apostle Peter went to the house of Cornelius and preached that Christ was raised from the dead on the third day (Acts 10:40). The apostle Paul stated that the buried Christ was raised on the third day according to the Scriptures (1 Cor 15:3). The high priests, the Pharisees, and Pilate knew about the third day (Matt 27:62–64).

Put differently, it is possible that the expression "on the third day" in the account of the wedding at Cana provokes thoughts about the resurrection of Christ. This possibility increases in light of the interpretation of the first sign presented below. It also increases because Christians connected the redemption of Christ with wedding symbolism. They perceived Christ as the groom (3:29) and the church as his bride. Even if one dismisses the symbolic connection between the third day and the resurrection of Christ, we argue that it would be difficult to avoid the connection between the wedding at Cana and the redemption of Christ.

God's interaction with human beings in the Old Testament began when he established marriage and officiated the wedding of Adam and Eve. Their presiding pastor was God himself. The children of Israel perceived this first wedding as a divine act and consequently developed important religious interpretations and social customs surrounding the marriage ceremony.[30] Although the uncritical endorsement of first-century customs is not necessary, understanding those customs does help us better understand the wedding at Cana.

A wedding was a covenant between two families or countries. Usually, the father of the groom would discuss the conditions of the marriage with the father of the bride. The groom's family would present gifts to the bride and her family as part of the engagement (see Gen 24:53). This was followed by a written agreement, but the couple was not yet allowed to consummate the marriage with sexual intercourse as husband and wife. The bride and groom continued to live apart, each in their parents' home, until the consummation day, which occurred during a week-long celebration (see Judg 14:10–12; Gen 29:21–27). The events of the celebration were as follows: the groom and his friends went to the bride's house; then, in a special bedchamber, he removed the veil covering her face and knew her as his wife. They would then spend the night in the bedchamber while the couple's friends and the bride's parents celebrated outside. In the morning, after the consummation of marriage, the best friends would check the bedchamber and linens in order to testify

---

30. Hazel Perkin, "Marriage, Marriage Customs," *BEB* 2:1405–10, edited by Walter A. Elwell (Grand Rapids: Baker Academic, 1988).

to the virginity of the bride. They would then present the bloodstained cloth to the parents of the bride (see Deut 22:17).[31] Later, the couple left the bride's house and went to the wedding feast at the groom's house.

It is important to imagine the wedding as accurately as possible. The bride, for example, did not wear a white dress in the first century. In 1406, Philippa of England was one of the first women in recorded history to wear a white wedding dress. In 1559, Mary Queen of Scotland was married in a white wedding gown, and later, in 1840, the white gown was popularized by Queen Victoria.[32] In Jewish first-century culture, brides wore blue or purple dresses as the groom and bride were treated as a king and queen. As his friends accompanied the groom to the bride's house, they played flutes, tambourines, and drums, and they sang, danced, pronounced blessings, and recited poetry on their way (see Ruth 4:11–12; Song of Songs 3:6–11; Ps 45).[33] Then the couple returned to the groom's house to continue the celebrations.[34]

A wedding was attended by three kinds of invitees: family members and friends, the poor, and the rich or dignitaries. First, family members and friends were expected to bring gifts, the value of which would be reciprocated when they hosted a wedding. For example, if a family member or friend gave a gift equivalent to one hundred dollars, they would expect a gift of at least one hundred dollars in return when they invited this family to a wedding in their family. To bring a gift of less worth was considered shameful. In other words, gifts given by family members and friends were considered to be a kind of social debt that would be returned on another happy occasion.

Second, the poor also attended weddings; they ate and drank freely but were not expected to give any gifts. Third, rich people or dignitaries were also invited and were expected to give large gifts according to their social status, usually wine. They gave unconditional gifts, expecting nothing in return. When Jesus appeared at the wedding, people wondered what his social status was and what kind of gift he would give. Some thought that he was a relative as his mother was in the kitchen helping with wedding arrangements, while others thought that he was poor and could not offer a gift.

In any case, the wine ran out, which was a serious problem in a first-century Jewish wedding. The reputation of the family was at stake. Reputation was more important than wealth. Furthermore, due to the corruption of certain people who used

---

31. Sadly, these oppressive customs continue to this very day in certain villages in Egypt!

32. Marcel Danesi, *The Semiotics of Love* (Cham, Switzerland: Palgrave Macmillan, 2019) 152.

33. W. S. Towner, "Wedding," *HBD* rev. ed., edited by Mark Allan Powell (Harper Collins: New York, 2011) 1125–26.

34. These details can help us better understand the parable of the ten virgins and the bridegroom who was late (Matt 25:1–13).

weddings to receive gifts and gain income without providing food, first-century rabbis responded with strict laws. If a person presented a gift at a wedding where there was insufficient food or drink, then that person could take the groom to court. If the latter was found guilty, he would be imprisoned.[35] Thus, the couple encountered a serious problem that could have destroyed their marriage. Their wedding could have been transformed from joy to sadness, and the status of the groom could have been overturned from a king to a condemned prisoner. However, as Jesus intervened and changed water into wine, the problem became an opportunity to reveal the glory of Christ, and, in so doing, he gave the couple a great, free, and unconditional gift. He asked the servants to fill the water jars to the brim to demonstrate that there were no tricks involved – no one could add any liquid to the filled jars. When Jesus transformed the water into wine, he gave them more than five hundred bottles of good wine, demonstrating that his gift was similar to those of great dignitaries. It was a free, unconditional gift that the couple would remember for the rest of their lives.

Christ solved a serious problem at the wedding, but he created another serious one. There was no longer water at the wedding. The water jars were used for purification, and the jars were large enough to contain the quantity of water needed for all the purification required. The people had to wash their hands, the utensils, and more. Some washed their hands before the meal, during the meal, and after it. Purification reflected their commitment to obey the law of Moses. How would the guests be purified? They had six water jars, one for every day.[36] They could rest from these rituals only on the Sabbath.

In order to better understand John's intentions, it might be helpful to look at the motif of water in the Gospel of John.[37] We encounter the water of baptism in John 1:29-34; in John 2:1-11, water is transformed into wine; in John 3:5, Jesus challenges Nicodemus to be born again from water and the Spirit; in John 4:7-15, Christ offers the Samaritan woman water that wells up into eternal life; in John 5:1-17, we encounter a sign next to a pool; in John 6:16-21, Jesus walks on the water; in John 7:37-38, Jesus relates the living water to the Holy Spirit; in John 9:7, Jesus asks the man born blind to go and wash in the pool of Siloam; in John 11:55, the text reminds us of the importance of cleansing; in John 13:1-20, Jesus washes the feet of

---

35. Neb Hayden, *When the Good News Gets Even Better: Rediscovering the Gospels through First Century Jewish Eyes* (Colorado Springs: David Cook, 2009) 44; Rhondra Crutcher, *That He Might Be Revealed* (Eugene, OR: Pickwick, 2015) 89; J. Duncan M. Derrett, *Law in the New Testament* (Eugene, OR: Wipf & Stock, 2005; orig. Darton, Longman & Todd, 1970) 228–46.

36. Matta El Meskeen (المسكين) الإنجيل بحسب القديس يوحنا [*The Gospel according to St John*] (Cairo: Dyr Alqdys Anba Mqar, 1990) 174.

37. Wai-Yee Ng, *Water Symbolism in John: An Eschatological Interpretation* (New York: Peter Lang, 2001).

the disciples; and in John 19:34, when Jesus is pierced, water and blood come out of his side. It seems that John is indeed interested in the water motif.

In John 2, the reference to water is part of a larger water motif that concerns the requirement of water for purification. The Bible informs us that there were six water jars for purification (2:6). Also, we know that the servants filled the jars to the brim and all the water was transformed into wine. Put differently, Jesus solved the problem of the absence of wine but created a new problem, the absence of cleansing water. This idea becomes more significant in light of its context, for the wedding at Cana in the first part of John 2 is juxtaposed with the cleansing of the temple — and Jesus's statements about its destruction and replacement — in the second part of John 2.[38]

It is thus legitimate to ask: If there is no cleansing water, how will people be purified? The Gospel of John presents several interconnected themes. When we trace some of these motifs through words, imagery, and other literary tools, then we have a better understanding. One of the important words in the story of the wedding at Cana is the word "hour." Jesus told his mother that his hour had not yet come (2:4) but, at the same time, he performed a sign that resolved the problem of the lack of wine. Why did he speak in such a way? Perhaps Jesus is indicating that the foundation of the coming messianic or Davidic age is not to be miracles but the "hour." The "hour" is a clear motif in the Gospel of John, connected to the glory of Christ, his suffering, death, resurrection, and the redemption of humanity, as mentioned explicitly in 7:30, 12:23–27, 13:1, and 17:1.

Reference	The Text from the NIV Translation
John 7:30	At this they tried to seize him, but no one laid a hand on him, because his hour had not yet come.
John 12:23	Jesus replied, "The hour has come for the Son of Man to be glorified."
John 12:27	"Now my soul is troubled, and what shall I say? 'Father, save me from this hour'? No, it was for this very reason I came to this hour."
John 13:1	It was just before the Passover Festival. Jesus knew that the hour had come for him to leave this world and go to the Father. Having loved his own who were in the world, he loved them to the end.
John 17:1	After Jesus said this, he looked toward heaven and prayed: "Father, the hour has come. Glorify your Son, that your Son may glorify you."

When we read the above texts together, we recognize that the motif of the hour in the Gospel of John is related to the cross as well as the glorification of Jesus

---

38. This is unlike the Synoptic Gospels, which place the cleansing of the temple at the end of the ministry of Jesus. See Matt 21:12–17 // Mark 11:15–19 // Luke 19:45–48.

through the cross. The "hour" becomes an indispensable foundation for the messianic or Davidic age and is the prerequisite for the new world order. The water of purification in first-century Pharisaic Judaism would not be transformed into the messianic wine without the dawn of the hour. The messianic activity that is centered on the hour becomes the starting point for rereading the major elements of John's perception of Pharisaic Judaism. Assuming this perspective in reading the first sign, we recognize that the glory of Christ would not be revealed without the cross as well as the resurrection. Therefore, it is important to stress that John presents signs, not miracles, and that these signs pave the way for a better understanding of the messianic age and the kingdom of God.

Signs alone are not enough to lead people to a saving faith or even to a discovery of the crucified God. Jesus performed many signs in Jerusalem on the Passover. Many believed in his name, but Jesus did not entrust himself to them (2:23–25). Nicodemus was interested in Christ because of the signs, but he could not discover the identity of the savior of the world (see ch. 3). In addition, the crowds saw many signs but were not satisfied and did not discover God (6:25–31). When the high priests and other first-century Jewish leaders met in a council to discuss the resurrection of Lazarus, they admitted that Jesus had performed many signs. Although they accepted that the signs were genuine, they decided to kill Jesus (11:47–53). Signs are not enough! The way to discover the glory of God is through the death and resurrection of the Messiah. Only this way will change history and offer to God the glory he deserves.

Put differently, Christ honored the request of his mother at the wedding at Cana, but he insisted on the way of the cross: "'Woman, why do you involve me?' Jesus replied. 'My hour has not yet come'" (John 2:4).[39] Jesus did not rebuke his mother but rather respected her desire. At the same time, he expressed his unbending commitment to revealing his glory through his crucifixion and resurrection. He rescued the couple in Cana from social humiliation without abandoning his commitment to the cross. The cross is the way to reveal the glory of God and a new world order in which changes start by the transformation of hearts, not mere behavioral changes. Thus, the "hour," or the death and resurrection of the Christ, becomes the lens through which we see the enhumanization of the second person of the Trinity. It also becomes the mindset or worldview that interprets the identity and works of the Christ. We can no longer understand the humanity of Christ only from the

---

39. The expression "woman" (*gynē*) is not derogatory. John uses it in 2:4; 4:21; 8:10; 19:26; 20:13, 25. John usually uses it to respectfully call upon a woman in trouble. For further information about the expression "woman" in John 2:4, see Jean-Bosco Bulembat, "Head-Waiter and Bridegroom of the Wedding of Cana," *JSNT* 30 (2007) 55–73.

perspective of his conception and birth. We must also consider his humanity in relation to the cross and resurrection.

In other words, Jesus was not only a Jewish baby; he was also the savior of the world. He was not only shaped by first-century Judaism; he also redefined many central components of Jewishness. He was the groom of the messianic age in whom the longings of Old Testament prophets were fulfilled. John the Baptist said, "I am not the Messiah but am sent ahead of him. The bride belongs to the bridegroom. The friend who attends the bridegroom waits and listens for him, and is full of joy when he hears the bridegroom's voice. That joy is mine, and it is now complete" (3:28–29). Christ, the groom, redeems his bride through the cross; thus, the motif of the hour is related to Christ, the groom. The connection between the sign of the wedding at Cana and the cleansing of the temple becomes clearer as we reflect on Christ, the groom, who redeemed us through the cross, where his body was broken and his blood was spilled. The signs in the Gospel of John must be connected to this central reality.

Only Jesus' death and resurrection provide a lasting meaning to his signs. John explicitly connects the death of Christ to signs. He quotes the Jews saying, "What sign can you show us to prove your authority to do all this?" (2:18). The response was the death and resurrection of Christ (2:19–22). For John, it is only from within this perspective on the death and resurrection of Jesus that the re-shaping in inclusive fashion of crucial aspects of Jewish identity makes sense. The dawn of the messianic age necessitates a radical re-evaluation of the nature of the temple and holy space, time, people, history, land, and life.[40]

Conclusion: Christ at the Center

I have pointed out that the Gospel of John presents a new world order in which the major components of Pharisaic Judaism are deconstructed and then reconstructed in relation to the centrality of the inclusive Christ. I have also pointed out the contextual implications of John's arguments in Israel/Palestine. The following are some salient points that we should highlight.

First, both Palestinians and Jews should avoid the temptation of employing the identity of Christ to make political gains. Christ is fully human and can represent both Palestinians and Jews. We cannot and should not understand the identity of Christ in an ethnically exclusive way. The Chalcedonian Christ is fully human and is inclusive. He does not exclude any nation. It is important for us to understand the

---

40. All these themes are explored further in Katanacho, *Reading the Gospel of John through Palestinian Eyes.*

nature of the Christ that we follow. He is not the Christ who rejects Palestinians or Jews or any other person. He is not the Christ who pushes people away, refusing to engage them, because God loves all nations. Every human being is created in the image of God. Therefore, we should respect everyone without exception. In fact, every human being is a gift from God. The value of human beings is not only related to our creation in the image of God but also to the incarnation in which humanity has been honored and elevated.[41] Humanity has also been elevated in the resurrection of Christ. Through Christ, the fallen creation has been transformed into a new creation. It is clear that Christ was born in a Jewish culture, but his human identity has redefined Jewishness in inclusive ways. Put differently, through Christ historical Jewishness has been reread in light of eschatological Jewishness. Christ is not only a historical Jew, he is also an eschatological Jew. Greater than any other Jew, he redefines Judaism in inclusive ways and has embodied its deepest hopes. He is fully human and can represent all human beings.

Second, our understanding of the Messianic age should not be divorced from the centrality of Christ. Any trustworthy Christian interpretation of the Old Testament should take into consideration how John – and perhaps the rest of the New Testament – has reread the Old Testament in light of the coming of Christ. Furthermore, our understanding of the temple, the Sabbath, the exodus tradition, the wilderness traditions, the children of Abraham, the holy land, and life itself should be shaped by the centrality of Jesus Christ. This centrality defines faith as well as hermeneutics – how we are to read and interpret Scripture. Since Christ is fully human, both Palestinians and Jews can see him as their hero and savior.

---

41. Khoury, (خوري). من أجل حدود مفتوحة بين الزمن والأبدية: الحضور المسيحي [*For an open border between time and eternity: The Christian presence*] 145.

RESPONSE TO KATANACHO

Madison N. Pierce

Dr. Katanacho offers a stimulating reflection on the Gospel of John. His reading from a Palestinian Israeli Christian perspective is certainly rather different than my Western, American perspective, and he has helped me to understand some of the questions that are important in his context, as well as some cultural details of which I was not aware. In the discussion that follows I will proceed through a very brief summary of what I take to be his major points, some things that I really appreciate, and some things that I might challenge. These latter two categories—the good and the less good—are accompanied by a number of questions that I hope provide a starting point for our conversation.[1]

Katanacho begins with a useful reminder to us about the fact that we read from a particular perspective. Our perspectives, he says, "exaggerate particular features while others denigrate specific traits." Further, he critiques those in his context who label their own perspective as "biblical" or "scriptural," as this implies that their reading of the text is correct; it implies that their reading is somehow divorced from bias. Some in my context have taken to this strategy also—and I likewise have been affected by the "biblical" view "[becoming] an abusive tool in the hands of some dominant [traditions]" that have called into question my own calling and ministry. I say this, not to distract from the paper at hand, but to acknowledge my own bias in keeping with the spirit of his paper.

Katanacho shares with us his experience of reading Scripture through "a Palestinian cultural lens" within a "Jewish majority." His reading, he says, "challenges ethnocentric or nationalist perspectives or interpretations." This leads him into a discussion about "Jewishness" with his important reminder that, at any single moment in history, there has not been one "Jewish culture," and to point backward 2,000 years and equate the "Jewishness" of today with the "Jewishness" of that day is all the more flawed.

---

1. Thanks are due to Stephen Chester for his feedback on an earlier version of this response.

Katanacho also briefly introduces the perceived problem of a negative representation of the Jewish people in the Gospel of John.[2] Though evidence throughout the Fourth Gospel is often cited, the strongest verse to this effect is John 8:44: "You belong to your father, the devil, and you want to carry out your father's desires." If *hoi Ioudaioi* is translated " the Jews" and no further historical, literary, or hermeneutical explanation is given, then the modern reader of John could conclude, as many have, that the Jews are ironically the enemies of the "one who comes in the name of the Lord" (John 12:12).[3]

In attempts to remedy this supposed anachronism and reduce anti-Semitic readings of John's Gospel, one trend has been to translate this term as "Judaeans,"[4] acknowledging that Jesus' trouble was isolated to the Jewish people in a particular region, rather than the whole people group. Setting aside the fact that this simply limits the potential for prejudice against an ethnic group to a particular region, a number of Jewish scholars have noted the damage done by "erasing" the Jews from Christian Scripture. Amy-Jill Levine says, for example: "The Jew is replaced with the Judean, and thus we have a *Judenrein* ('Jew free') text, a text purified of Jews ... So much for the elimination of anti-Semitism by means of changing vocabulary."[5] This discussion shows in part how, in my context, where Jewish people are a significant minority, my experience of this scholarly discussion is rather different indeed. Katanacho is worried about a Jewish majority—as well as a Jewish Jesus who will justify the displacement of Palestinians.

We will return to the test case of John 2 below, but let us turn now to the end of his paper where Katanacho advocates for an understanding of Jesus as a universal representative of humanity. The problem with that statement might not yet be perceptible, and so let me say it again: It is of utmost importance for Katanacho that Jesus is fully human. *Full stop.* This he says is the "Chalcedonian Christ." And although Katanacho identifies Jesus as one who is "Jewish" and also "born in Palestine," he says that "those who understand the identity of Jesus in exclusive, national, and ethnic ways are advocating a political depiction of Jesus that is contrary to the inclusive Christ promoted in the Gospel of John"—in addition to the potential of violating the

---

2. For a poignant summary of the history of this issue, see Adele Reinhartz, "The Vanishing Jews of Antiquity," *Marginalia: Los Angeles Review of Books*, June 24, 2014, https://marginalia.lareviewofbooks.org/vanishing-jews-antiquity-adele-reinhartz/.

3. For an early discussion on translating this term, see Malcolm F. Lowe, "Who Were the 'Ioudaioi?" *NovT* 18. 2 (1976) 101–30.

4. This prompted a lively debate. For a brief recent summary, see Wendy E. S. North, *A Journey Round John: Tradition, Interpretation and Context in the Fourth Gospel*, LNTS 534 (London: T. & T. Clark, 2015) 6–8.

5. Amy-Jill Levine, *The Misunderstood Jew: The Church and the Scandal of the Jewish Jesus* (New York: HarperOne, 2006) 160.

conciliar view of Christ formulated at Chalcedon. An "exclusive" Jesus, I think, is the primary error of what he labels "Pharisaic Judaism," the view to which he thinks John is responding. After rehearsing some of the ways that Jesus' cultural identity has been weaponized, Katanacho calls on us to "find our identity in [our Lord Jesus Christ] instead of conforming him to our identity." Indeed, outside its context, I have little to no disagreement with this statement, and yet within Katanacho's discourse, it serves a broader program that raises some questions. Now again, I grant that he reminds us of Jesus' ethnicity at a few key points in the paper but, largely, I felt a tension between an "inclusive" Jesus and a finite Jesus who had his own specific set of descriptors not unlike our own.

In light of all the details that John does *not* provide about the birth and earthly life of Jesus—such as his mother's name—we do know his religious tradition, and we know that tradition has thoroughly shaped how he presents himself in this narrative told by John. John locates Jesus within the writings of Moses (5:46) and Isaiah (12:41). Further, the chronology of John's Gospel is oriented around the religious festivals. In addition to nine references to the Passover (2:13, 23; 6:4; 11:55; 12:1; 13:1; 18:28, 39; 19:14) John also mentions the Feast of Booths (7:2) and the Feast of Dedication (10:22) among other Jewish rites. He is not simply a "savior" or a modern-day super hero invented for entertainment; he is a Jewish man anointed by God—the Christ. The significance of his coming is presented in the language of his religious tradition. This of course does not negate his coming on behalf of all humanity—in fact the idea of one as the representative of all comes from his religious tradition as well—but it does warrant attention.

Is it possible for us to celebrate the religious identity of Jesus without privileging a particular ethnicity? I raise this question even though this certainly seems reductionistic. This is particularly so when I consider the fact that, for me, though I hurt for my brothers and sisters in Palestine, it does not sting me the same way when I say that Jesus was Jewish. Even so, returning to prior discussions about how to represent the Jewish people, we simply cannot erase the Jews, and we certainly cannot erase the "Jewishness" of Jesus.

The test case for John's response in this paper is the Wedding at Cana in John 2. To give some background for this account in John, Katanacho provides his readers with some information about weddings. But in most cases, he provides no reference or clarification as to whether this describes first-century weddings, modern weddings, or weddings at some other point in human history. Since his primary evidence is references from Hebrew Bible, it seems unlikely that this information pertains directly to the first century, but those details are admittedly more relevant than the framework in place for this twenty-first-century Westerner.

Also, within this discussion, he provides us with several interesting cultural details, explaining the potential significance of the day of the wedding and various customs that underlie the narrative, for example, the potential legal implications for the host who does not furnish an adequate feast. He likewise explains the typical timeline, which includes a week-long celebration that culminates in the consummation of the marriage by the bride and groom. From his perspective, is the feast that accompanies this consummation what is presented in John 2?[6] After his discussion of weddings in antiquity, Katanacho reveals the detail that will be his focus: the water turned into wine was the water for purification. Those present at the wedding no longer have the means to pursue ritual purity—they no longer have the means to prioritize aspects of their Jewish heritage. Katanacho asks: "if there was no cleansing water, how would people be purified?" He then briefly develops the theme of water in the Gospel of John.[7] From my reading, this detail is not a focus in the narrative itself. Thus, the perceived problem of a lack of water is not explicit, and the symbolic interpretation of that lack of water is even less so.

Nevertheless, he argues that turning water into wine is in some way representative of the coming abundance at the messianic banquet,[8] which is part of Jesus' universal mission—his mission to *all* people. He was born a Jewish child, but he has come to save the world. To his credit, yes, of course, Jesus is the "light of the world," not the light of any particular ethnicity or nationality. John famously begins his gospel at the cosmic level—a view that led to him being represented by the eagle in early Christian literature and art. Further, John, in an argument akin to that of the apostle Paul, challenges the view that one is a "child of Abraham" on the basis of ethnicity (esp. John 8:39), and Jesus identifies himself in John as the reconstituted temple (esp. 2:21)—he is/contains the presence of God. These are just a few small examples of how Katanacho's thesis applies to the Gospel of John. Still, if space permitted, I would like to hear more about how John is "re-reading" biblical themes. This seems to be an important feature of Katanacho's argument, but how this works is not a part of the present discussion. I agree that a number of themes are christologically-appropriated in John, but what does that mean? This is an important question in my context.

Let us end with a discussion of interpretation more generally. I am grateful for the reminder of how our biases inform our interpretive decisions, but I would like

---

6. And if so, what does it mean that Jesus was a part of the, to use his language, "oppressive custom" of validating the bride's virginity?

7. He develops this idea further in Yohanna Katanacho, *Reading the Gospel of John through Palestinian Eyes* (Carlisle: Langham Preaching Resources, 2020).

8. So also D. A. Carson, *The Gospel According to John*, Pillar New Testament Commentary (Grand Rapids: Eerdmans, 1991) 174.

to hear more from Katanacho's perspective on when critical engagement with an interlocutor crosses the threshold. For example, in his presentation of this paper, Katanacho declared Western scholarship "irrelevant" to his readings of John. I respect his desire to disengage with what he perceives to be oppressive majority traditions, but I do not know where this leaves us in terms of a "fruitful" dialogue. My aim is for each of us to come closer to a more faithful interpretation of the Gospel of John, while respecting our very different locations. My background, for example, is a tradition that often marginalizes the voices of women; this was not the first time a man declared me "irrelevant." But I return to the table with the hope of a conversation.

THE JEWISH PEOPLE AND ERETZ YISRAEL: A JEWISH EVALUATION OF SELECTED CHRISTIAN THEOLOGICAL PERSPECTIVES

Yehiel Poupko

The Jewish Return to Sovereignty as a Problem for Christian Theology

At times it seems that there is more Christian theological thinking and writing about the return of the Jewish people to sovereignty in the ancient homeland of Israel than there is Jewish theological writing on the subject. Indeed, for a majority of the Jewish people and at least 90 percent of Israel's Jewish citizens, the establishment of the state of Israel has no religious significance.

It goes without saying that the Jewish people and Judaism are one of the most enduring topics of Christian theology over the past two millennia. Jewish faith affirmation requires no reference to Christianity. Christian faith affirmations inherently begin with statements about Judaism. The Jewish people have regularly presented a set of dilemmas for Christianity ever since its nativity. In each and every stage of Jewish historical and religious development over the past two thousand years, Christianity perceived new challenges to which it responded. Paul wrote several letters to explain why the very people of the flesh of Jesus had not accepted him. Augustine had to explain why, centuries after rejecting Christ, the Jewish people were still present. The Church in the Middle Ages had to explain not just the endurance of the Jewish people, but the flourishing of their religious civilization as well. Luther had a lot of trouble explaining why the Jews did not become Christian after his attempt at reforming the Catholic Church. His writings on that subject are less than pleasant. After the Enlightenment and the "emancipation" of the Jews, Protestant theologians in Western Europe could not understand why the Jewish people remained stubbornly distinctive in an "enlightened" Europe. With all the disabilities removed, there were American Christians who did not understand continued Jewish distinctiveness in an American Christian civilization that welcomed them. When the Jewish people no longer played their two-thousand years old traditional role in the Christian imagination, they returned to sovereignty in the ancient homeland. And of all the problems the Jewish people created for and presented to the world of Christian theology, none is greater than the return of the people, who two millennia earlier had rejected Jesus, to sovereignty in the ancient homeland of Israel. What have been the Christian theological responses?

A word or two is in order about the application of theology to current events. To be sure the faithful Jew and Christian regularly turn to the texts of the Hebrew Bible and the New Testament for wisdom, guidance, and inspiration in order to understand and respond to the world around them. Verses from the Hebrew Bible and the New Testament are regularly employed in the discussion of the Israel-Palestine conflict. While the inspiration for justice and righteousness on behalf of all who are suffering is a hallmark of both faith communities, the present circumstance in the land of Israel poses unique degrees of difficulty for the application of biblical text. The prophets of old speak eternal and absolute ideas, in the circumstance and the vernacular of their time. God speaks. Men and women hear. The message is precise. The challenge of course is to extract the idea and to apply it to the contemporary circumstance. The contemporary State of Israel is not ancient Israel of the First Temple period, eleventh century BCE to sixth century BCE, nor Judea of the first century, although there are important historical, genetic, familial, and communal continuities. In the absence of an explicit word of God to a prophet in the form of prophecy we can never be secure in our sense that we are assessing the contemporary situation as the ancient scriptural authors, and, more importantly, God, in whose name they speak, would have us do.

From a Jewish perspective the presentation of any theology is fraught with all sorts of difficulties. To present a theology is to presume to know the mind of God. In and of itself there are many risks here, one of them is hubris itself. This risk becomes greater when the presented theology attempts to grapple with contemporary events.

If one applies to the state of Israel biblical oracles addressed to the ancient people Israel, one has to be careful to do so with a sense of symmetry. One cannot simply apply the oracles of prophetic judgment thereto, while ignoring those of promise and restoration, including the land-promise to Abraham, Isaac, and Jacob. This is not a point that nearly two thousand years of Christian tradition has prepared Christians to perceive so clearly as they should. Classically, the Church tended to apply the oracles of judgment and doom to the Jews, the stiff-necked, unbelieving "carnal Israel" or "old Israel," who blindly crucified their own savior, but the oracles of promise and restoration to itself, the "new Israel," the beneficiary of divine love and grace, the "body of Christ" awaiting its promised glorification. Given this legacy of replacement, supersessionism, and defamation, it is an enormous challenge for

Christians to approach the Israeli-Palestinian conflict with an unclouded sense of the historical, political, social, economic, and military realities. The default position that their own Christian scripture and tradition suggests to them is just too ingrained and too available. It has a well-developed career. That position tempts them to conclude hastily that the Jews, ethnocentric, unethical, and grasping by nature, are once again exploiting or killing the innocent, in this case the Palestinian Arab. This may make for a good sermon or ten-second sound bite, but it does not reflect the complex history of Zionism or the history of the last two hundred years of Jewish life in the region, or the region's endemic internal problems. Worse, the prophetic sermon, this one-dimensional view, not only enables but re-energizes and re-analyzes the old supersessionist defamations that many of the Christian denominations righteously and courageously renounced in recent decades.

Criticism of policies of the Israeli government is surely no evidence of antisemitism, theological or other, but when those critiques are not comparative and contextual, but single out Israel, the telltale tradition is surely rearing its ugly ahead anew. This is all the more the case when Scripture is cited selectively and prejudicially, and the Jews are once again are made to fit into certain hoary Christian archetypes in defiance of the realities on the ground.

Premillenial Dispensationalism and the Response of Gary Burge

It is the purpose of this essay to present a Jewish appreciation of several types of Christian theological understanding about the Jewish relationship to the land. Some Christian theology about Israel is written in response to premillennial dispensationalism.

Essentially, without presenting in detail the Scofield Bible or the life of John Nelson Darby, and the Plymouth Brethren, premillennial dispensationalism holds that God has in this era, or dispensation, given up on the church. The second coming will now take place through Israel. As proof, the Jewish people have returned to Israel in order to make that possible. Of course, after the Rapture, Armageddon and the like, the Jewish people will either accept Christ or disappear. Insofar as it sees no future for the Jewish people, it is no different than many other Christian theologies in which the Jews are actors in someone else's drama. Truth be told the Jewish response to the claims of premillennial dispensationalism is no different than its response to the initial claims of Christianity two thousand years ago.

The claims of pre-millennial dispensationalism and responses to them ought to be an exclusively internal Christian matter. An assessment of this new theology (not even two centuries old) should be developed in an exclusively Christian setting. It should be none of our Jewish business. Yet, it is in Christian responses to premillennial dispensationalism that we find some of the most extensive and critical Christian theological writing about the Jewish people and the Land.

One type of response to the Jewish relationship to the land of Israel is covenantal disenfranchisement. This is the view of those who believe that with the coming of Jesus Christ and the Christian covenant, the Jewish people are disenfranchised, disinherited by God. The promises made to their father in the flesh, the Patriarch Abraham, are now transferred to the new, real, and true Israel, those who have come to Christ. The Jews who do not accept Christ are no longer the children of Abraham. They are disenfranchised. This view is presented in the writings of Gary Burge. Indeed, we are fortunate to have them presented in both a practical, as well as in a scholarly theological form. In his book *Whose Land? Whose Promise?* Gary Burge tells us that Paul "drawing again on that Old Testament notion of a remnant" argues "that Christian believers are the new remnant in God's working": *So too at the present time there is a remnant, chosen by grace* (Rom 11:5).[1] He proceeds to take up Paul's all-important question: "Has God rejected His people? By no means!" (Rom 11:1). Burge tells us that the key to understanding this is Rom11:2. God has not rejected His people whom He foreknew. Burge writes,

> The remnant is the body of believers within Israel who have kept faith with the covenant and God's purposes, and God knows who they are. Therefore God has been faithful to His covenant people because these people are found now within the Church. *Israel in Christ* (emphasis Burge's) is now heir to the great covenant history of the Old Testament.[2]

Burge expands upon this in another book, *Jesus and the Land*. He writes,

> Paul develops the picture of an olive tree as an image of God's people in history. It has many branches and, thus many people. Paul says that unbelieving Israel is like a branch broken off from the trunk of this tree. That is unbelieving Israel has been rejected (11:15) and "broken off" (11:20).[3]

He sums it up in this way:

> Therefore in Paul's theology he sees the Jewish people *outside of Christ* (emphasis Burge's) living at a loss and under judgment (Rom 11:21-22). They are branches broken off. Unenlightened and misdirected… Linked now to Hagar (not Sarah) and Mt. Sinai rather the heavenly Jerusalem (Gal 4:24, 26) . . .

---

1. Gary Burge, *Whose Land? Whose Promise? What Christians are Not Being Told About Israel and the Palestinians* (Cleveland, OH: Pilgrim, 2003) 185.

2. Burge, *Whose Land? Whose Promise?*, 186.

3. Gary Burge, *Jesus and the Land: The New Testament Challenge to 'Holy Land' Theology* (Grand Rapids: Baker, 2010) 88.

> There is hope, however. The Jewish people *outside Christ* (emphasis Burge) may return to their location in the economy of God should they embrace Christ.[4]

This idea of Burge's that only "Israel in Christ" is heir to the promises made to Abraham is fortuitously given expression not just in a scholarly theological work, but in a practical document as well. In an essay entitled "Christian Zionism, Evangelicals and Israel," which has been widely circulated in some mainline Protestant denominations, Burge sets forth and describes the five core beliefs of premillennial dispensationalism, also known as so-called Christian Zionism, in order to reckon with them. The first premillennial dispensationalist belief he treats is:

> Covenant: God's covenant with Israel is eternal and unconditional. Therefore the promises of land given to Abraham will never be overturned. This means that the Church has not replaced Israel and that Israel's privileges have never been revoked despite unfaithfulness.[5]

In commenting upon this core belief of Pre-Millennial Dispensationalism Burge writes,

> It would not be difficult to offer fatal criticisms of this theological framework . . . for instance the covenant's promises are conditional and their blessings are revoked when there is faithlessness. The Babylonian exile is the best example of this. But in addition the New Testament is making a stunning claim about genuine continuity between the covenants, that Christians are the children of Abraham and heirs of his promise.[6]

There is a striking similarity between premillennial dispensationalism and Gary Burge's theology about the status of the covenant made with Abraham and his children, the Jewish people. They both agree on one thing: the Jewish people will be disenfranchised; the covenant promise made to them by God in the Torah is taken away from them and given to those who have come to Christ. The only difference between the two theologies is the timing. For Gary Burge that happened two thousand years ago; for the premillennial dispensationalists it is just around the corner. There are just too many sources to cite in Roman Catholic and mainline Protestant documents affirming that the Jewish people are still in covenant with God; that this covenant is efficacious even in the context of the classical Christian hope and expectation that all humanity, including the Jews, but not just the Jews, will at some point come to Christ.

---

4. Burge, *Jesus and the Land*, 89.
5. Gary M. Burge, "Christian Zionism, Israel, and Evangelicals," 3 (christianzionim.org [accessed July 31, 2006]).
6. Burge, "Christian Zionism, Israel, and Evangelicals," 4.

Another parallel between Burge's theology and that of the premillennial dispensationalists is that they are both focused on end times and completing certain tasks in order for Christianity to soon realize its destiny. A feature of this aspiration is of course the use of the language and ideas of culmination and finality in a supernatural cataclysmic way. Burge writes,

> Just as the first century Church was forced to grapple with Jewish territorialism and nationalism, so too, the Christian Church today must do the same. This is our final assignment (emphasis mine).[7]

The Jews sinned once two thousand years ago, and in returning to sovereignty in the land of Israel are repeating that very sin. We know what happens when someone has some "final assignment" for the Jewish people. Burge joins the list of those millennialists, premillennialists, and others whose anticipation for the fulfillment of history necessarily involves some "final" cataclysmic event for the Jewish people.

The Particular and the Universal: The Theology of Naim Ateek

Another response to the Jewish return to Israel is the erasure of universalism. Palestinian theologian Naim Ateek takes up the idea of universalism in his writing about Israel. In his book, *Justice and Only Justice*, Ateek calls for a more mature understanding of God, in which God expresses concern for all peoples, not just Israel.[8] Ateek identifies three traditions in the Bible: the "nationalist," the "Torah-oriented," and the "prophetic." He considers the first two to be Jewish traditions and the third, while originally Jewish, is developed by Christianity. For Ateek, the "nationalist tradition" is found in the promises of God to Israel in the Bible, which Ateek sees as "very narrow" and "militaristic,"[9] because it emphasizes the land of Israel and God's special concerns for one people. The focus of the "Torah-oriented tradition" is somewhat more favorable because those who emphasize the study of Torah should have a fundamental religious obligation to reject political activity in favor of quietism and performance of the commandments. Nonetheless, this tradition is also described as tending "toward legalism and isolation."[10] Ateek claims that even Torah-oriented Jews have an insufficiently "mature" understanding of God because they also emphasize God's special relationship with Israel. According to Ateek, only the

---

7. Burge, *Jesus and the Land*, 114.
8. Naim S. Ateek, *Justice and Only Justice: A Palestinian Theology of Liberation* (Maryknoll, NY: Orbis, 1989) 92-97.
9. Ateek, *Justice and Only Justice*, 94.
10. Ateek, *Justice and Only Justice*, 95.

prophetic tradition truly reveals God. He argues that this is a late tradition, and the most evolved, because the focus is no longer on Israel, but on "all people."[11]

Ateek writes:

> The land that God has chosen at one particular time in history for one particular people is now perceived as a paradigm, a model, for God's concern for every people and every land . . .[12]

> The particular has become universal. The blessing of God's concern for one people is universalized to encompass every people and every land . .[13]

> To cling only to the understanding of God in those limited and exclusive passages is to be untrue to the overall Biblical heritage.[14]

> The tragedy of many Zionists today is that they have locked themselves into the nationalist concept of God. They are trapped in it and they will be freed only if they discard their primitive image of God for a more universal one.[15]

This assertion that "the particular has become universal" is at the very heart of the Jewish- Christian encounter. It is the argument of the New Testament and the new Israel against the Old Testament and the old Israel. However, because these ideas are central to the Christian teaching of contempt for Judaism and the Jewish people and contributed a necessary, but insufficient, cause two thousand years later to the destruction of European Jewry, the Catholic Church and the mainline Protestant denominations today view the Jewish people as having a divine vocation of their own, and do not denigrate the familial and particular nature of Israel's continued covenant with the one God. Ateek, as cited above, says that the modern state of Israel invokes

> An ancient promise – one that betrays a very exclusive and limited knowledge of God in one stage of human development – in order to justify their uprooting an entire people and expropriating their land in the twentieth century.[16]

In doing this Naim Ateek goes back to the first century. He explains why Christianity broke with Judaism. This is well-known. Ancient Israel is a people that professed a creed that is parochial, particular, and narrow; that believes that the one

---

11. Ateek, *Justice and Only Justice*, 97.
12. Ateek, *Justice and Only Justice*, 108.
13. Ateek, *Justice and Only Justice*, 108.
14. Ateek, *Justice and Only Justice*, 109.
15. Ateek, *Justice and Only Justice*, 109.
16. Ateek, *Justice and Only Justice*, 109.

God is theirs only and not available for all of humanity, for which they were punished with loss of their land and exile. This is an accurate description of the teaching of early Christianity and the church fathers about Judaism. Ateek emphasizes the universalist trends in the Bible. In doing so, he follows the anti-Jewish polemics of early and medieval Christians. He holds that since God is God of all the world, that He is as much the God of the Gentiles as of Israel, and therefore, any reading of the Bible that focuses on the particular covenant with Israel is wrong. For Ateek, this promise comes from what he calls the exclusive, narrow, or nationalistic parts of the Bible, the parts of the Bible that speak about the relationship between a "tribal" and an "ethnocentric" God and one people, and are therefore morally offensive.

Ateek treats the text of the Hebrew Bible and the Jewish people as certain passages in the New Testament and the early Church Fathers did some two millennia ago. Whatever in the text is addressed specifically to one people, Israel is at an inferior stage of God's revelation. This is improved upon by later prophets, and perfected by Jesus. Ateek uses the words of the prophets of ancient Israel to indict the state of Israel and the Jewish people, as did some early Christian polemics. For Ateek Jewish faithfulness is a scandal to *verus Israel*, the true Israel, Christianity. Judaism and the Jewish people are, in their very continuity, a blasphemy of particularism, a failure to understand their own purpose. Enduring Judaism is enduring particularism. For Ateek to continue this enterprise long after it has been repudiated by most Christian groups is not just anachronistic; it is to begin the teaching of the contempt of Judaism and the Jewish people all over again.

Naim Ateek takes that first century critique of Judaism and extends it to Zionism and to the state of Israel. He asserts that what is so odious about the Jewish return to the land of Israel is that the Jewish people in returning to their land, exercising sovereignty, building a majority Jewish culture are once again committing the sins of their ancestors two thousand years later. The very existence of Israel is an affront to the new covenant of Christianity. For a Christian it does not get much worse than that. For Ateek, as opposed to Burge, the Jews are not disenfranchised. Rather, their covenant is erased by being universalized.

Election and the Jewish People Today: The Theology of Mitri Raheb

Let us turn to the theological writing of another Palestinian theologian, Mitri Raheb, in his book *I Am a Palestinian Christian*. Raheb writes about the election of Israel in the Torah:

> Election, correctly understood, is therefore a promise to the weak, encouragement to the discouraged, and consolation to the desperate… Election is and

will always be God's action alone, which a human can never make exclusively his or her own, but which can be gambled away. Election by God is not "an eternal unchangeable decree" to which God "would be subject once and for all."[17]

Mitri Raheb writes that he does not believe that God's covenant made with Abraham and then with the Jewish people at Sinai continues after the coming of the Christ, nor can it apply in any way to the Jewish people today who are not "weak" or "desperate." I do not think I have to explain why this is unacceptable in virtually any contemporary Christian understanding of Judaism and of the continuity of the Jewish faith community in history. Raheb writes,

> I agree with Nicolas Walter, who writes: "In my opinion, Israel is not the "olive tree or the trunk", and certainly not the root, despite Jeremiah 11:16, for "Israel" is the branches of the olive—which have now—due to their non-acceptance of Jesus Christ—been in large measure removed (Rom 11:25b). Nor are the Gentiles the wild tree. Instead, the believers among the Gentiles are the newly grafted branches which have been removed from the "natural" wild tree, paganism. In my opinion, if one were to interpret the cultivated olive tree, its roots and the sap that flows into its branches and fruit, one would probably point first to God—to God's electing and promising, and the saving grace streaming from Him—but not identify it immediately with Israel. The election of the Gentiles should consequently be understood as a promise that has its roots and foundation solely in God's faithfulness (Rom 11:17–24).[18]

Whether the cultivated olive tree and its roots are to be identified primarily with Israel itself or with the God of Israel, the branches which Paul describes as being cut-off were "natural" to this tree (Rom 11:21, 24) and can be grafted back by God into "their own olive tree" (Rom 11:24). The attempt to distinguish sharply between Israel as the branches on the one hand and the tree from which they were cut on the other simply does not persuade as an interpretation of Paul's imagery. Mitri Raheb here subscribes to an understanding of Romans 11 that no mainstream Christian denomination (save possibly for some surviving Marcionites!) would embrace as its own.

---

17. Mitri Raheb, *I am a Palestinian Christian* (Minneapolis: Augsburg Fortress, 1995) 66-67, with quotation from Kurt Stürmer, "Auferstehung und Erwählung," BFCT 53 (1953) 161.

18. Raheb, *I am a Palestinian Christian*, 69 quoting Nicolaus Walter, "Zur Interpretation von Römer 9–11," ZTK 81 (1984) 172-95.

Perspectives on Covenant in Contemporary Lutheranism

Indeed, in an affirmation of 2002 from its Consultative Panel on Lutheran-Jewish Relations, the Evangelical Lutheran Church of America states,

> The living Jewish community of today — in North America, in Israel, and around the world — continues the heritage of biblical Israel and rabbinic Judaism in new and vibrant ways. While diversity has led to denominational differences among Jews, there remains a core communal identity and loyalty to the ancient faith. Often giving leadership in philanthropy and social justice causes, the Jewish community is a powerful partner with the church in living out God's call to be stewards of healing for the world.[19]

> Living in the new covenant given by God in Jesus Christ, we also affirm God's continuing faithfulness to the covenant with the Jewish people. Modern Judaism is a vibrant community with much to offer us in faith, ethics, and piety. Christians err if we dismiss Judaism as a misguided relic of the past.[20]

> From ancient Israel to our own day, Jews have lived in covenant with God as well. This is seen not only in the circumcision of Abraham and his offspring, but also, for example, in the kingship of David, the gift of the Torah at Sinai, and the appearance of the rainbow in the heavens. Israel's prophets were the ones who proclaimed God's faithful intent to establish a new covenant with the people, a living covenant "written on their hearts" (Jer. 31:33), even embodied in a "new heart" (Ezek. 36:26). This would not have to supersede the existing covenant understandings, but in continuity with them it would renew and extend Israel's hope and confidence in God's loving commitment.[21]

> *I ask then,*
> *has God rejected his people? By no means!*
> Rom 11:1[22]

Similarly, in a consultation document from 2001 the Lutheran World Federation (LWF) states,

> Yet all share in the heritage of biblical Israel that establishes the churches' bond to modern Jews and Judaism. In faithfulness to their calling in the gospel, the

---

19. Section 1, "Introduction: Judaism Then and Now," *Topics in Christian-Jewish Relations*, ELCA Consultative Panel on Lutheran-Jewish Relations, September 2002 (https://www.ccjr.us/dialogika-resources/documents-and-statements/protestant-churches/na/lutheran/elca2002).
20. Section 2, "Covenants Old and New," *Topics in Christian-Jewish Relations*.
21. Section 2, "Covenants Old and New," *Topics in Christian-Jewish Relations*.
22. Within *Topics in Christian-Jewish Relations* one or more biblical texts are quoted in boxes alongside the main text in support of the argument being made at that point. Romans 11:1 serves this function in Section 2, "Covenants Old and New."

churches will seek to discern the significance of this bond for the life and mission of the church. What we affirm is the validity of God's covenant with the Jewish people which has never been superseded.[23]

This reflects a concern that can be seen in other LWF documents from as long ago as 1969:

We as Lutherans affirm our solidarity with the Jewish people. This solidarity is legitimized in God's election and calling into being in Abraham's seed a people of promise, of faith, and of obedience peculiar unto him, a people whose unity will one day become manifest when "all Israel" will be saved. The Lutheran churches, therefore, may not appropriate the term "people of God" and "Israel" to the church in such a way as to deny that they applied in the first instance to the Jewish people. They may not assert continuity of the church with the covenant people of Abraham in such a way as to question the fact that present-day Judaism has its own continuity with Old Testament Israel (section 3).[24]

Finally, the 2016 Synod of the Evangelical Church in Germany made a declaration concerning the Jewish people and the proper sphere of Christian mission:

We conclude that: Irrespective of their mission in the world, Christians are not called to show Israel the way to God and his salvation. All efforts to induce Jews to change their religion contradict the confession of God's faithfulness and the continuing status of Israel as God's chosen people.[25]

The Jewish People and the Land in Contemporary Roman Catholic Theology: Gary Anderson and Richard Lux

I want to close with reference to the theological thinking of two Catholic scholars. The following excerpt comes from article published in 2009 in *The Christian Century* by the Catholic scholar Gary Anderson, who teaches at the University of Notre

---

23. "Antisemitism and Anti-Judaism Today. A Contribution to the Jewish-Christian Dialogue: A Consultation of the Lutheran World Federation, Dobogokö, Hungary, 2001" in *A Shift in Lutheran-Jewish Relations? A Lutheran Contribution to Christian-Jewish Dialogue with a focus on Antisemitism and Anti-Judaism Today*, edited by Wolfgang Greive and Peter N. Prove (Documentation No. 48; Geneva: Lutheran World Federation, 2003) 202 (https://www.lutheranworld.org/sites/default/files/dts-doc48-jewish-full.pdf).

24. *On the Theology of the Church's Relation to Judaism*, Committee on the Church and the Jews, Lutheran World Federation Commission on World Mission, Asmara, Ethiopia, April 1969 (https://www.ccjr.us/dialogika-resources/documents-and-statements/protestant-churches/int/lwf1969)

25. "A Declaration concerning Christians and Jews as Witnesses of God's Faithfulness," Declaration of the 12th Synod of the Evangelical Church in Germany, November 2016 (https://www.ccjr.us/dialogika-resources/documents-and-statements/protestant-churches/eur/ekd-2016nov9).

Dame. It is titled, "Does the promise still hold? Israel and the land: An essay and responses." Anderson writes,

> The return of the Jews to Israel has also posed a challenge to Christians. Ever since the days of Augustine, Israel's landlessness was commonly thought to be a punishment for the death of Christ. The events of the 20th century showed us where this type of thinking can lead. Happily, many Christians have moved beyond this position. The question now is whether we can move from an attitude of toleration to bold theological affirmation. It is hard to imagine what more fundamental promise to the people of Israel there is than that of the land. Certainly Paul must have presumed as much when he penned his letter to the Romans a few decades prior to the Roman invasion . . . Can we go one step further and say that the return to Zion in our own day is part of God's providential design? I believe we can. Does asserting this position require one to agree with all of the policies of the modern state? Obviously not.[26]

Curiously enough, what Gary Anderson presents is the only time in this paper that I am going to make reference to any Jewish religious thinking. What he writes is no different than mainstream pragmatic religious Zionism, which assiduously avoids the premature proclamation of a messianic era, and on the one hand gives thanks to God for faithfulness and on the other hand views the human creation of the present-day state of Israel as no different than the creation of any other democratic nation-state.

Finally, I want to turn to the thinking of Richard C. Lux, Professor of Scripture Studies at Sacred Heart School of Theology in Wisconsin. He is the author of *The Jewish People, The Holy Land, and the State of Israel: A Catholic View*. He writes,

> Nowhere in Paul's writings is the idea of the land of Israel *explicitly* mentioned. This is not surprising, since one of Paul's primary concerns was with the bonding together of his Gentile converts with the Jewish followers of Jesus. However, Romans 9-11 gives an eloquent defense of the continuing validity of God's covenant with Israel and its continuing election.[27]

This quote surely speaks for itself. He then builds upon it to discuss the meaning and significance that the land of Israel has had and can have for Christians. He writes,

> Catholics have often been called Sacramentalists, which means that we are a Church based on sacrament and word. She draws her life from the word in the

---

26. Gary Anderson, "Does the promise still hold? Israel and the Land: An Essay and Responses," *Christian Century* 126.1 (January 13, 2009) 25.

27. Richard C. Lux, *The Jewish People, The Holy Land, and the State of Israel: A Catholic View* (New York: Paulist, 2010) 49.

body of Christ and so herself becomes Christ's body. What is the meaning of Christ's presence here and how does this take place in Church?[28]

It is from this Sacramentalist perspective that Lux writes,

> In a reimaging of our relationship to the Holy Land we can say, 'As Christ is the sacrament of our encounter with God, the Holy Land is a sacrament of our encounter with Christ.'[29]

Lux bases this on the reality of the ministry of Jesus of Nazareth in the Holy Land and the venerated sites of his ministry as the object of Christian pilgrimage. Or, as the Apostolic Administrator, His Eminence, Pierbattista Pizzaballa once put it, "The sites of Christ's ministry in the Holy Land constitute the materialization of faith."[30]

Building upon this, Richard Lux seeks to describe a Christian, or Catholic, parallel to the Jewish people's attachment to the land of Israel. He writes,

> ... the relationship of *all* the Christian people to the Roman Catholic Church as an instrument and manifestation of covenant fidelity to God and the relationship of *all* the Jewish people to the State of Israel as an instrument and manifestation of covenant fidelity to God has a surprising and life- giving parity! In sum, the proposal that the state of Israel and the Roman Catholic Church are both covenantal institutional structures within which a fidelity to God can be lived out in concrete ways has some consequences.[31]

Conclusion: The Dangers of Theology

Having presented a few Christian theologies about the land of Israel and the Jewish people's return to sovereignty in the land of Israel, let me make a simple plea and call for a moratorium on theology. In the past two thousand years, not a single Christian prediction made about Judaism and the Jewish people came to be. In the past two thousand years most Christian theological writing about the Jewish people has had devastating consequences for the Jewish people, and I dare say, for Christianity itself. There is a deep Jewish aversion to the writing of theology. At risk is the sin of hubris itself in that theology seeks to present the mind of God and the will of God about contemporary events.

---

28. Lux, *The Jewish People*, 56.
29. Lux, *The Jewish People*, 60.
30. This perspective was one expressed by Pierbattista Pizzaballa in personal conversation with the author.
31. Lux, *The Jewish People*, 92.

RESPONSE TO POUPKO

Robert Cathey

A Question about the Israeli-Palestinian Conflict

I am grateful for the opportunity to respond to Rabbi Poupko's very interesting paper. Exploring his reflections has prompted me to ask one overview question and to make a modest proposal. My question is the following:

> Are theological-ethical issues raised by the Israeli-Palestinian conflict dialogical?

Some argue from experience that they are not. A colleague of mine who is a theological ethicist at a church-related university first shared this question and negative conclusion with me. My colleague directs a program that engages a diverse public audience in a wide array of social issues in order to work toward the common good. Their constituents include Christians, Jews, Muslims, and secular persons of good will. Over the years my friend learned they could foster good public dialogue on any issue with two exceptions: abortion and the Israeli-Palestinian conflict. On these two public issues, more heat than light was always generated regardless of whom they invited to speak, and one or more communities went home ready to disengage from others in dialogue.

Recently I tested this experience with the former president of an innovative seminary. She reported the same outcome in their public programs. Israeli-Palestinian issues tend to make partisans of us all. How one would even begin to set up the rules of engagement for such a dialogue seem elusive.

For example, take the following four observations:

1. There is no one historical record of the conflict that all sides agree on;
2. The vocabulary for naming the conditions on the ground differ;
3. Both Israelis and Palestinians see themselves in an existential conflict in which external actors and nation-states have taken sides with lethal consequences;

4. Peoples on both sides have been traumatized by the violence and consequences of the conflict.

My colleagues' experiences as social ethicists raises the question for us, how will we engage in discussion of these issues here at this conference, hoping for more light rather than merely more heat?

As an academic, I tend to assume that with good planning one can provide positive learning experiences about all manner of debatable issues. But in the case of the Israeli-Palestinian conflict, we run up against the limits of our different visions of justice, our different understandings of the conflict, our different goals for the outcome, and some deeply held theological convictions.

A Modest Proposal concerning the Israeli-Palestinian Conflict

This gridlock leads me to a modest proposal. Let me begin with a qualification. Some Christians tend to view the Israeli-Palestinian conflict through the lens of other conflicts, e.g., South Africa and the American civil rights movement. In my proposal below, I am not recommending that we reduce the Israeli-Palestinian conflict to the terms of the struggle for civil rights in the US.

In 1949, Howard Thurman published his best-known book, *Jesus and the Disinherited*.[1] The first chapter, "Jesus—An Interpretation," is the best known. Thurman identified the historical Jesus as a first century Jew among Jews who lived under Roman occupation. His life was one of solidarity with his own colonized people who lived with their backs up against the wall.

Thurman argues this is the Jesus whom many African Americans have identified with as their Savior who gives them strength to struggle against discrimination and deprivation. Like a modern-day Emerson, Thurman constructs from Jesus' life and teachings a spiritual-moral vision of life lived unbowed to oppression. At the same time, according to Thurman, Jesus' modern-day followers must resist the temptation to give into hatred that dehumanizes the oppressor into an object fit for revolutionary execution.

The following chapters of *Jesus and the Disinherited* lay out a philosophy of how one can resist oppression non-violently while not giving in to hate for the oppressor. They cover the topics of fear, deception, hate, and love. In the new documentary on Howard Thurman's life that premiered last spring, many veterans of the civil rights movement testify to the impact of Thurman's philosophy of non-violent opposition to oppression and the kind of love for one's fellow human beings that refuses hatred.

---

1. Howard Thurman, *Jesus and the Disinherited* (Boston: Beacon, 1976, 1996) 102.

What if in our times someone authored a work of spiritual-moral vision for those who resist the current conditions faced by Palestinians in the occupied territories and in other nations of the Palestinian diaspora? I imagine a book that taught a practical philosophy of non-violent resistance and at the same time how to avoid the temptations of anti-Semitism and anti-Judaism. For as some of us may know from experience, when we come to hate others, they gain a power over us that unleashes the worst aspects of our all-too-human condition.

Conclusion: Dialogue and Christian Theology

Both Rabbi Poupko and Adam Gregerman of St. Joseph University in Philadelphia have shown us through their scholarship how some Christian theologies about the modern nation of Israel often fall into the tropes of anti-Judaism and replacement theology.[2] Some of these theologies seem intended to undermine Jewish and Christian Zionist rationales for the existence of the modern state of Israel, not only to change Israeli policy and practice vis-a-vis the Palestinians. Such theologies are not the beginning of constructive dialogue. Our debates over theologies about the state of Israel sometimes function as a war of words we conduct on the sidelines beyond the conflict in Israel or Palestine. Our war of words often creates more partisans or merely preaches to the choir. How might we construct the terms of a dialogue between Jews, Christians, Muslims, and people of good will seeking pragmatic steps that might build toward a better future for all the diverse peoples of the region called Israel by some, Palestine by others?

---

2. Here is a sample of Gregerman's research on Christian theological approaches to land issues in Israel/Palestine: Adam Gregerman, "Old Wine in New Bottles: Liberation Theology and the Israeli-Palestinian Conflict," *Journal of Ecumenical Studies* 41.3-4 (2004) 313–40; Adam Gregerman, "Comparative Christian Hermeneutical Approaches to the Land Promises to Abraham," *Cross Currents* 64.3 (2014): 410–25; Adam Gregerman, "Is the Biblical Land Promise Irrevocable?: Post-Nostra Aetate Catholic Theologies of the Jewish Covenant and the Land of Israel," *Modern Theology* 34.2 (2018) 137–58.

COMMUNITIES OF FORGIVENESS: A PALESTINIAN CHRISTIAN PERSPECTIVE[1]

Rula Khoury Mansour

Introduction

Christian forgiveness is much more than an individual experience involving the speaking of words and the healing of inner emotions; it is a social relationship. God works in the lives of forgivers through a community that makes the practice of forgiveness full of meaning.[2]

In this paper, I will present the argument that for a successful forgiveness process to take place, community is essential. It provides the place of belonging that everyone desires and needs, and in that sense the community can offer support to its members — both offenders and offended — by bearing the burden of wrongs done together, as the Apostle Paul exhorted us: "Bear one another's burdens, and thereby fulfill the law of Christ" (Gal 6:2).

In order to explain the significance of the community in the forgiveness process, I will describe forgiveness in two different settings: theological and cultural. Theologically, I will describe forgiveness in a Western evangelical theology (using Miroslav Volf's theology, which was created in an individualistic Western culture). Culturally, I will give an account of forgiveness in a communal culture, choosing my own culture: the Palestinian Middle Eastern community. This is for two reasons: first, Palestinian Middle Eastern cultural proximity to the Bible's own context and second, it is my own culture, which I believe has amazing themes that we as followers of Christ can learn from.

---

1. Some of the literature review and ideas in this paper are taken from chapter 7 of my book *Theology of Reconciliation in the Context of Church Relations: A Palestinian Christian Perspective in Dialogue with Miroslav Volf* (Carlisle, UK: Langham Monographs, 2020). Used with permission.

2. See Miroslav Volf, *Free of Charge: Giving and Forgiving in a Culture Stripped of Grace* (Grand Rapids: Eerdmans, 2005) 214.

According to Karl Barth, "culture means humanity";[3] therefore if humanity is a gift from God then culture is also a gift from God. Yu argues, "All culture, no matter how inadequate, aims to achieve a certain degree of wholeness for human existence. The wholeness of humanity however can only be found in the fulfilment of humanity as the image of God,"[4] namely, us. Culture is not static. Elements of culture may be transformed or filled with new meanings and take on new expressions. Culture is constructed as we select particular items from the shelves of our past and present. In this way cultures can be seen to change; they are borrowed, blended, rediscovered, and redefined.[5]

After I present forgiveness in a culturally Palestinian model (*sulha*) and in a Western evangelical model, I will compare them and make the proposal that for successful forgiveness processes first, community should have an active role and, second, forgiveness should have external expressions in addition to internal ones.[6]

Forgiveness and Community Setting

Forgiveness is often described as a shift in *feelings*, *attitudes*, and *behavior* toward the offender. The process of forgiveness begins as an internal process of overcoming any negative feelings towards the offender such as resentment, anger, avoidance, and revenge.[7] Some suggest that forgiveness involves trying to replace any negative feelings towards the offender, with feelings of compassion and love for the offender,[8] and even a desire for "friendship,"[9] and thus, the intrapersonal process of shifting in attitude and emotions may progress to the interpersonal process of restoration

---

3. Karl Barth, "Church and Culture" in *Theology and Church: Shorter Writings* (New York: Harper & Row, 1962) 338, as cited in Carver Yu, "Culture from an Evangelical Perspective," *Transformation* 17.3 (2000) 82

4. Yu, "Culture from an Evangelical Perspective," 82.

5. Joane Nagel, "Constructing Ethnicity: Creating and Recreating Ethnic Identity and Culture," *Social Problems* 41.1 (1994) 162.

6. It is noteworthy that forgiveness does not simply equate to reconciliation. It is an essential element in reconciliation, but reconciliation is incomplete without justice and embrace.

7. Everett Worthington Jr., "The Pyramid Model of Forgiveness: Some Interdisciplinary Speculations about Unforgiveness and the Promotion of Forgiveness," in *Dimensions of Forgiveness: Psychological Research and Religious Perspectives*, edited by Everett Worthington Jr. (Laws of Life Symposia Series Vol. 1; Philadelphia: Templeton Foundation, 1998) 108.

8. Robert Enright, Suzanne Freedman, and Julio Rique, "The Psychology of Interpersonal Forgiveness," in *Exploring Forgiveness*, edited by Robert D. Enright and Joanna North (Madison: University of Wisconsin Press, 1998) 46–62; Jeffrie Murphy and Jean Hampton, *Forgiveness and Mercy* (Cambridge: Cambridge University Press, 1988); Trudy Govier, *Forgiveness and Revenge* (London: Routledge, 2002).

9. Nigel Biggar, "Forgiveness in the Twentieth Century: A Review of the Literature 1901–2001," in *Forgiveness and Truth*, edited by Alistair McFadyen and Marcel Sarot (Edinburgh: T. & T. Clark, 2001).

of broken relationships.[10] Forgiveness can also be seen as a shift in *behavior*, such as seeing forgiveness as a *craft* that is practiced throughout a person's lifetime by constantly shifting attitudes and behaviors for the sake of others and community.[11]

A community can be seen as a group of people with a shared culture and language who live together and feel connected through their common values and experiences. Members feel a sense of community when they feel that they belong to one another, that they are important to one another, and that they can meet each other's needs.[12] In order to honor its transcendent values, a community will choose certain events to become part of its collective heritage, and will often represent these events in the community's symbols. Certain tragic events within a community with stories of redemption and courage became community stories that represent the community's values and traditions.[13]

Communities have been seen to be more cohesive when community leaders and members simultaneously influence each other. Social scientists have found that trust is a key aspect of influence, which happens through the community's use of its power. In order for a community to have trust that will evolve into justice, there needs to be order (community norms and rules), decision making capacity, authority based on principle (rather than person), and group norms.[14] In addition, love, intimacy, and cohesiveness have been seen by social scientists to operate simultaneously from the individual to the group and from the group to the individual. This happens when order, authority, and justice create the right atmosphere for the exchange of power.[15]

A community makes decisions and acts according to its shared beliefs, empowering its members to communal actions whether for good or bad. Individual attitudes and behavior within the community differ from those in another interpersonal setting, because the member acts as a part of a community (although he or she may not represent the attitude of the whole community). History is full of examples of group members who were empowered by one another to display revenge and violence, but we need more examples of how a community can empower its members to display empathy, acceptance, and forgiveness.

---

10. For some, forgiveness is incomplete or has not happened at all if this intrapersonal process does not become interpersonal.

11. Gregory Jones, *Embodying Forgiveness: A Theological Analysis* (Grand Rapids: Eerdmans, 1995).

12. David W. McMillan and David M. Chavis, "Sense of Community: A Definition and Theory," *Journal of Community Psychology* 24.4 (1986) 6–23.

13. David W. McMillan, "Sense of Community." *Journal of Community Psychology* 24.4 (1996) 323.

14. McMillan, "Sense of Community," 315-25.

15. McMillan, "Sense of Community," 320.

In order for a community to be strong, members need to be able to interact with each other and have shared experiences. When members honor each other and each invests in the community, an increased spiritual bond can grow among the members.[16]

It is reasonable to conclude that the community is the natural place for providing forgiveness and embrace for its members — especially those offended and the offenders; simply, forgiveness in the community is like "bearing one another's burden."[17] Christian forgiveness is a response to God's forgiving love, it involves crafting communities of *forgiven* and *forgiving* people.[18] To discover what it means to be *forgiven forgivers* depends on the richness of one's communal habits and the practices of grace-filled Christian communities.[19]

Communal societies, such as those of the Middle East, Africa, Asia, and Latin America, place high value on the network of interpersonal relationships within a community, encouraging their members to communal actions. Therefore, injuring an individual means hurting the entire community. These injuries will expand if not repaired and forgiven.[20] On the other hand, forgiving strengthens communal bonds and restore relationship.[21]

In what follows I will present forgiveness in *sulha*, the Palestinian Middle Eastern communal approach, and in Volf's Western theological model, I will compare them and make a proposal.

Forgiveness in the Palestinian Middle Eastern Tradition: The *Sulha* Model

What is *Sulha*?

Sulha means peace in Arabic. It also means "resolution" or "settlement" or "fixing" generally, in problem solving. *Sulha* is a ceremonial-covenant meal of reconciliation. Though not mentioned specifically, this ancient tradition could be seen as present in many covenantal ceremonies in Scripture. Some examples are the covenant meal of reconciliation between Jacob and his father-in-law Laban;[22] the ceremonial meal the

---

16. McMillan and Chavis, "Sense of Community: A Definition and Theory," 14–15
17. Jones, *Embodying Forgiveness,* 271; Galatians 6:1–2.
18. Gregory Jones, "Crafting Communities of Forgiveness," *Interpretation* 54 (2000) 122.
19. Jones, "Crafting Communities of Forgiveness," 126–31. Jones refers to Jas 5:12–20 to point to activities that form and sustain Christian community as the body of Christ.
20. Elias Jabbour, *Sulha: Palestinian Traditional Peace-making Process* (Montreat, NC: House of Hope, 1993).
21. Miroslav Volf, *Free of Charge.*
22. Genesis 31:52–54.

father prepared for the Prodigal Son;[23] Jesus' invitation: "Behold, I stand at the door and knock. If anyone hears My voice and opens the door, I will come in to him and dine with him, and he with Me."[24] In the Lord's Supper Jesus chooses the fellowship meal of the Passover to celebrate God's redemption of his people. In addition, for thousands of years, Eastern cultures throughout Asia and Africa perceived sharing a meal together as a sign of genuine fellowship and a symbol of peace.

Sulha, the Palestinian Middle Eastern model of reconciliation, makes use of a unique mix of local variants of mediation and arbitration techniques to help transform inter- and intra- communal conflicts from revenge to forgiveness.[25] *Sulha* does not recognize the Western-based differentiation between mediation and arbitration, but rather makes use of both approaches when needed.[26] *Sulha* is still used to this day, sometimes in the absence of state jurisdiction and at other times alongside state judicial procedures, but it does not replace an individual's responsibility, which is subject to trial by the state legal system.

The communal approach to conflict is based on the view that hurting an individual means hurting the entire community.[27] *Sulha* "stresses the close link between the psychological and political dimensions of communal life through its recognition that injuries between individuals and groups will fester and expand if not acknowledged, repaired, forgiven, and transcended."[28] As ritualized behavior, *sulha* produces the space for retrieving dignity when lost. As an interpersonal strategy, *sulha* allows for micro-level relationship repair with the capability for macro-level impact.[29] *Sulha* does not address the source of conflict but does re-adjust communities for peaceful coexistence and keeping the status quo. Such views of social order are represented and retold repeatedly in the minds of *sulha* participants.[30]

23. Luke 15:11–31.

24. Revelation 3:20.

25. On the mediation side, *sulha* strives to reconcile differences between the disputants' clans; on the arbitration side, the decision of the *jaha* is final and binding (Jabbour, *Sulha*).

26. Doron Pely, "Where East not always meets West: Comparing the *Sulha* Process to Western Style Mediation and Arbitration," *Conflict Resolution Quarterly* 28.4 (2011) 427–40.

27. Jabbour, *Sulah*.

28. Laurie King-Irani, "The Power of Transformation and The Transformation of Power: Rituals of Forgiveness and Processes of Empowerment in Post-War Lebanon," in *Traditional Cures for Modern Conflicts: African Conflict "Medicine,"* edited by I. William Zartman (Boulder: Lynne Rienner, 2000) 131, quoted in George E. Irani and Nathan C. Funk, "Rituals of Reconciliation: Arab-Islamic Perspectives" in *Peace and Conflict Resolution in Islam: Precept and Practice*, edited by Abdul Aziz Said, Nathan C. Funk, and Ayse S. Kadayifci (Lanham, MD: University Press of America, 2001) 182.

29. Mneesha Gellman and Mandi Vuinovich, "From *Sulha* to *Salaam*: Connecting Local Knowledge with International Negotiations for Lasting Peace in Palestine/Israel," *Conflict Resolution Quarterly* 26.2 (2008) 127–48.

30. Sharon Lang, "*Sulha* Peace-making Process and the Politics of Persuasion," *Journal of Palestine Studies* 31.3 (2002) 52–66.

The connection between the internal cohesiveness of the Arab family and community and *sulha* is crucial. "The collective responsibility of the extended family or the community in Arab culture toward all its members is one of the main factors that makes *sulha* work."[31] It is important to recognize that in the same manner that the family or the community may be the key to resolving conflicts, they could also cause the eruption or quick expansion of conflicts.

The Stages of the *Sulha* Process

Sulha has six stages:

1. *Jaha:* forming the *Sulha* committee

The *jaha* includes only elderly men. The *jaha* draws its power from its members' positions in the community and from a disputant's authorization.[32] The *jaha* includes an "unbiased insider with on-going connections to the major disputants as well as a strong sense of the common good and standing within the community."[33] They are not neutral outsiders, since they are familiar with the history, norms, and customs of the community.[34] They are selected for their honesty, experience, intelligence, status, leadership in the community, and age (as older community members are highly respected in Arabic society);[35] in other words, the *jaha* represents the community.[36]

The role of the *jaha* is to urge the offended family, on behalf of the offender, to seek reconciliation through *sulha* instead of revenge. A unique characteristic of the *jaha* is its ability to act as "anger or shock absorbers," with great tolerance and patience, when listening to family members of disputants who are often filled with sadness and bitterness. As Jabbour, a long-time dispute resolution practitioner within

---

31. Jabbour, *Sulha,* 69.

32. Doron Pely, "Resolving Clan-Based Disputes using the "*Sulha*" the Traditional Dispute Resolution Process of the Middle East." *Journal of Dispute Resolution,* 63.4 (2008) 80–88.

33. George Irani and Nathan Funk, "Rituals of Reconciliation: Arab-Islamic Perspectives." *Arab Studies Quarterly* 20.4 (1998) 61.

34. Mohammed Abu-Nimer, "Conflict Resolution Approaches: Western and Middle Eastern Lessons and Possibilities," *American Journal of Economics and Sociology,* 55.1 (1996) 35–52.

35. Gellman and Vuinovich, "From *Sulha* to *Salaam.*"

36. Women are not allowed to serve in the *jaha,* and the *sulha* does not contain any formal mechanism designed to provide for the concerns of women. However, Doron Pely, "Women in S*ulha* – Excluded yet Influential: Examining Arab Women's Formal and Informal Place in Traditional Dispute Resolution, within the Patriarchal Culture of Northern Israel's Arab Community," *International Journal of Conflict Management* 22.1 (2011) 89–104 examines the role of women within *sulha* and finds that women's informal influence extends throughout the process, from the pre-*sulha* stage of venting to the *sulha* agreement.

the Palestinian community says, venting is fundamental in *sulha*: "Grief work must be enabled by the *jaha* to make way for peace."[37]

2. *Taffwid*: initiating the *Jaha*

To act officially, representatives of the offender's family contact a member of the local *jaha* and provide the *jaha* with a *taffwid* — that is, an irreversible written authorization to act on their behalf to contact the victim's family and conduct the *sulha*. The *taffwid* contains the commitment of the offender's family to obey whatever verdict the *jaha* reaches.[38] By giving written authorization, the psychological, emotional, and communal burden of the conflict is shifted from the parties to the *jaha*, namely: *the community*.

3. *Hodna:* ceasefire agreement

The *sulha* process begins after the *taffwid* is given. The *jaha*'s first goal is to convince both families of offended and offender to accept a temporary ceasefire and promise not to take revenge or confront the other side.[39]

4. *Atwa*: payment of good faith

The *sulha* process demands a symbolic payment from the offender's family to the offended's, as determined by the *jaha*. The *atwa* is in addition to any payment made by the offender's family to ensure its agreement to obey the *jaha*'s final decision. When the victim's family receive the *atwa*, the *hodna* goes into effect.[40]

5. The *Jaha*'s investigation

Investigation generally takes place via private discussions with representatives of the disputants and witnesses. The *jaha* must not expose information given by witnesses as it could damage the reputation of the *jaha* and the community's trust in them as credible mediators.[41]

6. The *sulha* ceremony

The verdict is determined and participation in post-ceremony activities is required to ensure the durability of the agreement. If the offender has already taken responsibility, the *jaha*'s only determinations are the amount of compensation to be paid and conditions for reconciliation. This includes paying a huge amount of

---

37. Jabbour, *Sulha*, 46–47
38. Pely, "Resolving Clan-based Disputes." 82.
39. Jabbour, *Sulha*, 34.
40. Jabbour, *Sulha*, 35.
41. Pely, "Resolving Clan-based Disputes," 84.

compensation for the victim's family and many times (in murder cases) the offender's family is asked to leave the village for some years or even permanently. If the dispute did not arise out of violence, the *jaha* does not assign guilt. A mediated agreement, agreeable to each side, is crafted and memorialized in writing;[42] it is then read at a public ceremony and signed by representatives from each side. Afterwards the *jaha* and notable community members sign the agreement as well. A rejection of the verdict is considered a severe infraction of the process, an insult to the *jaha* and a loss of face for all involved.[43]

External Public Expressions in *Sulha*: Forgiveness is Seen

Forgiveness cannot be adequately discussed as an abstract concept; it should take local form and therefore it must be contextualized. Forgiveness and honor (which I will elaborate next) are the main basis of the socio-cultural assumptions employed within *sulha*.[44] In the *sulha* process, several external expressions of forgiveness are seen:

1. Ceremony in the village center: When the *sulha* agreement is ready, disputants' families and the wider community are invited to the final *sulha* ceremony outdoors in the village center, as the restoration of honor requires public viewing.[45] In murder cases, the most senior representatives of the disputing families tie a symbolic knot in a "peace flag." The white cloth flag represents both forgiveness by the victim's family and submission of both families to the authority of the *sulha* committee.[46]

2. Heavy silence: The final *sulha* ceremony is usually punctuated by a "heavy silence"[47] and is a scene of temporary humility by both parties — the offender's family humbly accepts the wrongdoings and offers compensation on behalf of their family member, and the bereaved family respectfully forgives the offender's family as an act of humility.

3. Three symbolic acts: The final ceremony is centered on forgiveness, peace, and compromise for the greater good of society. *Sulha* ceremonies involve three symbolic acts:

---

42. At this point, there are no further negotiations or appeals allowed in relation to its contents.
43. Jabbour, *Sulha:* Pely, "Resolving Clan-based Disputes"; Gellman & Vuinovich, "From *Sulha* to *Salaam.*"
44. Jabbour *Sulha*, 56.
45. Lang, "*Sulha* Peace-making Process and the Politics of Persuasion," 58.
46. Pely, "Resolving Clan-based Disputes," 85.
47. Jabbour, *Sulha*. 55.

(a) *Musafaha*, a handshake between the disputants validates the peace for all those present and absent.[48]

(b) *Musamaha*, a declaration of forgiveness by the victim's father.

(c) *Mumalaha*, a ceremonial meal that ends the *sulha* process. The sharing of a meal indicates the reversal of the tragedy and the restoration of peace.[49]

4. Venting ritual: In *sulha*, the venting ritual aims to start the process of channeling the emotions of the victim's family. It is given large cultural support in order to help position them into the communally preferred option of conciliation and forgiveness.[50] In her discussion of *sulha*, Sharon Lang describes the venting process and the underlying social rationale as "reverse *musayara*" (reverse social etiquette and ingratiation). This refers to the practice whereby the *jaha* treat the victim's family, from the beginning to the end of the *sulha* process, with the great respect normally given to high status persons. Lang explains this process as a performative reversal of the standard patron-client relationship common in Arab society: "In relationships of patronage (*wasta*) the client's request for a favor is flattering for the patron, and each *wasta* favor can be seen as a transaction wherein honor flows from the client to the patron."[51] In the venting process the *jaha* symbolically turn this relationship on its head (reverse *musayara*) by pleading with an ordinary family to grant them a favor, namely to forgive rather than to seek revenge. This reverse positioning is exceptionally flattering for the offended, humiliated family. The family is temporarily placed in a position of "patronage" over the most respected men in the community. Such a process calms the feelings of humiliation further and in a sense contributes to honor restoration.

5. Honor tools: *Sulha* is the only culturally authorized means to provide an alternative to the path of vengeance. In *sulha*, honor plays a major functional, ritualistic, and emotional role. Interveners and disputants use honor tools during each of *sulha's* stages so that the option to forgive gradually replaces the drive to avenge.[52] If, eventually, honor is increased and forgiveness replaces revenge, there will be an agreement. The use of honor tools continues after the agreement, with honorable

---

48. The larger community is taking the role of an observer, rather than that of an active witness to the resolution.

49. Irani and Funk, "Rituals of Reconciliation," 65.

50. Jabbour, *Sulha*.

51. Lang, "*Sulha* Peace-making Process and the Politics of Persuasion," 55.

52. Honor tools such as: the ceremony, the apology, compensation, praises to the offended family, the venting process, the offended family starts the ceremony process (under the protection of the white flag the offender family are welcomed to join the reconciliation ceremony).

figures noticeably used in actions designed to guarantee the endurance of the agreement.[53]

Sulha provides a culturally appropriate means for restoring values and demonstrates that cultural symbols and rituals are necessary for societal construction of peaceful coexistence.[54] In the Holy Land, *sulha* is a method of communicating both the need to "resolve a conflict" as well as creating a future-oriented socio-political relationship in which different communities can live together in harmony.[55] Even if done with resentment, the final sharing of a meal is the ritualized performance of sharing vital nutrients that counts, "Sincerity is irrelevant because by participating in the *sulha* the actors enmesh themselves in a web of social relations that will constrain them to observe the peace."[56]

The honor tools, venting ritual, heavy silence, public acknowledgement of wrongdoings, *sulha* verdict (partial justice, restitution, and material reparation) ceremony in the village center, and the three symbolic acts of handshake, declaring forgiveness, and sharing of a meal indicate the reversal of the tragedy and the restoration of peace. Coexistence, mutual toleration, and respect are established. These are external public expressions of forgiveness which happened *gradually*. Forgiveness is seen and heard publicly with the whole community and the disputants present.

Sulha has amazing themes. Nonetheless it lacks some aspects that would make its reconciliation closer to what I call a "diplomatic reconciliation"; an ethical response which echoed some of the major concerns of Palestinians, notably living in a relational, closely intertwined community, and in an unforgiving traumatized environment. By walking a fine line between conflicting demands and possibilities, this "diplomatic reconciliation" allowed them to cooperate and live together in some kind of social order.[57] However, this diplomatic reconciliation can become genuine reconciliation. Genuine reconciliation could be achieved as a result of working through the public expressions of forgiveness, though not necessarily in a linear structure. Despite the dangers of rigidity, describing processes of forgiveness in this

---

53. Doron Pely, "Honor: The *Sulha's* Main Dispute Resolution Tool," *Conflict Resolution Quarterly* 28.1 (2010) 73.

54. Gellman and Vuinovich, "From *Sulha* to *Salaam*."

55. Daniel L. Smith, "The Reward of Allah." *Journal of Peace Research*, 26.4 (1989) 385–98.

56. Lang "*Sulha* Peace-making Process and the Politics of Persuasion," 64.

57. See Rula Khoury Mansour, *Theology of Reconciliation*, 146. *Sulha* has a few weaknesses. First, *sulha* intervenes only *after* the conflict has exploded. Second, the values of honor and forgiveness, that are foundational to the *sulha* process, can also prevent or obstruct the process of reaching a just resolution; by reinforcing the unequal power balance that exists between the two parties. Third, *jaha* lacks the resources and professional background fully to understand the causes of disputes, and instead treats the symptoms. Finally, and most importantly, God has no clear role in *sulha* although the *sulha* committee includes religious dignitaries.

manner increases awareness of what might help in the full achievement of forgiveness, and would open possibilities for internal divine forgiveness which will lead into genuine reconciliation.

Forgiveness in the *Sulha* Model

How is forgiveness understood in the Palestinian context (*sulha*)? How might culture or religious beliefs influence forgiveness both in understanding and enactment? As we have seen, forgiveness in *sulha* has the following characteristics:

1. Forgiveness is mostly initiated by community representatives (the *jaha*) aiming at achieving social order and peace in the community. This process will shift the burden of the wrongdoing from the disputants to the community.

2. Forgiveness is conditional on achieving reconciliation.

3. Forgiveness in *sulha* is obligatory. The victim's family *has* to forgive — both as a ritual and practically. This act of reconciliation is binding.

4. It has a declaratory nature and transforms forgiveness from a private to a public affair covering past, present, and future generations. Its aim is to transform revenge to forgiveness through the tool of public restoration of dignity.

5. Forgiveness takes place in a triangle which includes the community, the family of the offended, and the family of the offender. This forgiveness is human, not divine.

6. It is a decision that is made externally and it demands the participation of the whole community with the rituals, because without this restoration of dignity would fail.

7. Described in this way forgiveness in *sulha* can be viewed as a change in attitude and behavior by the offended, or by both offended and offender. Forgiveness is seen as an *invitational act by the community* which leads to a bilateral process of forgiving and embracing. Given the fact that *sulha* is conditioned by achieving reconciliation, forgiveness is mainly identified as a *bilateral process*.

After introducing forgiveness in the Palestinian Middle Eastern culture, I will move to explain forgiveness in a Western evangelical theology.

Forgiveness in a Western Evangelical Theology: Volf's Theology of Forgiveness

Understanding God's Forgiveness

According to Volf to forgive is to name wrong in the sense that it entails it, but the heart of forgiveness is not naming and blaming. Forgiveness is a special kind of gift, and by forgiving we release others from the burden of their wrongdoing.[58] As for Christians, forgiving always takes place in a triangle involving the wrongdoer, the wronged person, and God. If we forgive because God forgives, then we should forgive as God forgives by echoing God's forgiveness. Thus, to understand our own forgiveness we should understand God's.[59]

In understanding how God forgives, Volf highlights the difference between doing justice and forgiving. He argues, "To be just is to condemn the fault and, because of the fault, to condemn the doer as well. To forgive is to condemn the fault but to spare the doer. That's what the forgiving God does."[60] But God does not merely spare sinners the penalty for sin, God also separates their sin from them.[61] Our unforgiveness, explains Volf, may make manifest the fact we have not allowed ourselves to receive and be shaped by God's forgiveness.[62]

In sum, to receive forgiveness means to receive both the accusation and the release from debt. To receive release from debt, we simply believe and rejoice in gratitude for the generous gift. To receive the accusation, we confess our offence and repent.[63]

---

58. Volf, *Free of Charge*, 130.

59. Volf, *Free of Charge*, 130–131.

60. Volf, *Free of Charge*, 141.

61. God can do that because: first, Christ who died for our sins is one with God, and second, Christ who died for our sins is also one with humanity. It is because of Christ's union with humanity that God can separate sinners from their sin (Volf, 146). Volf mentions two effects of the union with Christ: (1) we are freed from the power of sin and the life we live is God's life in us; (2) God does not count our sins to us but instead counts to us Christ's righteousness (2 Cor 5:17). So, in fact, God does not only forgive us; he transforms us into Christ-like figures (Volf, *Free of Charge*, 148–51).

62. This is how Luther explained forgiveness in the Lord's Prayer, "The outward forgiveness that I show in my deeds is a sure sign that I have the forgiveness of sin in the sight of God. On the other hand, if I do not show this in my relations with my neighbor, I have a sure sign that I do not have the forgiveness of sin in the sight of God and am still stuck in my unbelief." See *Luther's Works* 31:150, edited by Harold J. Grimm (Philadelphia: Fortress, 1957) as cited in Volf, *Free of Charge*, 156).

63. Volf, *Free of Charge*, 153.

How Should We Forgive?

Volf explains, we should forgive because 'saving' our enemies matters more to us than punishing them,[64] just as God re-established communion with us by forgiving our sin. We cannot forgive exactly as God does, but because we were created to be like the God who forgives we should imitate God in our own way as an instrument of God.[65] Since God is in us and Christ lives through us, God forgives and we make God's forgiveness our own and so pass it on.[66] To forgive means doing the following activities:

1. To condemn: condemnation and blame are intrinsic to the process of forgiveness, "we accuse when we forgive, and in doing that, we affirm the rightful claims of justice."[67]

2. To not shrug off: we should forgive primarily for the other's sake, not our own, as a gift we give to the one who has wronged us. Emotional healing is not the main purpose of forgiveness.[68]

3. To release debt: (a) not to press charges against the wrongdoer, (b) to forego the demand of retribution, (c) to absorb the injury, (d) to blame but not to punish.[69]

4. To release from guilt: punishment cannot release us from guilt. Only forgiveness can. "Christ didn't only bear our punishment on account of his oneness with God; Christ also separated us, the doers, from our evil deeds and released us from guilt on account of his oneness with humanity."[70] Those who forgive see the forgiven offenders as innocent, not guilty.

5. To forgive indiscriminately: "God's forgiveness is not reactive—dependent on our repentance."[71] It is original and conditioned by nothing on our part.

6. To apologize and repent: to apologize is to say we are sorry for committing the wrongdoing and for causing suffering. We also commit ourselves to not repeating the wrong in the future and repairing the damage. For an apology to be honest,

---

64. Volf, *Free of Charge*, 162.

65. Volf, *Free of Charge*, 161 argues, "Revenge multiples evil, retributive justice contains evil—and threatens the world with destruction. Forgiveness overcomes evil with good. Forgiveness mirrors the generosity of God whose ultimate goal is neither to satisfy injured pride nor to justly apportion reward and punishment, but to free sinful humanity from evil and thereby re-establish communion with us ... this is the gospel in its stark simplicity—as radically countercultural and at the same time as beautifully human as anything one can imagine."

66. Volf, *Free of Charge*, 165.
67. Volf, *Free of Charge*, 166–69.
68. Volf, *Free of Charge*, 168.
69. Volf, *Free of Charge*, 169–70.
70. Volf, *Free of Charge*, 172
71. Volf, *Free of Charge*, 179–80

repentance must be truthful. In the Christian sacrament of confession, repentance of the heart accompanies confession of the mouth. The only way to freedom from the wrongdoing leads through repentance and confession, through apology.[72]

7. Restitution: repentance will prove sincere only if the wrongdoer is willing to repair what wrongdoing took away from the victim.[73]

8. To reconcile: we forgive in hope that forgiveness will bring repentance, reparation, and restoration of relationships.[74]

Forgiveness is an important factor in the God-humanity restoration.[75] We forgive because we love even our enemies. This love that motivates forgiveness, "pushes forgiveness not just from exclusion to neutrality, but from neutrality to embrace."[76] Forgiveness is embedded in a way of life that is committed to overcoming evil by doing good.[77]

How Can We Forgive?

Volf argues we have the *power* and the *right* to forgive. Since every wrong committed against a creature is a sin against the creator, God has the power to forgive all sins,[78] and He has already forgiven sinful humanity.[79] When we forgive, we make God's sending of the "forgiveness package" our own. This is why we have the power to forgive, "Whether the package will be received depends on the recipients, on whether they admit to the wrongdoing and repent."[80] We too have the right to forgive because God has forgiven. We do not have that right on our own, "But we have the right and the obligation to make God's forgiving our own — to forgive on our part what has already been forgiven by God," so we have a derivative authority. Without this

---

72. Miroslav Volf, *Flourishing: Why we need Religion in a Globalized World* (New Haven, CT: Yale University Press, 2015). Volf, *Free of Charge*, 182-83 explains that without faith and repentance we are not forgiven because, "forgiveness is stuck in the middle between the God who forgives and humans who don't receive." Repentance is a necessary consequence of forgiveness and not a condition of forgiveness, but it does help make repentance possible (183–86).

73. Volf, *Free of Charge*, 187.

74. Volf, *Free of Charge*, 188–89.

75. Volf points out that, in Scripture (Rom 5:1) peace is not the absence of war. Peace is the flourishing of the community and its people and "Peace with God is our delight in communion with God . . . God forgives by indwelling us and indwells us by forgiving us" (*Free of Charge*, 189).

76. Volf, *Free of Charge*, 189.

77. Volf, *Free of Charge*, 189.

78. Volf, *Free of Charge*, 196.

79. Volf, *Free of Charge*, 197.

80. Volf, *Free of Charge*, 197.

authority, the bible could not urge us to forgive and God's warning not to be forgiven if we do not forgive others would only mock us.[81]

Regarding the relationship between God's forgiveness and ours, Volf illustrates the idea that God forgives, and we take this divine forgiving and put our own signature under God's. This activity is God's work, so when we forgive it is Christ who forgives through us.

How can we let that echo become full of our own real voices? Volf proposes that when things go well forgiveness gives birth to forgiveness. When things go ill forgiveness remains barren. That's the impotence of forgivers; they can "knock at the door" by forgiving and wait, "trusting that the Spirit of the resurrected Christ will make the seed of their forgiveness bear fruit."[82]

In relation to the burden of mending relationships resting on the shoulders of victims, Volf agrees that although it is unfair for victims to bear it, they should.[83] We bear the burden of forgiveness because: first, Christ forgave in such a way, and second, when we are forgivers "we are restored to our full human splendor. We were created to mirror God."[84] However, as long as victims do not forgive (due to death, mental illness) even if we have received God's forgiveness we will have to live with a small wound of unforgiveness. In the world to come, all partial forgiveness will be made complete.[85] Forgiveness is a social relationship, not an act of a solitary individual. God works in the lives of forgivers "not through the isolated decision of self-enclosed individuals but through a life lived in response to the God of grace and through a community that makes the practice of forgiveness meaningful."[86]

Volf advocates an *unconditional* view of forgiveness; it is unilateral and is a process within a person and between persons.[87] A unilateral act aiming at response so that it is always interpersonal, like giving, has the structure of giving and receiving. Ideally, forgiveness is also bilateral.[88] Therefore we forgive, even without repen-

---

81. Volf, *Free of Charge*, 199.

82. Volf, *Free of Charge*, 205.

83. Volf, *Free of Charge*, 209 explains, "Because that's what it means to be followers of Christ. Forgiving the unrepentant is not an optional extra in the Christian way of life; it is the heart of the thing."

84. Volf, *Free of Charge*, 209.

85. Volf also explains that we should always forgive humbly and provisionally. Sometimes what we considered to be an offence against us is actually an offence that we need to apologize for more than we need to forgive. We do not need to know exactly what was the nature and extent of the offence, argues Volf, since God knows, and "we join God in forgiving" (*Free of Charge*, 211).

86. Volf, *Free of Charge*, 214.

87. For advocates of *conditional* forgiveness, forgiveness is bilateral. It is modelled after God's forgiveness, which is conditional upon repentance. It should include remorse, confession, and restitution. Without repentance, the offended is obligated to withhold forgiveness. For conditional forgiveness, reconciliation automatically follows forgiveness.

88. The central question is whether that bilateral relation has a nature of the exchange of some

tance. To do that, "We shield the tender plant of forgiveness from the frigid winds that blow from unrepentant perpetrators, and we nourish it with the food of God's goodness."[89] Even when offenders are unrepentant, we can and should forgive. There are better ways to protect ourselves than the refusal to forgive. For Volf, forgiveness is not a reaction to something but the beginning of something new.

A Cultural Critique of Volf's Theology of Forgiveness in Light of Palestinian Culture (*Sulha*)

Sulha functions as a social mechanism for the promotion of forgiveness. When a conflict breaks out, dignitaries recruit the victim's family into the *sulha* process, achieve a ceasefire, and generally convince the disputants that their honor will be restored and increased if they forgive much more than if they seek vengeance. In a public reconciliation ceremony, dignitaries become communal guardians of the reconciliation.[90] The final ceremony is centered on forgiveness, peace, and compromise for the greater good of society. In *sulha* forgiveness is obligatory, since only with forgiveness can the torn social fabric be mended. "*Sulha* is first and foremost based on forgiveness. If the offended side does not forgive, there will be no *sulha* and there will be no peace,"[91] and in a similar way Volf states that forgiveness is the only solution to vast conflicts. Forgiving strengthens communal bonds and restores relationship.[92] However there are several differences between forgiveness in *sulha* and in Volf's theology:

1. Conditional: Forgiveness in *sulha* is *conditional* on achieving reconciliation; it is a bilateral process of forgiving. For Volf forgiveness is *unconditional*; it is a unilateral process and unconditioned by repentance.

2. Formality: *Sulha* involves *external* public expression of forgiveness. Cultural *symbols and rituals* are necessary for societal constructions of peaceful coexistence. The *sulha* ceremony involves the three main symbolic rituals of *musafaha* (the hand shake), *musamaha* (declaring forgiveness), and *mumalaha* (the ceremonial meal). Forgiveness in Volf's theory does not involve any ritual or formality; it is an *internal* private process.

---

kind of equivalents (so that forgiveness is dependent on adequate repentance and if repentance is not there then forgiveness is withdrawn) or whether it has the nature of a gift—Volf advocates the latter.

89. Volf, *Free of Charge*, 209.

90. Leaders from different religions are always present at the reconciliation ceremony to symbolize the coming together of the community.

91. Jabbour, *Sulha*, 31.

92. Volf, *Free of Charge*.

3. Community: In *sulha*, forgiveness is initiated by the community. Forgiveness demands the participation of the whole community in its rituals, otherwise restoration of honor will fail. In *sulha* forgiveness is human not divine;[93] it is a mostly external, decisional, and communal process that takes place in a triangle consisting of the offender's family, the offended family, and the community. Without the involvement of the community, *sulha* fails. Given that religious dignitaries are part of the *sulha* process, it is likely God has a role in this process,[94] however it is not a clear role as in Volf's concept of forgiveness. Volf's definition of forgiveness is as a divine gift; it is a human, internal, decisional, and individualistic process (compared to *sulha*) and takes place in a triangle of the individual offender, the individual offended, and God. "Take God away," Volf argues, "and the foundations of forgiveness become unsteady and may even crumble."[95]

4. Restoration of Dignity: Volf's theme of forgiveness does not require the public restoration of dignity as in *sulha*, although for Volf it is part of a "larger strategy of overcoming evil with good and bringing about reconciliation."[96] Volf speaks about the restoration of a lost human identity, an individual's own "dignity"; in his words "When we are forgivers we are restored to our full human splendor."[97] For Volf the good is primary and dignity is secondary. In *sulha*, it is also related to the primacy of the good, however, restoration of dignity is a significant tool to achieve forgiveness.

5. Declaratory Binding Nature: The *sulha* ceremony transforms forgiveness from a private affair to a public formal one involving the community and multiple witnesses. It covers past, present, and future generations. The formal text in the *sulha* ceremony says: "This peace is valid for all those who are present here, and all those who are absent, for every embryo in the womb of its mother or for every sperm from the back of the father."[98] This means the community (in particular the victim's family) has a ritualistic and practical obligation to forgive, though, of course, not the duty to *forget*, and that the act of reconciliation is binding for all of the victim's "circles of responsibility."[99] Compared to *sulha*, Volf's forgiveness is binding by virtue of an

---

93. It means that human beings, apart from acknowledging or invoking deity, still do practice forgiveness, which is a necessary invention for living, but not a process of transcendence as in Volf's theology of forgiveness.

94. Sayings such as "God is the forgiver," "God forgives him," and "God helps us forgive" are heard in *sulha*.

95. Volf *Free of Charge*, 131. I am aware that Volf distinguishes between social agents and social arrangements. While he argues the latter are important, his focus is on social agents. However, in Arab culture this distinction cannot be so easily made.

96. Volf, *Free of Charge*, 217.

97. Volf *Free of Charge*, 209.

98. Jabbour, *Sulha*, 53.

99. Doron Pely "When Honor Needs Trump Health and Safety Needs," *Negotiation Journal*, 27.2

internal personal obligation to imitate God and not a declaratory external obligation made binding by the community the way we see in *sulha* rituals. Volf's forgiveness covers past, present, and future. For him, God works in the lives of forgivers through a life lived in response to God and a "community that makes the practice of forgiveness meaningful."[100]

In *sulha*, the victims absorb the wrongdoing to maintain the social order and communal peace and be freed from *shame*. However, for Volf, the victim should absorb the wrongdoing in order to transform the wrongdoer and to release him from the burden of *guilt*; the same way God has freed us from sin's *guilt*. The goal is a community of love.

The practical meaning of forgiveness in *sulha* is, first and foremost, *pacification* and the decision not to seek revenge, and also restoration of relationships on different levels. The psychological component of forgiveness means the disputants will not view the "others" as enemies but will treat them as equal members in the community and rise above the dispute and its memory of conflict. If a member of the victim's family does not forgive the offender and his clan, any revenge from his side will bring dishonor on his family, and community, and the regional dignitaries who signed the forgiveness agreement. Even though Volf's forgiveness is aimed at stopping the circle of revenge and restoring relationships and is connected with the affirmation of common humanity, it is not about the affirmation of common belonging to a specific group. Volf's forgiveness has the primacy of the good over dignity.

In sum, forgiveness processes in *sulha* are initiated by the community. Forgiveness is obligatory; its aim is to transform revenge into forgiveness through the tool of public restoration of honor. This forgiveness is human; not divine. It is a decisional and external process. It demands the participation of the whole community in its rituals; without this, restoration of dignity will fail. It has a declaratory nature and transforms forgiveness from a private to a public affair covering past, present, and future generations. The victim's family has both a ritualistic and practical obligation to forgive. This act of reconciliation is binding. Practically forgiveness in *sulha* is a pacification, which also includes restoration of relationships.

Volf's definition of forgiveness, like *sulha's*, is decisional and a process needing to be nurtured and is usually initiated by the offended. While in *sulha* forgiveness is human, and conditional on achieving reconciliation, Volf's forgiveness is divine and human, an internal and private process; it is unconditional and yet it aims at the reception of itself in repentance and restitution and is not complete until that

---

(2011) 205–25.

100. Volf, *Free of Charge*, 214.

happens;[101] its aim is not pacification but restoration of the offended and the offender to the communion of love. It is a social event and it involves God, the offended, and the offender who can receive forgiveness by repentance, apology, and restitution. The community has a role in encouraging forgiveness, but not a role in 'imposing' forgiveness or becoming guardians of its practical application as in *sulha*.

Forgiveness in Volf's Theory and the *Sulha* Model: A Comparison

Volf	*Sulha*
Obligatory	Obligatory
Unconditional	Conditional
Internal process	External process (rituals)
Private individualistic process	Public communal process
Initiated by the offended	Initiated by the community
Burden on the offended	Burden on the community
Takes place in a triangle of offender, offended, and God	Takes place in a triangle of the offender's family, offended family, and community
Restoration of lost human dignity	Restoration of a group dignity
Binding by virtue of a personal obligation to imitate God	Declaratory binding by community
Divine and human	Human

Discussion and Proposal

Community is essential for a successful forgiveness process. Sometimes the reason we do not forgive is that we live in an unforgiving culture or community; as social beings we are shaped by our environment. Our choices and desires often echo the choices of the community to which we belong and the wider culture in which we live. When our culture and communities become litigious, forgiveness starts making less sense.[102] In order to forgive effectively, we need an environment in which forgiveness is valuable and nurtured. Seemingly, if there is no modelling of forgiveness, acceptance, and empathy in the external environment, then the capacity of individuals to forgive is weakened. This also includes the ability to forgive ourselves both as

---

101. According to Volf, *Free of Charge*, "We forgive because Christ has forgiven us and because Christ forgives through us" (206).

102. Volf, *Free of Charge*, 212.

offenders or offended, as this is related to being embraced back into the community. Community members help one another to love and forgive. As we saw in *sulha*, in communal life, offenders and offended are not left alone to carry the heavy burdens of shame, guilt, and forgiveness. Therefore, I believe the process of forgiveness should be seen as mutually supportive and promoted especially in church settings, where proper forgiveness and reconciliation will benefit both the church community and individuals.

Wrongdoings harm offended, offender, and a whole community,[103] and since we can neither undo nor disregard wrongdoing, we need to do the hard work of forgiving in a community setting. Paul urged the community of the Corinthian church to forgive the offender,[104] both as a community and as individuals within the community. The offender hurt the church community by his wrongdoing. When he apologized, the church should forgive him and embrace him back into the community of believers and not exclude him. Paul had to rebuke the Corinthian church twice: first, for not disciplining the individual who had sinned,[105] and second when the church had gone too far in the punishment.[106] Many churches have a similar difficulty of knowing when and how to discipline individual offenders.

It is the church's responsibility as a *community of love* to exclude a wrongdoer (in the case of persistent sin) and to re-embrace the repentant. Condemnation is not forgotten when forgiveness is offered; we accuse when we forgive. Disciplinary punishment does not contradict forgiveness; "disciplinary measures" (deterrence, prevention, or rehabilitation) are compatible with forgiveness since they aim to bring a better future.[107] Thus, combining forgiveness with disciplinary measures will remove obstacles from the past to create conditions for peace in the present.[108] Punishment often serves as a tool for protecting and restoring *shalom*.[109]

---

103. "If anyone has caused grief, he has not so much grieved me as he has grieved all of you to some extent—not to put it too severely" (2 Cor 2:5 NIV).

104. 2 Corinthians 2:7.

105. 2 Corinthians 2:9.

106. 2 Corinthians 2:6.

107. Volf, *Flourishing*, 178. Volf explains that retribution and reprobation are the two main rationales for punishment strictly understood. Forgiveness is incompatible with retribution (one purpose of punishment) because to forgive is to forego retribution. But forgiveness is compatible with reprobation, for to forgive is to implicitly condemn the forgiven deed.

108. Volf, *Flourishing*, 178.

109. *Shalom* is a Hebrew word meaning "peace." It denotes the presence of harmony and wholeness, of health and prosperity, of integration and balance. *Shalom* is when everything is as it ought to be and thus, it combines into one concept the meaning of justice and peace. See Chris Marshall, *Little Book of Biblical Justice: A Fresh Approach to the Bible's Teachings on Justice*, The Little Books of Justice and Peacebuilding Series (Intercourse, PA: Good Books, 2005) 12–13.

Paul instructed the Corinthian church first to *forgive and comfort/encourage* the offender rather than continue with the discipline,[110] since the punishment by the majority was sufficient,[111] and second, to *confirm their love* for the offender, since the purpose of Christian discipline is to save and restore, not merely to punish.[112] Discipline that goes beyond the stage of "godly sorrow" may create two problems: first, it becomes punitive and non-redemptive.[113] Second, Satan can take advantage of an unforgiving legalistic attitude to create division and conflict in the church.[114] In the absence of forgiveness, exclusion may worsen the conflict; dissatisfaction and bitterness could lead to revenge and divisions.

What Can We Learn from *Sulha* for an Effective Forgiveness Process?

After looking at forgiveness in both cultural and theological models, and in order to be able to practice forgiveness effectively, I suggest that, (1) the *community* should have an active role in forgiveness processes and, (2) forgiveness should have *external expressions* in addition to internal. My suggestion is also a proposal to adjust Volf's theory as I elaborate below.

It is noteworthy that I do not suggest adopting *sulha* simply as it is, but to learn from the following themes and adapt them accordingly.

The Community

I suggest adding the community as an essential participant in the forgiveness process through combining Volf's triangle of God, offender and offended, with the *sulha* triangle as follows:

As discussed, forgiveness in *sulha* takes place in a triangle consisting of the offender's family, the offended's family, and the community:

---

110. 2 Corinthians 2:7.
111. 2 Corinthians 2:6.
112. 2 Corinthians 2:8.
113. 2 Corinthians 7:10.
114. https://www.biblegateway.com/resources/commentaries/IVP-NT/2Cor/Church-Discipline-Forgiveness

Forgiveness in *Sulha*

Community

Offended's family   **Offender's family**

Volf's theory of forgiveness takes place in a triangle of the offender, the offended, and God:

Forgiveness in Volf's theory

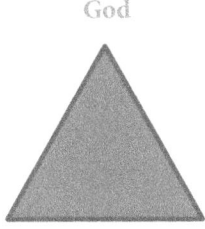

God

Offended   Offender

The outcome of my proposal will be that forgiveness takes place not in a triangle but in a rhombus as follow:

Proposed model

God

Offended **& Family**   Offender **& Family**

Community

I found several advantages to including the community as a fundamental participant in the process of forgiveness. The community helps to remove the obstacles and builds the bridge toward forgiveness by the following actions:

1. Bearing the burden of the wrongs done together. When the community actively participate in the forgiveness process, the psychological, emotional, and communal burden of the conflict will shift from the parties to the community, who has the ability to act as an "anger absorber." As the community plays an active role in the process of forgiveness it can offer support to both the offended and offender within the community, by bearing the burden of wrongs done together in the process of redeeming past offences, forgiving the offender, and healing broken relationships. In this way, the heavy responsibility of forgiving and restoring relationships rests not only on the shoulders of the wronged and the wrongdoer but will also be carried by the community. Even so, forgiveness is an act that involves a person's heart, and therefore the community can encourage and aid the process of forgiveness, but it cannot ultimately forgive in place of the individual of whom forgiveness is required.

2. Using forgiveness and inclusive language. The letter of James clearly teaches on the power of language (the tongue) both to destroy and to heal.[115] Community leaders carry influence as they use the language of forgiveness. The language of forgiveness that community leaders use is necessarily on behalf of, and for the sake of, the community. The use of inclusive language (such as "we") among the community can help to encourage the community members to practice forgiveness.

3. Seeking and sustaining justice. The community can put pressure on the offender to encourage him or her to repent and repair the damage. The community can be the best guardian to sustain justice and ensure the durability of the agreement post-conflict, as well as becoming the witness in whose presence reconciliation takes place. The book of James emphasizes the importance of being open and honest with each other in order to name sin.[116] James invokes mutual accountability and support where members are required to speak truthfully with the erring person, for the sake of both the community and the erring person. This will be effective if there is a high level of trust, mercy,[117] and community practices.

4. Restoring and embracing. The community holds the potential to have a powerful restorative influence in the life of its members. This could happen through, first, healing the shame of both offender and offended by welcoming them back and restoring what was lost, and second, through helping them to move from the painful past to a hopeful future, and to overcome present and future challenges.

---

115. James 3:1–12.
116. James 5:19–20.
117. James 2:13.

For example, community leaders may need to raise awareness through influencing community members in order to change certain attitudes or to change problematic behaviors toward either the offender or offended.

External Expressions

When the community becomes active in the forgiveness process, the process becomes more publicly visible and as forgiveness is seen and heard, it therefore becomes "binding." In addition to the community element, there are various other aspects from *sulha* that I suggest should be included in order to encourage a successful forgiveness process: (1) formality, (2) venting, and (3) the restoration of dignity. When practiced within the community these aspects are effective. I will discuss each aspect in turn:

1. Formality. A community uses music, songs, symbolism, and rituals to express spiritual or eternal values, such as love, integrity, and compassion. These shared values live on in the spirit of the community for generations.[118] While forgiveness may begin as an intrapersonal initiative (as in Volf's theory) it is worked out both intrapersonally and interpersonally in the community, as it is expressed in public rituals, religious practices, and collective activities, as seen in the *sulha* ceremony. As I elaborate below, churches could make use of internal and external resources and practices, in order to lead each party to realize forgiveness, even though it may be imperfect:

Ceremonial-covenant meal. I suggest that a declaration of forgiveness could be framed by formal, ritualized public action, culminating with the Lord's Supper followed by a common meal. In the early church, the Lord's Supper and a common meal were not clearly separated. The Lord's Supper is an appropriate ritual for the community to confirm the completion of the process of forgiveness, because it celebrates God's reconciliation with us as the foundation of human reconciliation. The Aramaic word for forgiveness has the root of "table," which, according to Augsburger, is a perfect picture of how Christ transformed the sharing of a meal (table) into a symbol of realized forgiveness. The older brother of the prodigal son did not join his father at the table because he did not want to forgive.[119] Eating a meal together is also an actual sign of forgiveness and reconciliation in the *sulha* ceremony; it is a ritual that transforms forgiveness from a private matter into a public, formal, and binding one that involves the church community and multiple witnesses.

---

118. McMillan, "Sense of Community."
119. David Augsburger, *Helping People Forgive* (Louisville, Westminster John Knox) 13.

Church practices. Church practices can also provide ritualized, formal, and public action for promoting forgiveness and redeeming the remembrance of past sorrow. Repeated church rituals like communion, foot washing, singing, praying, and studying the bible together, along with various other creative practices, are helpful for multiple reasons. First, it gains the community's involvement. Second, it provides a space for interaction that can encourage the move beyond offence in order for bilateral forgiveness and reconciliation to take place. Third, these church practices also provide a way for members to experience a partial redemption of past sorrow and wrongdoing as these practices happen repeatedly and thereby contribute to the transformation and reshaping of the memories of the offended. Studying Scripture allows the Word of God to work in their minds and hearts in reshaping their memory. In taking communion they are reminded of the promise of redemption as an eschatological reality and they receive a renewed awareness of a partial redemption now. Singing brings people together in unity; there is a responsibility to both perform and to listen which open us to God, to one another and to ourselves.[120] Singing fills space in ways that draw more voices to take part with no sense of crowding, "a performance of abundance as new voices join in with their own distinctive tones... the music is both outside and within them, and it creates a new vocal, social space of community in song."[121] Finally, these activities are important when it comes to sustaining Christian forgiveness because they focus on God's love, as we repeatedly remember that we are both forgiven and forgivers each time we confess, sing, pray, read Scripture, and eat together.

2. Venting. Volf's theory of forgiveness does not provide practical ideas of how resentment and revenge transform into compassion toward the offender. I suggest that venting can play an important role in the forgiveness process. This is because, first, venting names and condemns the wrongs. Second, it allows negative feelings such as hatred, resentment, and pain to be expressed, in order to then transform them into tolerance and compassion. Third, venting is a vital factor in redeeming past sorrow. It provides a space for anger to be publicly expressed, thereby enabling the reversal of dignity violation through a public acknowledgement of the moral standing of the offended — a form of symbolically removing the humiliation that the offence has caused the offended to feel in the eyes of the community. Freeing the offended from fear and humiliation caused by the offence then makes the future possible. These aspects are vital for forgiveness to be achieved. In order for this process to be effective, it is important that this process is overseen by a third-party who

---

120. Gregory Jones, "Crafting Communities of Forgiveness," *Interpretation* 54 (2000) 121–34.

121. David Ford, *Self and Salvation: Being Transformed* (Cambridge: Cambridge University Press, 1999) 121 as cited in Jones "Crafting Communities," 132.

can act as "anger absorber." Since to forgo revenge and resentment does not necessarily remove shame, it is also important to add another element, namely dignity restoration.

3. Dignity restoration. In order to remove shame, I suggest adding dignity restoration to the forgiveness process. Dignity is important to every human being and any threat provokes a strong reaction. Publicly affirming the dignity of the other in the community context is vital in restoring broken relationships, and essential for healing the pain — especially when dignity violations caused the conflict in the first place.[122] In the *sulha* ritual, dignity restoration plays a key role in achieving forgiveness. *Musayara* is the name for the practice whereby the community (*jaha*) treats the victim's family with the great respect normally given to high status persons, and this continues throughout the whole *sulha* process from beginning to end. The *jaha* temporarily places the family in a position of "patronage" over the most respected men in the community. This aspect is important in helping to remove any remaining feelings of shame and humiliation, in contributing to dignity restoration, in *healing shame* as the offended is embraced back into right relationship and community, and finally in ensuring that revenge is transformed into forgiveness.

Conclusion

Forgiveness is not an act of a solitary individual. God works in the lives of forgivers through a community that makes the practice of forgiveness significant. When the church community plays an active role in promoting forgiveness through engaging in forgiveness processes and Christian practices, this will shape a way of life in which we learn to live peacefully with one another even during suffering and conflicts. "There is a craft of forgiveness that Christians are called to learn from one another and particularly from exemplars, as we seek to become holy people."[123] When forgiveness is practiced in such a way then forgiveness becomes not a private act but a part of a larger strategy of overcoming evil with good and bringing about reconciliation.[124]

In our churches we need more collective practices that symbolize the redemption of past wrongdoing for both offender and offended, into a hopeful new future. External public forgiveness processes and practices support rebuilding the church community and its values, as well as encourage and increase forgiveness.

---

122. Donna Hicks, *Dignity: Its Essential Role in Resolving Conflict* (New Haven: Yale University Press, 2011).

123. Jones, "Crafting Communities of Forgiveness," 125

124. Romans 12:21; Volf, *Free of Charge*, 217.

RESPONSE TO MANSOUR

Jeffrey Anderson

I am extremely grateful for the chance to reply to this excellent and practical paper by Dr. Rula Mansour. She has skillfully integrated the western more individualistic approach to forgiveness (focusing on the work of Miroslav Volf) with a Palestinian communal approach known as *sulha*. Her presentation demands moving from curiosity to action; this is something that fits well with how I think about ministry

I must admit that I started reading thinking, "Maybe this is a culturally appropriate way to address the conflict in the region at least on a small and grass roots level . . ." Not knowing if this is the case, I asked two residents of the Holy Land, Orthodox Rabbi Hanan Schlesinger and my Messianic Israeli friend, Lisa Loden whether this would be similar to Jewish thought. Both replied to my question by saying that they found the paper to be highly engaging but that the approach in Jewish theology is focused on the sin of the individual and actions related to that sin and thus, there would not be culturally similarity.

This caused me to realize that I could not merely look at this work as something for "out there" but rather this is something that I need to look at with a view to my own culture and my own contexts as someone who is from North America but who is involved with the Middle East in every day of my working life. As a person whose vocational life has been involved with the local, national, and global setting of the church, I soon found three specific applications that I believe would be valuable in developing further ideas contained in this document.

The first area of interaction is with local churches that are facing conflict. Sadly, conflict is a reality in too many churches. It is not limited to a certain size, denomination, or style of church. One of the keys to the outlined process is trust. In working with churches over the years conflict is often the result of broken trust. Those congregations that did forgive, recover, and move forward often had a broker of trust that was able to bridge the gap. The principle of wisdom and trustworthiness illustrated by Mansour through the *jaha* would need to be adjusted for a North American setting to encompass a broader inclusion of gender and age. The problem with conflict in most congregations is that the primary desire is to put the conflict in the past. While we do not typically identify as a shame culture, more often than not, the weaker party in a conflict ends up leaving because of awkwardness and shame. Dr. Mansour rightly impresses the importance of dignity for all parties.

The second relational context in which I think this proposal could assist the church is in relation to the Indigenous and First Nations peoples of Canada and the USA. Our record of interaction is generally lacking, with few positive images. For this to work the church would need to submit to a process that may shine a light into some very dark places, but we could see some amazing healing. In 2007 the government of Canada formalized a residential school settlement. In 2008 the Prime Minister of Canada invited the Grand Chief of First Nations Peoples to the floor of Parliament (not ever done during a sitting parliament) and offered an unreserved apology.[1] Between 2007 and 2015 the Truth and Reconciliation Commission heard over 6500 stories.[2] While not resolving all grievances by any means, the offended party was put into a new position within Canadian society; no longer that of mere victim. The church of Jesus Christ has an opportunity to right a societal wrong to which we have contributed both knowingly and unknowingly over many years.

The third relational setting that this proposal brought to mind was that of our friends in the Holy Land. On one side of an imposing wall we have a dark history of anti-Semitism toward the Jewish people. One of the most difficult parts of visiting Yad Vashem, the Holocaust museum, is to see the quotes of some of our theological heroes; quotes that make us squirm if we let them settle in our minds. But there is the other side of that wall where our brothers and sisters in Christ along with the majority Muslim culture suffer due to both our actions and inactions. Too many times I have been asked questions like "Why do our evangelical brothers and sisters hate us?" Too many times I have heard believers (and I mean dedicated Bible-believing people) say things like "Palestinians are terrorists, aren't they?" or "Palestinians are the modern Philistines." Like the four carrying their paralyzed friend to Jesus in Mark 2 we need to see that it is we who need to be brought to Jesus for forgiveness. Maybe if we would take more seriously the importance of community in forgiveness the result could be a celebratory feast that builds community and builds bridges that are not subject to the political or physical barriers we often use as excuses not to address a long standing wrong.

---

1. "Statement of Apology to former students of Indian Residential Schools," *Indigenous and Northern Affairs Canada Website,* assessed August 15, 2019, https://www.aadnc-aandc.gc.ca/eng/1100100015644/1100100015649.

2. "About the Truth and Reconciliation Commission," *Crown-Indigenous Relations and Northern Affairs Canada Website,* assessed August 15, 2019, https://www.rcaanc-cirnac.gc.ca/eng/1450124405592/1529106060525#chp1.

I end by returning to my starting point; I am grateful for the way Dr. Mansour has presented an integrated approach to forgiveness that combines the important work of God with the work of the community. I pray that our church will do the hard work necessary to follow this much needed path of integration.

THE UNKNOWN PATH: MARTIN BUBER'S ZIONISM AND THE MAKING OF A VEXED, ATYPICAL CHRISTIAN ZIONIST

Joel Willitts

Buber would remain an atypical Zionist throughout his life.[1]

I'm sympathetic toward Zionism and have been for a long time. I guess you could call me a Zionist. Zionism is an inheritance. My ecclesial background—once in the Sunday School our teacher drew a chart and talked to us about the end times, about rapture, the tribulation and the great white throne judgment. We were dispensationalists. And both my undergraduate and graduate institutions were thoroughgoing Dispensational and Zionist. Although for most of those formative years, I did not know enough either to name the institutions as Zionist or even to know what Zionism was. Zionism was just the way it was. Of course, it didn't stay that way.

During my MPhil and PhD at Cambridge, I read lots of Second Temple Jewish literature. Because of it, I became convinced dispensationalism did not prove adequate to explain the Bible's eschatological program. I parted ways with my inheritance. At that time, too, I came to understand more of the complexity of the Israeli-Palestinian conflict. Also, my knowledge of Zionism widened, though at the time I wasn't sure what I believed. Largely, I think because of the stigma Zionism carried. I intentionally decided to put the question on hold until I had time to research it. I never spoke about Zionism or the Israeli-Palestinian conflict because I felt ignorant on the issues. It has been only recently that I've spent time reading as much as I could on the topic.[2]

---

1. Paul R. Mendes-Flohr, *Martin Buber: A Life of Faith and Dissent*, Jewish Lives, (New Haven; London: Yale University Press, 2019) 90.

2. Among the books I read are these: Ehud Barak, *My Country, My Life: Fighting for Israel, Searching for Peace* (New York: St. Martin's, 2018); Ian Black, *Enemies and Neighbors: Arabs and Jews in Palestine and Israel, 1917–2017* (New York: Atlantic Monthly Press, 2017); David Brog, *Reclaiming Israel's History: Roots, Rights, and the Struggle for Peace*, Kindle ed. (Washington, DC: Regnery Gateway, 2017); Martin P. Bunton, *The Palestinian-Israeli Conflict: A Very Short Introduction*, First edition (Oxford: Oxford University Press, 2013); Shalom Goldman, *Zeal for Zion: Christians, Jews, & the*

My Ph.D. work was on the Gospel of Matthew and while working on Matthew's Messianism, I came to the conclusion that Matthew harbored territorial expectations of Israel's restoration which were tied to his presentation of Yeshua as the Davidic Messiah.[3] I was surprised to discover that a Yeshua-believing-Jewish community in the late first century harbored hopes for a territorial restoration. I completed my Ph.D. freshly sympathetic to Christian Zionism, though not the Zionism of the cartoonish proponents in the late twentieth and twenty-first centuries in American evangelicalism and beyond. What I discovered, much to my surprise, was a biblically rooted foundation for a Christian belief in the territorial restoration of Israel in the eschatological age—"at the renewal of all things" (*tē palingenesia*; Matt 19:28).[4] Zionism had a biblical foundation in the New Testament.

Several years ago, Gerry McDermont invited me to participate in a symposium on Zionism he had organized on Christian Zionism because of my conclusions from Matthew's Gospel. I was still uncertain on where I stood on the issue but was honored to be invited. The presentation later became my chapter in the book *The New Christian Zionism* edited by Gerry.[5] The essay was a development from my published

---

Idea of the Promised Land (Chapel Hill: University of North Carolina Press, 2009); Micah Goodman, *Catch-67: the Left, the Right, and the Legacy of the Six-Day War*, trans. Eylon Levy (New Haven: Yale University Press, 2018); Daniel Gordis, *Israel: A Concise History of a Nation Reborn* (New York, NY: Ecco, 2016); Daniel Gordis, *The Promise of Israel: Why Its Seemingly Greatest Weakness is Actually Its Greatest Strength* (Hoboken: John Wiley & Sons, 2012); Alan Hart, *Arafat, A Political Biography* (Bloomington: Indiana University Press, 1989); Francine Klagsbrun, *Lioness: Golda Meir and the Nation of Israel* (New York: Schocken, 2017); David Landau, *Arik: The Life of Ariel Sharon* (New York: Alfred A. Knopf, 2013); Michael B. Oren, *Six Days of War: June 1967 and the Making of the Modern Middle East* (New York: Ballantine, 2003); Ilan Pappe, *The Ethnic Cleansing of Palestine* (London: Oneworld, 2006); Ilan Pappe, *A History of Modern Palestine: One Land, Two Peoples*, 2nd ed. (Cambridge; New York: Cambridge University Press, 2006); Ilan Pappe, *The Forgotten Palestinians: A History of the Palestinians in Israel* (New Haven: Yale University Press, 2011); Ilan Pappe, *The Biggest Prison on Earth: A History of the Occupied Territories* (London: Oneworld, 2017); Anshel Pfeffer, *Bibi: The Turbulent Life and Times of Benjamin Netanyahu* (New York: Basic Books, 2018); Abraham Rabinovich, *The Yom Kippur War: The Epic Encounter that Transformed the Middle East* (New York: Schocken, 2004); Barry M. Rubin and Judith Colp Rubin, *Yasir Arafat: A Political Biography* (New York: Oxford University Press, 2003); Tom Segev, *One Palestine, Complete: Jews and Arabs under the Mandate* (New York: Metropolitan, 2000); Tom Segev, *1967: Israel, the War, and the Year that Transformed the Middle East* (New York: Metropolitan, 2007); Tom Segev, *A State at Any Cost: the Life of David Ben-Gurion* (London: Apollo Library, 2019); Anita Shapira, *Israel: A history*, translated by Anthony Berris (Waltham: Brandeis University Press, 2012); Anita Shapira, *Ben-Gurion: Father of Modern Israel*, translated by Anthony Berris, Jewish Lives, (New Haven: Yale University Press, 2014); Ari Shavit, *My Promised Land: the Triumph and Tragedy of Israel* (New York: Spiegel & Grau, 2015).

3. Joel Willitts, *Matthew's Messianic Shepherd-King: In Search of the Lost Sheep of the House of Israel*, BNZW 147 (Berlin; New York: Walter de Gruyter, 2007) 157–73.

4. The whole verse is instructive for thinking about the restoration of Israel territorially: "Yeshua said to them, "Truly I tell you, at the renewal of all things, when the Son of Man is seated on the throne of his glory, you who have followed me will also sit on twelve thrones, judging the twelve tribes of Israel." Cf. Willitts, *Shepherd-King*, 147, 120.

5. Joel Willitts, "Zionism in the Gospel of Matthew," in *The New Christian Zionism*, edited by

thesis *Matthew's Messianic Shepherd-King: In Search of the Lost Sheep of the House of Israel*.⁶ In the conclusion of the chapter I wrote,

> The Matthean Jesus did not redefine a concrete view of Israel's restoration into something else. The elements of a restored *turfed* Davidic Kingdom remain present for Matthew and were expected in the indeterminate future. In this way, Matthew stood firmly within his late first-century Jewish historical and social context. Matthew held to the hope for Israel's territorial restoration and believed it would be realized as a consequence of Jesus' life, death and resurrection.⁷

Thus, I've come to be more with Zionism than against, although I have tensions, reservations, concerns about the Israeli State. In my chapter in the *New Christian Zionism*, I fell short of a full-throated endorsement the State of Israel. I ended the chapter with reference to the eminent Michael Wyschogrod (1928–2015) whom I quoted in the epigraph. Wyschogrod's friendly, but still ambivalent, sentiment about the State of Israel with which I deeply resonate.⁸ He wrote,

> In our time, the people of Israel has returned to its land. Was it justified in doing so? Does this return signal the beginning of the redemption promised by God or is it a human act of will resulting from impatience and the secularization of Jewish consciousness? These are difficult questions to answer and will ultimately be answered by history. But whatever the answer to these questions may be, they concern only the issue of whether we should have waited longer. *But that sometime Israel will return to the land which it has been promised by God cannot be in question because God has so promised*.⁹

The last lines of my chapter read:

> In Wyschogrod's wise counsel, a full judgment in the present should be suspended because only history will ultimately answer the questions of legitimacy. But what is in question neither for Matthew nor for me is the eternal link between the land and people of Israel in God's eschatological purposes: the people as well as the land have a future.¹⁰

Gerald McDermott (Downers Grove, IL: InterVarsity, 2016).

6. Willitts, *Shepherd-King*, 147.

7. Willitts, "Zionism," 139.

8. Renown historian of Judaism, philosopher and theologian and leader in Jewish-Christian dialogue movement. For a through introduction to his life and thought consult Kendall Soulen's two essays in Michael Wyschogrod and R. Kendall Soulen, *Abraham's Promise: Judaism and Jewish-Christian Relations* (Grand Rapids: Eerdmans, 2004)

9. Wyschogrod and Soulen, *Abraham's Promise*, 102–3, emphasis added.

10. Willitts, "Zionism," 139.

In the same essay, Wyschogrod further elaborated on themes in the passage quoted above particularly, God's promise of the land, the inevitability of Israel's return to the land and the legitimacy of the State of Israel; additionally, he now spoke of the presence of Arabs in the land:

> No claim to the Land of Israel other than the Jewish claim is divinely validated. And this is so even if this was the wrong time to reestablish Jewish sovereignty and if, therefore, God is temporarily interposing another people between Israel and its Land. The people who have come to dwell in the Land during the estrangement of Israel from its Land have been drawn into the vortex of a theological drama not of their making. Their pain must be felt by Israel and the compassion that is the deepest dimension of Jewish consciousness must be brought to bear on the problem. But none of this can obscure the eternal link between Israel and the Land, a link that must, sooner or later, be reestablished.[11]

Four elements emerge from Wyschogrod's thinking in these two passages:

1. Jewish political-national sovereignty, that is to say the modern State of Israel, may in fact not be the fulfillment of God's promise of the territorial restoration of Israel; it's legitimacy as such is an open question.

2. There is an unbreakable and inseparable bond between the land of Palestine and the people of Israel.

3. Arabs in both the present and for generations past as well as those before, the Christians and the Romans, are and were interlopers, albeit unknowingly so, until God reconstitutes Israel in the Land.

4. Wherever suffering is caused by the immigration and settlement of Jews in Palestine, Zionists must exhibit solidarity, empathy and compassion as well as the deeds associated with them.

I largely agree with these points, although I take issue with numbers three and four. First, Christian Zionist arguments that attempt to prove the illegitimacy of an Arab claim to the land strikes me as foolish for two reasons. One, it is not possible to quickly sidestep the obvious fact that Arabs have lived in the land of Palestine for a millennium since the Muslim conquests of the seventh and eight centuries. Such history as theirs gives them the right to claim the land as their own.[12] Two, only in the nineteenth and twentieth centuries did Jews begin to colonize Palestine in great

---

11. Wyschogrod and Soulen, *Abraham's Promise*, 103.

12. Contra Brog, *Reclaiming*, ch. 2 (39–58). Hugh Kennedy (*The Great Arab Conquests: How the Spread of Islam Changed the World We Live In* [Philadelphia: Da Capo, 2007], 93) writes, "By 640 the whole of Syria, apart from one or two towns, had come under Islamic rule."

numbers, although there remained "important Jewish communities" even after the Bar Kokhba Revolt through modern times."[13] Therefore both Jew and Arab have legitimate claims to the land. The superiority of the Jewish claim, while *irrevocable* (Rom. 11:29) should not *at present* invalidate the Arab claim. Equally an Arab claim can in no way supersede the Jewish claim, while in the present they have claim to the land. Palestinian Arabs, then, have the right to live in a geography that cultivates their human flourishing. At present they do not.

The fourth point doesn't sit well with me either. Wyschogrod infers what I make plain: Jewish empathy and compassion is to be shown to Palestinian Arabs who the Jewish State has displaced, occupied or made to suffer in some other way. It's tantamount to bloodying someone's nose with a punch and then offering a handkerchief and an icepack.

As I will soon describe, the "peaceful infiltration" has been nothing of the sort. The State of Israel was born in War and has survived on a war footing ever since. Still Israel is a vulnerable State. It is surrounded by Arab countries and terrorist factions committed to its harm. Without a strong military, Israel would not have survived eight decades. There's no question Israel deserves the right to protect herself. What is more, Israel has attempted to negotiate peace on several occasions since 1948. But each time the attempt was rebuffed by the Palestinian leaders.[14]

The two issues of Israel's right to the whole land in the present and the inability or unwillingness to own the damage done to Palestinians through its militarism have put me in a bind. It's impossible to resolve with my Zionist sympathies. I'm vexed. What is more, two additional problems have emerged for me that have deepened my vexation.

This essay will unpack those two problems as well as introduce an unknown path for a vexed Zionist living in the second decade of the twenty-first century. I will show that Christian Zionism has a blind spot and an exegetical Catch-22. Further, I explain Martin Buber's Zionism and suggest his is a path worth considering for a twenty-first century vexed Christian Zionist.

I hope this essay, which advocates for an atypical Christian Zionism in the Bubarian pattern, invites an honest, more self-aware, and ambivalent Christian Zionism that must bear the ambiguities, tensions, and contradictions that inescapably

---

13. Brog, *Reclaiming*, ch 1 (15–36); Kennedy, *Arab Conquests*, 66.

14. The closest a peace plan was reached was in 2000 between Yasar Arafat and Ehud Barak at Camp David with Bill Clinton's mediation. From the Palestinian perspective the rejection of those plans was for good reasons—among the reasons for rejecting the plans were that the proposals were designed and brokered by Israel's sponsor the US. And the construct of the plans did not mean real statehood.

beset it because, on the one hand, the complex identity of the Jewish State, and on the other, the witness of Scripture.

Christian Zionist's Blind Spot

Blind Spot /ˈblīn(d) spät/ *noun*

1. the point of entry of the optic nerve on the retina, insensitive to light.

2. an area where a person's view is obstructed.

"the angle rearview mirror eliminates blind spots on both sides of the car"

Ari Shavit, in his recent book *My Promised Land: The Triumph and Tragedy of Israel*, tells a potent story of the massacre and explosion of the village of Lydda during the 1948 war by the IDF (Israel Defense Forces). Shavit, an Israeli and a former columnist for the *Haarezt*, has written a disturbing recount detailing the events which led to the massacre and the expulsion of all of the city's Arab residents.[15]

On a hot summer day in July of 1948, the IDF surrounded the city of Lydda—now the city of Lod in central Israel just east of Tel Aviv, Ben-Gurion Airport. In less than an hour in a barrage of artillery fire the city was in Israeli hands and more than 100 civilians were killed in the invasion including women and children and the elderly. By evening the city was squarely in the hands of the IDF having taken key positions in the city center. They also confined thousands of civilians in the Great

---

15. See also Shavit's article "Lydda, 1948" in the New Yorker: https://www.newyorker.com/magazine/2013/10/21/lydda-1948. For more information on the events in 1948 in Lydda, see also https://en.wikipedia.org/wiki/1948_Palestinian_exodus_from_Lydda_and_Ramle. For a largely corroborating treatment of the events see Ilan Pappé's discussion in *The Ethnic Cleansing of Palestine* (London: Oneworld, 2006) 166–69. Pappé draws on a different set of sources. He depends on a 1998 article in *Journal of Palestinian Studies* by sociologist Salim Tamari. Tamari's work depends on interviews conducted with Spiro Munayar, a resident of Lydda and an eyewitness of the events. See also the discussion in Black, *Enemies and Neighbors*, 125–26. Black confirms a detail that Shavit describes related to Ben-Gurion's role in the expulsion. The order to expel the residents was on the order of Ben-Gurion according to Yitzhak Rabin, the commander of the operation (called Operation Dani). Ben-Gurion waved his hand and barked "Remove them." The details of Shavit's recounting of the events on July 11 and 12, 1948 has received stiff criticism in some reviews most substantive is Martin Kramer's review https://scholar.harvard.edu/files/martinkramer/files/what_happened_at_lydda_kramer.pdf. Kramer's rebuttal however has suffered a harsh blow by Segev's account of the events. He shows the involvement of Ben-Gurion and Israel's best-known commanding officers: Moshe Dayan, Yigal Allon, and Yitzhak Rabin. Segev confirms Ben-Gurion's wave of hand in a "manner that Rabin interpreted as directive to expel them." Segev also discusses the report of the incident by Shmaryahu Gutman, the military governor of Lidda. Gutman is the same source Shavit used to write about the events in Lidda. Segev writes, "The battle for Lod was a difficult one; the IDF encountered opposition. At one stage the Israeli forces succeeded in confining thousands of the city's men in. mosque. They were permitted to leave and return to their homes, on condition that they and their families leave the city within a few hours" (A State, 440).

Mosque, the small mosque, and in St. George's cathedral. "By evening, Zionism has taken the city of Lydda."[16]

The next day, at noon, the fog of war caused the misidentification of two military Jordanian armored vehicles resulting in the death of two hundred civilians. Shavit writes

> The soldiers shoot in every direction. Some throw hand grenades into homes. One fires an antitank PIAT shell into the small mosque. In thirty minutes, at high noon, more than two hundred civilians are killed. Zionism carries out a massacre in the city of Lydda.[17]

The next day, in the monastery of St. George, negotiations proceeded between the city fathers of Lydda, anxious about the citizens of the city, and the military governor who wanted the residents out of the city but without having a direct expulsion order from his superiors. When the negotiation concluded, the governor achieved his goal. In fear for the lives of the people of Lydda, the leaders of the city agreed to depart the city en masse. In the end, in fact, the negotiations went so well for the governor that the city fathers *requested* to leave their homes and their city. Shavit reports the sinister nature of the negotiations. He writes,

> Gutman [military governor over the city] feels he has achieved his goal. Occupation, massacre and mental pressure have had their desired effect. At the end of the day, after forty-eight hours of hell, he does not quite order the people of Lydda to go. Under the indirect threat of slaughter, Lydda's leaders *ask* to go.[18]

Photograph by Joel Willitts

---

16. Shavit, *Promised Land*, 107.
17. Shavit, *Promised Land*, 108.
18. Shavit, *Promised Land*, 122.

The residents of Lydda are given less than two hours to gather whatever they can carry and leave the city. They began a march. Fifty thousand Palestinian Arabs in all, including the residents of the neighboring city of Ramla marched in a long column toward the east.

Ian Black calls what happened in Lydda the "biggest atrocity of the war."[19] That is, perhaps, alongside the massacre in Deir Yassin earlier in April of 1948, where 110 villagers were murdered by the Irgun. To be fair, the action in Deir Yassin was conducted by Etzel and Lehi, radical and unauthorized militia groups, was vehemently condemned by the Jewish Agency Executive which had been the state-in-waiting until the Declaration of Independence just a month later on May 14, 1948. While the known atrocities in the War of Independence of 1948, also referred to as the "ethnic cleansing," are relatively few, the news of even a couple of massacres had "the positive effect," from the point of view of Israel, of causing mass flight of Palestinians from their homes and towns and cities, fearing a similar fate if they stayed.[20]

The story of Lydda was not an anomaly. It was a species of military tactics performed by the IDF before and during the War of Independence. Shavit reports an interview with the Shkaryahu Gutman, military commander over Lydda. The commander said "'[the] general instruction to Palmach headquarters was that war presented a one-time opportunity to solve the Arab problem.'" Yigal Allon [operational commander], said, "'they [Arabs] must not remain or else there would not be a state,' reported the brigade commander. Allon further stated, according to Shavit's interviewee, 'wherever you fight, Arabs should not remain.'" After reporting this interview, Shavit concluded, "So it was in Tiberias and Safed, so it was in the villages of the Galilee, so it was in the villages of the Valley of Lydda—Iraba, Daniyal, Gimszu, Dahariya and Haditha." The brigade commander emphatically denied, however, an explosion order was ever given. But there was no need for one. "In many cases [of expulsion of Arabs] there was no need to issue an explicit order to expel Arabs—the spirit of the message conveyed by the commander in chief was sufficient."[21] No order was given, but Lydda was no more.[22]

---

19. Black, *Enemies and Neighbors*, 125.

20. Eugene Rogan (*The Arabs: A History* [New York: Basic Books, 2009], 259) writes: "Time and again, contemporary accounts make reference to townspeople and villagers across Palestine taking their loved ones and abandoning their homes and possessions out of fear of another Dar Yassin [and Lydda]." Photo is taken from the New Yorker article on Lydda: https://www.newyorker.com/magazine/2013/10/21/lydda-1948, accessed 1/6/2020.

21. Segev, *A State*, 418.

22. Ilan Pappe (*Ethnic*) presents a well-researched and argued case that there was a comprehensive plan by the new Israeli State to systematically take over, occupy villages and cities and expel the Arab population. Similarly, Ian Black (*Enemies and Neighbors*, 115–16.) writes, "The predisposition to population transfer and the tactical military considerations in fast-moving circumstances inclined

Shavit wrestles with how to make sense of Lydda as a Zionist. He voices his struggle with the ambiguities and the tensions looking face to face with facts:

> Lydda is our black box. In it lies the dark secret of Zionism. The truth is that Zionism could not bear Lydda. From the very beginning there was a substantial contradiction between Zionism and Lydda . . . [We] should have known that Lydda was an obstacle blocking the road to the Jewish state and that one-day Zionism would have to remove it . . . For half a century it succeeded in hiding from itself the substantial contradiction between the Jewish national movement and Lydda . . . Then, in three days in the cataclysmic summer of 1948, contradiction struck, and tragedy revealed its face. Lydda was no more.[23]

One may not agree with how Shavit has assimilated Lydda into his Zionism, but he is one of the few Israelis who have raised such things as Lydda, things that are left unspoken in Zionist circles. Toward the end of the chapter, he questions,

> Do I wash my hands of Zionism? Do I turn my back on the Jewish movement that carried out the deed of Lydda? . . . I'm not only sad, I am horrified. For when one opens the black box, one understands . . . the conquest of Lydda and the explosion of Lydda were no accident. The were an inevitable phase of the Zionist revolution that laid the foundation for the Zionist state. Lydda is an integral and essential part of our story. And when I try to be honest about it, I see that the choice is stark: either reject Zionism because of Lydda or accept Lydda along with Zionism.[24]

The last sentence is provocative. It's how Shavit has come to terms with his Zionism. He's accepted Lydda. The deplorable actions of Israel's military and politicians those few days in July 1948 cannot be disregarded or forgotten; they force a decision on you.

I followed Shavit to Lydda on a trip to Israel recently. I was by myself. I hired a car and drove to the depressed city of Lod. It is clear that the city has seen better days. With Shavit's book in hand, I visited the big Mosque. I visited the Greek Orthodox Monastery of St George's. I talked to some folks in the monastery. They gave me an orange soda drink. I asked them if they knew what had happened here in 1948. They said they did, but not too much. We talked about it for a bit. I thanked them for the drink and took leave. There were a few barely readable signs around

---

Haganah commanders towards removing Arabs, given the opportunity . . . No high-level Jewish political discussion is known to have been held to explicitly discuss expelling Arabs, but many expulsions unquestionably took place. And the results, in the end, mattered far more than intentions—and the nuance of later historiographical controversy" over whether expulsions were a strategy or a happenstance of war ("born out of war, not by design"—Benny Morris). See also Segev, *A State*, 416–21.

23. Shavit, *Promised Land*, 108.
24. Shavit, *Promised Land*, 131.

the square identifying the buildings that lay in rubble. It feels like the town square is frozen in time.

Photograph by David S. Boyer / Corbis

It was eerie to be there at the very spot, envisaging the chaos, brutality, fear and the forced flight. I tried to imagine a column of 30,000 people, men, women and children, marching to the east, marching to nowhere. Marching nowhere with only what they could carry. Being in Lod brought the tragedy to life for me. Shavit's description of the events provided an orientation from which I could identify most of the physical elements that remained. It also helped me identify with the tragedy. I cannot now remember why I picked up and read *My Promise Land*, but I thank Ari Shavit for introducing me to Lydda. The events that happened there in the middle of July 1948 haunt me.

What does a Christian Zionist do with a Lydda? How will they assimilate Lydda into their Zionism? How will I? These are vexing questions.

Shavit's account showed me Christian Zionism's "black box." Lydda's story presents a contradiction to the noble narrative of the War of Independence. It reveals actions taken by the IDF to systematically conqueror villages and towns and expel residents.

After offering numerous qualifications along the way while reporting the story of Lydda, the Zionist apologist David Borg is still forced in the end to write:

> As with Deir Yassin, there is a general consensus that the Israelis committed war crimes in Lydda. Upwards of three hundred of Lydda's residents were killed in the fighting, including many unarmed civilians. By their own testimony, it's

clear that some Israeli soldiers overreacted to perceived dangers and failed to distinguish between civilians and combatants. There are even reports that some soldiers intentionally shot wounded prisoners and civilians. Then came Israel's largest and most brutal expulsion. The town's residents—including the very old and the very young—were forced to walk over ten miles in the July heat without sufficient water or food. "Quite a few," and possibly "dozens" died on the way.[25]

I was unaware of Lydda's story. I'm certain there are a lot more Lydda stories to learn. There are many, too many, to be dismissed as exceptions that prove the rule. This part of the Zionist story is troubling for me. Say what you like about the anti-Zionist historian Ilan Pappé, there is simply too much evidence for expulsions to be dismissed as bad history or leftist, anti-Zionist propaganda.[26]

The story of Lydda and its ramifications make my mind spin. Christian Zionism, Lydda, my beliefs. I'm vexed by the tensions, the extremes, the harm, the complexity, the confusion. Is Ari Shavit's either/or the only Zionist option: "Zionism could not bear Lydda . . . If Zionism was to be, Lydda could not be. If Lydda was to be, Zionism could not be?"[27] When I reflect on the events that transpired in Lydda, how do I incorporate it into a Christian Zionist framework? I know Israel is not perfect. I know there is room to criticize decisions they make. But does Lydda fall under the exception clause? I want to know what I'm supposed to do with Lydda! Nobody talks about it. *Lydda is Christian Zionism's blind spot.* Now the exegetical Catch-22.

Christian Zionist's Exegetical Catch-22

catch-22 noun, often capitalized
\kach-ˌtwen-tē-ˈtü, ˈkech-\
plural **catch-22's** or **catch-22s**

1. a frustrating situation in which one is trapped by contradictory regulations or conditions.

2. any illogical or paradoxical problem or situation; dilemma.

3. a condition, regulation, etc., preventing the resolution of a problem or situation; catch.[28]

---

25. Brog, *Reclaiming*, 145.
26. Ilan Pappe, *The Biggest Prison on Earth: A History of the Occupied Territories* (London: Oneworld, 2019); Pappe, *Ethnic*; Pappe, *History*.
27. Shavit, *Promised Land*, 108.
28. Definition taken from https://www.dictionary.com/browse/catch-22?s=t.

The Acts of the Apostles begins with important accounts of Yeshua's post-resurrection appearances. Luke tells us that Yeshua gave "many convincing proofs" that he was alive (1:3a) that he appeared to them forty days "speaking about the kingdom of God" (1:3b) that at one time during these days, Yeshua told them not to leave Jerusalem until they received the "promise of Father . . . not many days from now," by which he referred to the gift of the Holy Spirit (1:4). Then, Luke records the final exchange between him and his disciples:

> When they had come together, they asked him, "Lord, is this the time when you will restore the kingdom to Israel?" He replied, "It is not for you to know the times or periods that the Father has set by his own authority. But you will receive power when the Holy Spirit has come upon you; and you will be my witnesses in Jerusalem, in all Judea and Samaria, and to the ends of the earth."[29]

The dialogue is quite straightforward. The Jewish believers in Yeshua asked a question of Yeshua that the immediate literary context implies was a reasonable one to ask (1:6). Yeshua then responded taking issue with their preoccupation with calculating times and commissioned them to bear witness (1:7-8).

Kingdom

Taking notice of the earlier report that Yeshua spent forty days with the disciples "speaking about the kingdom," one must have a very low view of the disciples to think that after hearing Yeshua talk about the kingdom for forty days, they would ask an uninformed and confused question about the very center of Yeshua' teaching. It would be a much fairer interpretation in light of the context to give these men the benefit of the doubt. Once more, what kind of teacher does one imagine Yeshua to be after all; if, after all the time (3 years + 40 days) with his disciples, they would still not yet comprehend what he meant by "the kingdom."

There are not a few commenters who seem to conclude that Yeshua is correcting or redefining the concept of "kingdom" for the disciples[30.] What is at issue in the disciples' question?

---

29. All Scripture references in this essay come from the NRSV unless my own translation.

30. Cf. David G. Peterson, *The Acts of the Apostles*, edited by D.A. Carson, PNTC, (Grand Rapids: Eerdmans, 2009) 109-10; Mikeal Carl Parsons, *Acts*, Paideia, (Grand Rapids: Baker Academic, 2008) 28; F. F. Bruce, *The Book of the Acts*, Rev. ed., NICNT, (Grand Rapids: Eerdmans, 1988) 35-36; Craig S. Keener, *Acts: An Exegetical Commentary Introduction and 1:1—2:47* (Grand Rapids: Baker Academic, 2012) 684. Richard Pervo (*Acts: A Commentary*, edited by Harold W. Attridge, Hermeneia, (Minneapolis: Fortress Press, 2009) 41) writes, "Literary tradition allowed pupils ask dull or inappropriate questions so that teachers could promulgate the correct view." In line with my view, see John B. Polhill, *Acts*, edited by David Dockery, vol. 26, NAC, (Nashville: Broadman & Holman, 1992) 84) and Ben

"Lord, in this time, will you restore the kingdom to Israel?"[31]

The NRSV translates this one Greek sentence into two sentences or clauses:

6b "Lord, is this the time,

6c *when* you will restore the kingdom to Israel."

The Greek proposition is one sentence comprised of a prepositional phrase, a subject, an object and an indirect object. In this case a more literalistic translation would have been preferable over dynamic equivalency, because by doing the latter, the reader loses the ability to see the placement of the preposition relative to the main verb. Luke frontloaded the prepositional phrase imparting to it emphasis. The pay dirt of this discussion is the question the disciples are asking is about the timing of the kingdom's arrival.

Thus, having no special interest in addressing the subject of the kingdom, Luke apparently reasons a reader will assume that the kingdom in question is the kingdom Yeshua taught and preached (Luke 4:18–19; 43; 8:1; 9:2, 11, 27, 60; 10:9, 11; 11:2; 22:29[32]); which is also the kingdom preached later in Acts.[33] What does Luke-

---

Witherington III (*The Acts of the Apostles: A Socio-Rhetorical Commentary* (Grand Rapids: Eerdmans, 1998) 110) writes—and I quote him at length:

> no indent of the Spirit in "not many days" prompts the question, "Is this the time when you will restore the kingdom to Israel?" (*v. 6*). It is a natural question not only in view of the connection in Luke's thought between the pouring out of the Spirit and the coming of the kingdom, but also because of the speculations in early Judaism about the restoration of the land (cf. Sir. 48:10, the LXX of Mal. 3:23). In terms of Lukan theology, what this verse shows is that while Luke does believe that the coming of the Spirit inaugurates the kingdom, he does not believe that that is all there is to be said about the kingdom. This verse suggests that God will one day fulfill his promises to Israel, in fact that God has already set that time and determined the interval before it by his own authority, but that human speculation about the timing of such an event is unfruitful, since only God knows that timing and he is not revealing it to mortals. What this also shows is that Luke believes, not surprisingly, that many early followers of Yeshua believed in the restoration of the control of the land to Israel (cf. Luke 24:21).

31. My translation. The preposition receives the emphasis in the question. This is demonstrated by the emphatic position of *ei en tō chronō toutō* ("if in this time") in the sentence: *kyrie, ei en tō chronō toutō apokathistaneis tēn basilean tō Israēl*. The topic of "the kingdom" is not in question here; but rather the kingdom's timing.

32. Luke 22:29 is of particular importance: and "I assign to you, as my Father assigned to me, a kingdom, that you may eat and drink at my table in my kingdom and sit on thrones judging the twelve tribes of Israel."

33. Mark Kinzer ("Zionism in Luke-Acts," in *The New Christian Zionism*, edited by Gerald McDermott [Downers Grove, IL: InterVarsity Press, 2016], 163) makes this point: "The language of the apostles' question to Yeshua in Acts 1:6 is thus echoed by Peter's speech to the people of Jerusalem in Acts 3, with the same meaning in both cases: Peter tells the Jerusalemites that the kingdom will be restored to Israel (as a central and essential element in the "restoration of all things about which God spoke by the mouth of His holy prophets") when they acknowledge Yeshua as Israel's returning [Davidic] king. This echo implies that Peter has not interpreted Yeshua's answer in Acts 1:7–8 as a rejection of the legitimacy of the question."

Acts reveal about the kingdom? A messianic kingdom of David. A restored kingdom of Israel consisting in both a restored people and a restored land.

A messianic kingdom springing up from the Davidic promise of 2 Samuel 7 and 1 Chronicles 17 and prophecies like Isaiah 11 and Second Temple Jewish texts, besides the New Testament, like *Psalms of Solomon* 17–18. The kingdom these envisaged was a concrete, stuff-of-this-earth kingdom with a government, capital and borders.[34] The kingdom, according to the Chronicler, who had a thoroughgoing Davidic interest, equates the kingdoms of the Lord, David and of Israel. Two texts that illustrate this phenomenon are 1 Chron 22:5: "And of all my sons, for the LORD has given me many, he has chosen my son Solomon to sit upon *the throne of the kingdom of the LORD over Israel.*" And 2 Chron 13:8 "'And now you think that you can *withstand the kingdom of the LORD in the hand of the sons of David,* because you are a great multitude and have with you the golden calves that Jeroboam made as gods for you?'"[35]

It is evident that it is this kingdom to which Gabriel was referring when he said of Yeshua to Mary:

> He will be great and will be called the Son of the Most High. And the Lord God will give to him the throne of his father David, and he will reign over the house of Jacob forever, and of his kingdom there will be no end" (Luke 1:32–33).

And what Mary herself stated:

---

34. Although Munther Isaac (*From Land to Lands, from Eden to the Renewed Earth* [Cumbria, UK: Langham Monographs, 2015], 111–21) rightly emphasizes the metaphorical-theological aspects of the geographical borders of the Promised Land, he does not sufficiently account for the borders of the Davidic kingdom which are primary for both Jewish Scripture and Second Temple Judaism. The Davidic census in 2 Sam 24:5–7 presents the most expansive manifestation of the territory of Israel in history. In describing those borders, Yohanan Aharoni (*The Carta Bible Atlas*, 4th ed. [Jeruslaem: Carta, 2000], 79–80) writes, "There are three main elements ... discernable within it: Israelite population, conquered kingdoms; and vassal kings. At the center of the Empire stood the tribes of Israel and Judah ... the Cannanite-Amorite regions ... around these lay the conquered and tributary kingdoms." What is more, Martin Hengel ("Ioudaia in the Geographical List of Acts 2:9–11 and Syria as "Greater Judea"," *BBR* 10.2 [2000]: 171) has concluded that the Davidic Empire was used "as a model and about all determined the geogrpahy of messianic expecdtations." James M. Scott (*On Earth as in Heaven: The Restoration of Sacred Time and Sacred Space in the Book of Jubilees*, JSJSup 91, [Leiden: Brill, 2005], 175) has pointed out that in Jubilees, which is not known to have a Davidic messianic perspective, the borders of Israel are drawn along a Davidic-Solomonic territorial ideal. Finally, Markus Bockmuehl (*Jewish Law in Gentile Churches: Halakhah and the Beginning of Christian Public Ethics* [Grand Rapids: Baker, 2003], 63–64) has suggested that the Jewish expansions in the Hasmonenan period may relfect the "idea of the restoration of the Jewish land." For a more wideranging treatment of the subject, see Willitts, *Shepherd-King*, 162–68. The paydirt of all of this is Isaac's purely metaphorical understanding of the borders of the Promised Land is wholly insufficient to account for the evidence in biblical and post-biblical Jewish literature.

35. See Similarly Munther Isaac, *From Land to Lands, from Eden to the Renewed Earth* (Cumbria, UK: Langham Monographs, 2015) 107.

> He has helped his servant Israel in remembrance of his mercy, according to the promise he made to our ancestors, to Abraham and to his descendants forever (Luke 1:54–55).

And what Zechariah proclaimed:

> And you, child, will be called the prophet of the Most High; for you will go before the Lord to prepare his ways, to give knowledge of salvation to his people by the forgiveness of their sins (Luke 1:76–77).

And what Anna of Asher rejoiced about when she met the child:

> At that moment she came and began to praise God and to speak about the child to all who were looking for the redemption of Jerusalem (Luke 2:38).

These passages at the beginning of Luke establish the identity and vocation of Yeshua right through the two-volume work. Yeshua is the Davidic messiah come to restore concretely the kingdom of David. Of Anna's statement, Richard Bauckham states,

> Her [Anna of Asher] importance in Luke's narrative is to ensure that the Israel whose hopes of messianic restoration are so fully represented in Luke's first two chapters is truly Israel as a whole, northern tribes as well as southern, exiles as well as inhabitants of the land.[36]

I have argued elsewhere that Jewish messianic expectation—where David is the primary messianic figure—reveals that the claim of the mantel of the new Davidide demands the presence of the concomitant elements of the reconstitution of Israel's twelve-tribe league and territorial restoration in the shape of the kingdom of David. *There is no evidence of an eschatology, in which David is central, that is not stuff-of-earth, concrete and Israel-centric.*[37] Luke clearly is situated in this traditional milieu in view of the birth narratives.

That is by no means to say the conception of Davidic restoration relates *merely* to the territory of Israel narrowly defined as the tribal allotments. Neither does it exclude broad settlements of non-Jews within the restored twelve-tribe borders, however they be defined. Furthermore, within the mental conception of the restoration of David's monarchy, "Israel" is the name of the *realm* under David's hegemony; "Israel" in this sense reflects David's own kingdom which encompassed not only the tribal allotments, but also the territories beyond it.[38] In the prophetic tradition and

---

36. Richard Bauckham, "The Restoration of Israel in Luke-Acts," in *Restoration: Old Testament, Jewish, and Christian Perspectives*, edited by James M. Scott, JSJSup (Leiden; Boston: Brill, 2001) 458.

37. Willitts, *Shepherd-King*, 147, 170–73.

38. The extent of the borders of David's Empire is revealed in the census in 2 Sam 25:4–8.

the subsequent Jewish literature for which David play a key role in restoration, David's government was expected to stretch from Jerusalem within the borders of the tribal allotments to the ends of a renewed earth.[39] "Israel" is inclusive of the nations without diminishment of the Jewish territorial particularity.

Neither revision nor contradiction of concrete Davidic expectations are evidenced in the teaching of Yeshua in the four Gospels or in the Apostolic witness to him.[40] One *cannot* take up the new Davidide without the political-national freight that comes with him.

Time

The disciples ask Yeshua if the kingdom is to be restored to Israel *at this time*, now. Yeshua's response takes the form of seven propositions (amplified):

1. Do **not** concern yourself with the times and seasons [7a];

2. <u>*because*</u> ("which") the Father has fixed [7b];

3. **But** you will receive power [8a];

4. *when* (ptcp) the Holy Spirit's presence is given [8b];

5. <u>*so that*</u> (*kai*) you will bear witness of me in Jerusalem [8c];

6. *and moreover* (*kai*) in Judea and Samaria [8d];

7. *and moreover* (*kai*) to the whole world [8e].[41]

---

39. Willitts, *Shepherd-King*, 147, 170–71.

40. John's Apocalypse knows nothing of a reinterpreted kingdom. Quite to the contrary, it imagines an Israel-centric restored creation. Metaphorically it places, at the center of the new creation, the city of Israel's God and his Davidic messiah. A restored Davidic Jerusalem comes down and rests *on* a place on the earth. Although it comes from the heavens, it is a city on the earth, a Jewish city as its king is Jewish. However, now it is a city free of hierarchy and free of ethnic hostility whose walls have gates that are never closed. Where both the nations and Israel move freely in and out reconciled with creation (Rev 21:22—22:5). The ethnic identities of the peoples are retained as Yeshua' is. The implication of these observations is that Israel never loses its role in God's work on the earth. Israel's God and Israel's messiah are seated at the center of the city that is at the center of the new creation.

41. (1) As we saw, the dialogue begins with a one sentence *question* (6b) the answer follows in five propositions (7a, 7b, 8a, 8b, 8c). (2) The *response* to the question is in 5 parts. Starting from bottom to top, propositions 8c, 8d and 8e are connect by the conjunction "and" (*kai*) in this case signifying a *progression* from one region to another expanding outward. 8d and 8e assume the verb from 8c. Bearing witness in Jerusalem; bearing and witness in Judah and Samaria; and bearing witness in the whole world. Propositions 8c-e are the *resultative*. Bearing witness is the outcome of the presence of the Holy Spirit. The Spirit's power manifest in them *results* in witness. (3) The relationship between 8a and 8b is determined by adverbial participle *epelthontos* and is *temporal* ("when"). The relationship between these propositions is similar to that of 6a and 6b. The reception of power depends on the arrival of the Holy Spirit. (4) Verse 8's propositions are related to the two in verse 7 by the emphatic conjunction "but" (*alla*). The first two propositions (7a and 7b) are part of a syntactical structure in which one proposition is negated by the second proposition: *ouch . . . alla* ("not this . . . but that"). The *negative*

For my purpose here, the most important observation is the "not"/"but" construction comprising propositions 1, 2 and 3 (7a–8a). The construction represents a logical relationship between propositions in which one is negated, while another is affirmed: "*Not* this . . . *but* that." I've pointed this out to highlight the significance of the syntactic device. The construction structures the argument of the contrasting pair. When it is taken into account it is clear that Yeshua is negating *the disciples' focus on chronology* while affirming the expectation of the power that will come for mission. ["do *not* concern yourself with times and seasons . . . *but* you will receive power"]. Yeshua has created a collision between two expectations: an expectation of fulfillment of Davidic prophesy and the expectation to receive God's power through the Holy Spirit. Thus, the construction does not signal a replacement of a concrete stuff-of-this-earth kingdom expectation for empowered mission.

A close reading of the three verses demonstrate that the disciples' question was legitimate, and Yeshua's response honored their Israel-centric political-national and territorial understanding of the kingdom. Nevertheless, and likely to their great amazement, Yeshua switched gears on them redirecting their aims. Yeshua reoriented their priorities from *chronology* to *missiology*, toward Spirit-empowered witness to what God has done in and through Yeshua (Acts 3:20–21).

To me, frankly, in view of the literary contextual evidence I presented, it stretches imagination to its breaking point to interpret Yeshua' response in 1:7–8 as a correction of the disciples' understanding of the nature of the kingdom implied in their question (1:6).

We can draw two conclusions from the discussion of Acts 1:7–8: (1) the disciples' kingdom expectation is what Yeshua taught them; and (2) Yeshua's answer is a negation of computation, not a negation of Davidic kingdom expectation. Another way of putting it, albeit a step beyond the text, is *let the Father do statecraft; you do mission*.

The exegesis of Acts 1:6–8 places the Christian Zionist in a bind, I think. For a Christian Zionist, Acts 1:6–8, on the one hand, securely fastens down in the solid bedrock of the New Testament the commitment to a future territorial, political-national, Davidic "state" of Israel. One could hardly find a firmer biblical justification for Christian Zionism than Acts 1:6–8.

---

option is stated first followed by its antithesis, the *positive* alternative (8a–b). Yeshua' answer to the disciples' question goes something like this: "not time, but witness." (5) The two propositions in verse 7 are related by the conjunction relative conjunction *ous* "that/which." The connection between the two is causal. The "time and seasons" are the effect of God's action. There is an emphasis on with the repetition of the term *chronos* in verse six and seven: *ei en tō chronō toutō*["if in this time"] (v. 6) *ouch hymōn estin gnō*nai *chronous hē kairous* ["it is not for you to know the times or the seasons] (v. 7).

On the other, however, proper exegesis of Acts 1:6–8 should give a Christian Zionist whiplash. Certainty turns into perplexity. Luke's Yeshua shifts the ground under a Christian Zionist's feet. It seems the disciples were asking their question with the expectation of a positive response from Yeshua—they were expecting a yes. What they received instead was what amounted to a wink and dizzying redirection. Thus, the Christian Zionist's Catch-22.

Christian Zionist's Exegetical Catch-22	
Eretz Israel is an irreducible element of Israel's kingdom and, therefore, also an irreducible part of the kingdom restored to Israel through the reign of Yeshua, Son of David	The restoration of Israel in *Eretz* Israel should not be the concern of Yeshua's disciples at this stage in the unfolding of Israel's redemptive story.

Acts 1:6–8 indicates that while a Christian Zionist can be secure in their biblically grounded belief in the concrete nature of the restored kingdom of Israel in the future, Christian Zionism should not promote or lobby for or defend or justify the political-national and territorial interests of the Jewish state. *Bearing witness not statecraft.*

I cannot say if any other Christian Zionists have wrestled with this dilemma. But it has been a weighty vexation for me.

The difficulties I articulated I have with elements of my Zionism captured through those two passages of Wyschogrod, and in view of the Blind Spot and the Catch-22 I have just articulated, I am vexed Zionist. In seeking some useful resource for thinking about Zionism, I was introduced to Martin Buber. Buber's Zionism has much it can teach. If for no other reason than to become aware of a different sort of Zionism. Both heralded and vilified, Buber was ardently committed to the kind of Zionism he believed was true to its central principle. There is much to be learned for this unknown Jewish Zionist. I have found him to be a guide down a different path.

Martin Buber, the Atypical Zionist

Buber would remain an atypical Zionist throughout his life.[42]

In the early 20th century Martin Buber (b 1878, d 1965) was a vexed Zionist, vexed by the Zionism of his time; vexed by the very same things that vex likeminded Zionists. Paul Mendes-Flohr writes of Buber "His ongoing anguish would lead him . . . to be deeply ambivalent toward the Zionist project."[43] Buber's writings related to the relationship between Jews and Arabs have been collected by Paul Mendes-Flohr

---

42. Mendes-Flohr, *Life*, 90.
43. Mendes-Flohr, *Life*, 131.

in the volume *A Land for Two Peoples*. The essays span the length of his career (1918–1965). They reveal a man with relentless conviction and a tenacity to speak truth prophetically to Zionist leaders. Even though his voice was marginalized, Buber exercised significant influence until his death. The mainstream Zionist ends and the means to those ends greatly concerned Buber.

He wrote extensively about what he thought was contrary to a biblically Jewish mission and ethic. Buber saw the Jewish state created, developed and maintained at the expense of Palestinian Arabs. He was adamant that Jews and Arabs must live together with each other and not merely alongside. Cooperation and equal share in the economic prosperity of the Land was necessary. In his writings, he spoke presciently about the future character of the State—much of which has materialized. He did, however, accept it as his own, while continuing to advocate for issues that most concerned him.

I contend that Martin Buber opens a new path, an unknown path, for Christian Zionism. He models a Zionism, that, in the words of Paul Mendes-Flohr, was "atypical." Because of the similarities between his time and our own, his example is relevant, as if he were alive today.

Martin Buber in 1896, age 18, was first introduced to Zionism, while a student at the university of Vienne. He found in it a way to be in solidarity with the Jewish people without traditional Jewish religiosity, that is, apart from the Rabbinic tradition.[44] Paul Mendes-Flohr writes, "Zionism provided a revolutionary, secular alternative for maintaining Jewish national consciousness and solidarity."[45] Soon after becoming an adherent to Zionism, he and his cousin founded a local Zionist Jewish Students Association in Leipzig, where he was then attending University becoming its first officer. This would represent the beginning of Buber's leadership in the Zionist movement.

At 22 years-old, Buber's intellectual and spiritual life coalesced with his Zionism. He began to understand Zionism as a "Jewish renaissance." Summarizing Buber's perspective, Mendes-Flohr writes:

> The renaissance to which Zionism refers is born of "painful" understanding of *gault*, the torment of two thousand years of exile that has allowed the so-called custodians of tradition—the rabbis—to shackle the Jews "with the iron chains" to a "senseless tradition."[46]

---

44. Mendes-Flohr, *Life*, 22.
45. Mendes-Flohr, *Life*, 22.
46. Mendes-Flohr, *Life*, 25.

Buber's Zionism was a cultural nationalism, in the line of Ahad Ha'am,[47] which put him outside the mainstream for the rest of his life as Herzl's political Zionism eclipsed other forms.

Buber became an influential leader in the World Zionist Organization. His initial leadership was affirmed and promoted. That was to change, however, after controversy at the Fifth Zionism Congress in 1902. Buber, at the head of a group called the "young Zionists," came into conflict with Zionism's established leaders, most notably Theodore Herzl the father of political Zionism. He was ostracized after and in 1905 withdrew from all his work with the Zionist World Organization and was never to be involved with it again.[48]

Buber wrote prolifically across many disciplines, though he is known primarily as a philosopher. His most well know work is *I and Thou*,[49] which if I may say makes absolutely no sense to me! He lived in Germany until making *ailyah*, immigration to Palestine, in 1938 at the age of sixty. He remained an outspoken and influential leader and activist within the Zionist movement until his death in 1965. The last published work of his life at 87 was "A Time to Try just two years before the June 1967 and the Six Day War.[50] In the short essay, Buber wrote:

> Undoubtedly the fate of the New East depends on the question whether Israel and the Arab peoples will reach a mutual understanding before it's too late We do not know how much time is given to us to try.[51]

Buber's Opposition

Whatever initially was Buber's agenda for cultural Zionism in the early years of the 20th century, for the rest of his life he was embroiled in a fight which he thought was for the very soul of Zionism. In 1918 he wrote, "If we do not succeed to erect an authoritative [Zionist] opposition, the soul of the movement will be corrupted maybe forever."[52] Continuing to come to terms with the establishment the State in 1948, Buber wrestled with its implication, having spent three decades attempting to impede its realization. Buber possessed an uncommon resiliency and doggedness. What is more, he was able to adapt to changing circumstances over which he had

---

47. For information on Ahad Ha'am see https://www.britannica.com/biography/Ahad-Haam.
48. Mendes-Flohr, *Life*, 40.
49. Martin Buber, *I and Thou*, 2d ed. (New York: Scribner, 1958)
50. In Buber's last published work before his death, he was to continue to advocate a reconciliation between Arab's and Israel in "The Time to Try." See Paul Mendes-Flohr, *A Land of Two Peoples: Martin Buber on Jews and Arabs* (Chicago: Chicago University Press, 1983) 303–5.
51. Mendes-Flohr, *Land*, 304; 1965, "The Time To Try."
52. Mendes-Flohr, *Land*, 37–38; 1918, "State of Cannons, Flags, Military Decorations."

no power. In the following passage, Buber both expresses his rejection of idealist thinking, a kind of mindset which is unwilling to accept and adapt to what is *now* past for what is *today* present.

> I have accepted as mine the State of Israel, the form of the new Jewish Community that has arisen from the war. I have nothing in common with those Jews who imagine that they may contest the factual shape which Jewish independence has taken... He who will truly serve the spirit must seek to make good all that was once missed; he must seek to free once again the blocked path to an understanding with the Arab peoples.[53]

The passage touches on four issues within Zionism against which Buber contented: (1) political nationalism (statehood), (2) militarism, (3) expansionism, and (4) the Jewish-Arab relations.

Jewish Statehood

> *We must face the fact that most leading Zionists (and probably also most of those who are led) today are thoroughly unrestrained nationalists (following the European example) imperialists, even unconscious mercantilists and idolaters of success*[54]

> *That which, in Zionism, deserves the name "ideal" ...*
> *is the aspiration for national rehabilitation, regeneration.*[55]

For decades Buber decried political nationalism. "He was unyielding in his objection to the Zionist quest for political sovereignty."[56] Buber "harbored the fear that Zionism might very well degenerate into unalloyed political nationalism."[57] He believed "Zionism was not the founding of a state but true human community."[58] He distrusted nationalism and the nation state.[59] He said, "Any national state in vast, hostile surroundings would mean premeditated national suicide."[60]

His voice was drowned out by the furious march toward a political state, however. He bemoaned David Ben-Gurion's leadership—the leader of the Histadrut and later the Jewish Agency and the first prime minister of Israel—which was "succeeding

53. Mendes-Flohr, *Land*, 292–93; 1958, "Israel and the Commahd of the Spirit."
54. Mendes-Flohr, *Land*, 37; 1918 "The State of Canons, Flags, and Military Decorations?."
55. Mendes-Flohr, *Land*, 248; 1949, "Should the Ichud Accept the Decree of History."
56. Mendes-Flohr, *Life*, 233.
57. Mendes-Flohr, *Life*, 112.
58. Mendes-Flohr, *Life*, 129.
59. Mendes-Flohr, *Life*, 112.
60. Mendes-Flohr, *Land*, 211; 1947, "The Bi-National Approach to Zionism."

at [creating political nationhood] to a terrifying degree."[61] Buber said the nationalistic form of Zionism "blasphemes the name of Zion."[62] "It is nothing more than one of the crude forms of nationalism which acknowledges no master above the apparent (!) interest of the nation."[63] He, nevertheless, remained a fervent Zionist. He had the rare capacity to hold the "troubling ambiguities of Zionism's [nationalistic] aspirations" along with his opposition to those very aspirations. They must be embraced, nevertheless, as a creative challenge, if Judaism is *to cease being an ethereal disembodied entity, devoid of concrete expression.*"[64] One can see here Buber's phenomenological commitments. Judaism, to be fully realized, must be enfleshed in ethnically distinct bodies in a communal existence experiencing the rhythms of a cultural tradition in the land of ancestors.

Buber opposed the 1917 Balfour Declaration—Lord Balfour's letter stating that the United Kingdom supported the founding of a national Jewish homeland in Palestine—because it connected, he asserted, "the Zionist project to British colonialism."[65] Buber named the error of choosing to ally with a western colonial power was an act which sabotaged the Zionist effort by creating the impression that it was an agent of imperialism.[66] Mendes-Flohr comments, "Buber's fears had been especially aroused by . . . the Balfour Declaration, which aligned the Zionist project with British colonialism." [67] Mendes-Flohr notes further Buber's rejection of the Balfour Declaration put him at odds with most other Zionists, even his allies.[68]

From another angle, Buber opposed the Balfour Declaration because British imperial backing would legalize Jewish acquisition of Arab Land holdings. He wrote in 1920, "Extensive holdings [by Arab Land holders] cannot subsist forever in opposition to planned national settlement. But what could they do against the Balfour Declaration?"[69] In a letter to one Hugo Bergman in 1918, Buber wrote, "We must face the fact that most leading Zionists (and probably also most of those who are led) today are thoroughly unrestrained nationalists following the European example, imperialists, even unconscious mercantilists and idolaters of success." [70] It is worth

61. Mendes-Flohr, *Life*, 249.
62. Mendes-Flohr, *Land*, 221; 1948, "Zion and 'Zionism.'"
63. Mendes-Flohr, *Land*, 221–22; 1948, "Zion and 'Zionism.'"
64. Mendes-Flohr, *Life*, 112.
65. Mendes-Flohr, *Life*, 113.
66. Mendes-Flohr, *Land*, 199–40; 1939, "Concerning Our Politics."
67. Mendes-Flohr, *Life*, 113.
68. Mendes-Flohr, *Life*, 113; 1939, "A Letter to Gandhi."
69. Mendes-Flohr, *Land*, 43; 1920, "At This Late Hour."
70. Mendes-Flohr, *Land*, 37–38; 1918, "A State of Cannons, Flags, and Military Decorations."

finishing the quotation because it shows just how committed Buber was to fighting political nationalistic Zionism.

> If we do not succeed to erect an authoritative [Zionist] opposition, the soul of the movement will be corrupted, maybe for ever. I for my part am determined to commit myself totally to this cause, even if this should affect my personal plans . . .[71]

Buber also rejected the Partition Plan voted on by the UN on November 29, 1947. The Partition Plan divided Palestine into two states, one Arab and one Jewish. Buber and the group *Ichud* ("unity") an organization which promoted coexistence between Arabs and Jews, rejected the plan in fear of war between the two peoples. What is more, the "feverish haste" to create a state was foolish, he believed, arguing that the state, if there need be one, should develop organically. He wrote

> We must clearly declare what is necessary for us and what is not necessary. We need time and freedom for our enterprise, and not in order to gain the upper hand, we need *aliyah*, settlement and communal independence, not in order to become stronger than others, but solely that we shall be able to shape our lives. In order to do this, there is no need for a Jewish state; rather, there is need of a treaty [with the Arabs] based on faith.[72]

Militarism

Won't we be compelled, and I mean really compelled, to maintain a posture of vigilance forever, without being able to breathe? ... "Everyone with one of his hands wrought in the work, and with the other held his weapon" (Nehemiah 4:11)—that way you can build a wall, but it's impossible in that way to build an attractive house, let alone a temple.[73]

And when this hollow peace is achieved, how then do you think you'll be able to combat the "spirit of militarism."[74]

Inextricably linked to nationalism is militarism. As with the former so with the latter, Buber exposed the insanity of creating a militarized state. There were different aspects of militarism that Buber denounced. First, he condemned it because militarism begets militarism. Buber lamented that extreme elements of government could leverage the fear of national extinction to promote further military expansion.

---

71. Mendes-Flohr, *Land*, 37–38: 1918, "A State of Cannons, Flags, and Military Decorations."
72. Mendes-Flohr, *Land*, 219; 1948, "A Fundamental Error Which Must Be Corrected."
73. Mendes-Flohr, *Land*, 238; 1949, "Facts and Demands: A Reply to Gideon Freudenberg."
74. Mendes-Flohr, *Land*, 238; 1949, "Facts and Demands: A Reply to Gideon Freudenberg."

What is more, militarism could very well become the ethos of Israeli identity and patriotic duty. He wrote:

> When this hollow peace is achieved, how then do you think you'll be able to combat the "spirit of militarism," when the leaders of the extreme nationalism will find it easy to convince the young that this kind of spirit is essential for the survival of the country?[75]

He also rejected militarism because it derailed the project of Jewish renewal, which was for him Zionism's *sine qua non*. Buber makes this point in this excerpt from the essay "Facts and Demands: A Reply to Gideon Freudenberg." Buber vividly paints the likely outcome of militarism should it win the day. From our historical context, Buber's reference to the building a wall is startling.

> The battles will cease—but will suspicion cease? Will there be an end to the thirst for vengeance? Won't we be compelled, and I mean really compelled, to maintain a posture of vigilance forever, without being able to breathe? Won't this unceasing effort occupy the most talented members of our society? Won't the work of Jewish revival in which we are engaged undergo intense suffering, suffering of the most dangerous kind? "Every one with one of his hands wrought in the work, and with the other held his weapon" (Nehemiah 4:11)—that way you can build a wall, but it's impossible in that way to build an attractive house, let alone a temple.[76]

Finally, Buber believed the victory of militarism would mean the end of Zionism. He wrote, "Against my will I participate with my own being, and my heart trembles like that of any other Israeli. I cannot, however, even be joyful in anticipating victory, for I fear lest the significance of Jewish victory be the downfall of Zionism."[77] Buber here could be referring either to the downfall of a noble Zionism or the defeat of the Jewish State in a war against the Arabs of Palestine and those around the State of Israel.

Expansionism

Jews and Arabs both have a claim to this Land, but these claims are in fact reconcilable as long as they are restricted to the measure which life itself allots, and as long as they are limited by the desire for conciliation.[78]

---

75. Mendes-Flohr, *Land*, 238; 1949, "Facts and Demands: A Reply to Gideon Freudenberg."
76. Mendes-Flohr, *Land*, 238; 1949, "Facts and Demands: A Reply to Gideon Freudenberg."
77. Mendes-Flohr, *Land*, 223; 1948, "Zionism and ,Zionism."
78. Mendes-Flohr, *Land*, 123;1939, "A Letter to Gandhi."

Buber freely acknowledge how the Jewish settlement in the Palestine impacted the Arabs. He was one of the few who were willing to admit it publicly. Such admittance would undermine the propaganda of political Zionism. Strikingly Buber referred to the Jewish settlement as "a conquest by peaceful means." He said further:

> The finest people among us did not pretend to remain guiltless and unsullied in our national struggle for survival. Inasmuch as we came here to ensure a place for our future generations, we were perforce reducing the space for future generations of the Arab nation. Yet our intention was to sin no more than was absolutely necessary in the endeavor to obtain our objective.[79]

He also called the settlement colonialism, albeit a colonialism of a different kind. In an essay in 1939 titled "Concerning our Politics," he develops the concept of two types of colonialism, one should be rejected and other accepted. The former, called "expansive" by Mendes-Flohr, names the colonialism of the middle of the 19th century by European powers. The purpose of this colonialism was to expand a country's political power into other smaller nations in order to accomplish their aims. In such a colonial setting the colonialist backs up its presence with superior military technological force the likes of which the colonialized could not compete. This type should be rejected according to Buber.

The latter, which Mendes-Flohr names "concentrative," refers to a colonialism whose aim is the concentration of a "scattered nation lacking a nucleus" and "has no military power to fall back upon in the hour of need." Mendes-Flohr writes, "Concentrative colonialism . . . does not intrinsically serve an imperial power, but merely seeks to concentrate anew the members and moral and spiritual energies of a scattered, forlorn people. Zionist settlement in Palestine—with its emphasis on the return of the Jews to the soil and the renewal of their social and cultural autonomy—is thus fundamentally an undertaking in concentrative colonization."[80]

Buber envisaged the Jewish settlement in Palestine as a "peaceful conquest" and a colonialism of a different order. The characterization of the return to the Land is grounded in his Zionist conviction that Jews had a right to return to it. "Zionism affirms the right of the Jewish nation to return to its own country and put roots there,"[81] he was to say. Elsewhere Buber stated,

> Zionism is a late form assumed by a primal fact in the history of mankind, a fact of reasonable interest . . . This fact is the unique connection of a people and a country . . . Driven out of their promised Land, this people survived nearly two millennia by their trust in their return, in the fulfillment of the

---

79. Mendes-Flohr, *Land*, 271.
80. Mendes-Flohr, *Land*, 137; 1939, "Concerning Our Politics."
81. Mendes-Flohr, *Land*, 84; 1929, "The National Home and National Policy in Palestine."

promise, in the realization of the idea. The inner connection with this Land and the belief in the promised reunion with it were a permanent force of rejuvenation for this people.[82]

Further Buber wrote,

> A Land about which a sacred book speaks to the sons of the Land is never merely in their hearts, a Land can never become a mere symbol . . . it would be a vain metaphor if Mount Zion did not actually exist. This Land is called "Holy"; but this is not the holiness of an idea, it is the holiness of a piece of earth.[83]

Mendes-Flohr balances Buber's clear view of the right of the Jews to return to the Land, with a recognition of the place for Arabs, "Buber remained firm in his support of his people's return to the Land of Israel . . . Buber was equally certain that the Jewish claim need not negate the rights and national aspirations of the Arabs of Palestine."[84] Zionist leaders, particularly David Ben-Gurion, said something to this effect at an early stage. But it became clear soon enough that they were hallow statements of propaganda.[85] Thus, the genuine interest in Arab rights and aspirations made Buber among the unique in the Zionism of the time. Israel's right to the Land meant neither territorial nor population supremacy. Buber recognized the settlement must ultimately be good for Arabs:

> And let us state openly that the situation of our settlement includes the lives of the Arab inhabitants of the country, whom we do not intend to expel, and that therefore we must include them in our undertaking if we really wish to conquer the specific confusion which exists here.[86]

He would maintain throughout this life that the early decisions by the Histadrut and Jewish Agency exasperated what had already become a conflict as the Arabs watched waves of Jews immigrating. They realized that the implications of immigration and the growing Jewish settlements and protested and at times with extreme violence.[87] Because of errors of both omission and commission, Buber lamented, "cooperation is only possible on the basis of genuine trust, and we have trampled a thousand buds of trust. Certainly, the task has become several times more difficult

---

82. Mendes-Flohr, *Land*, 181; 1946, "The Meaning of Zionism."
83. Mendes-Flohr, *Land*, 117; 1939, "A Leter to Gandhi."
84. Mendes-Flohr, *Land*, 22, "Introduction."
85. Segev (*A State*, 219.) quotes Ben-Gurion, "'According to my moral outlook, we do not have the right to discriminate against even one Arab child, even if such discrimination would obtain for us all that we seek.'"
86. Mendes-Flohr, *Land*, 85; 1929, "The National Home and National Policy in Palestine."
87. Particularly the Arab uprisings of 1921, 1928, 1929 and 1936.

than it was."[88] Elsewhere he would reflect, "But despite all the obstacles in our path, the way is still open for reaching a settlement 'together with' [the Arabs]. What I do not know is that if we do not attain [such a relationship], we will never realize the aims of Zionism."[89] Buber idealistically believed mutual interest in the Land and mutual cooperation in its development would create a shared community of Arabs and Jews. From this perspective, Buber's apologia to Gandhi, he wrote,

> We have been and still are convinced that it must be possible to find some form of agreement between this claim and the other; for we love this Land and we believe in its future; and, seeing that such love and such faith are surely present also on the other side, a union in the common service of the Land must be within the range of the possible. Where there is faith and love, a solution may be found even to what appears to be a tragic contradiction.[90]

Buber and the *Ichud* advocated for a bi-national state in Palestine. They envisaged a social structure that would be mutually beneficial sharing the responsibility for the government of the state. Such a state would allow for independence and autonomy for each nation; each having responsibility for their own particular communal interests and needs, while in addition, cooperating in areas of common concern. Speaking for the *Ichud*, Buber states, "we describe our program as that of a bi-national state—that is, we aim at a social structure based on the reality of two peoples living together . . . this is what we need and not a "Jewish State."[91] As you see, Buber also believed that a Jewish state was not the right way forward. In a more lengthy quote Buber explains more fully what the *Ichud* envisages:

> A bi-national socio-political entity, with its areas of settlement defined and limited as clearly as possible, and within addition economic cooperation to the greatest possible extent; with complete equality of rights between the two partners, disregarding the changing numerical relationship between them; and with joint sovereignty founded upon these principles—such an entity would provide both people with all that they truly need. If such a state were established neither people would have to fear any longer domination of the other.[92]

In a bi-national state, there were no expansive and aggressive territorial interest. Territory was shared between the nations based on the needs of each nation.

---

88. Mendes-Flohr, *Land*, 141–42; 1932, "Concerning Our Politics."
89. Mendes-Flohr, *Land*, 91; 1929, "The National Home and National Policy in Palestine."
90. Mendes-Flohr, *Land*, 120; 1939, "Letter to Gandhi."
91. Mendes-Flohr, *Land*, 211; 1947, "The Bi-National Approach to Zionism."
92. Mendes-Flohr, *Land*, 199; 1947, "Two Peoples in Palestine."

David Ben-Gurion could not avoid the issue of binationalism. But the topic frustrated and baffled him. Tom Segev comments that Ben-Gurion found the German Jews' liberal mindedness "exasperating," especially those that advocated a binational state.

> "Does this man not see himself as a Jew?" he responded to an article by Martin Buber. "If not, he has no business intervening in what the Jews are doing. If he is a Jew, he should act like one." At another opportunity he said that Buber had the "psychology of a servant." He warned the advocates of binationalism that "If you reach an agreement with the Arabs, you will be in Hitler's camp."[93]

If we are generous with Buber's naivete and blindness, we need to place him appropriately in the turbulent times for Jews in the early 20th century. From his writings, Buber sought a just relationship with the Arabs. He truly believed in the Jewish right to return to the land that meant living alongside the Arabs. Shared care for the land would make Palestine a land flowing with milk and honey. And for this, he was a unitary voice in his generation.

The Arab Question

> *For me this [Arab] question became the [moral] touchstone of Zionism . . . It has, alas, become increasingly clear to me that in this respect the Zionist Organization has failed utterly.*[94] *These of course are the Arabs, who have dwelt in this Land for something like thirteen hundred years.*[95] *What distances us from the Arabs is our national arrogance?*[96]

As was suggested in the previous section, the issue which caught Buber's ire most was the Jewish relationship with the Arabs. Mendes-Flohr comments, "Buber remained firm in his support of his people's return to the Land of Israel . . . he was equally certain that the Jewish claim need not negate the rights and national aspirations of the Arabs of Palestine."[97] The topic of the Arabs in the land was tellingly labeled "The Arab Question." Buber was deeply concerned about those who were already in Palestine before Jewish settlement. He was one of the few willing to see and bear witness to the real impact of Zionism on the Arab inhabitants, although even as late as 1941 Ben-Gurion would insist that Arabs and Jews can co-exist because of the "country

---

93. Segev, *A State*, 309.
94. Mendes-Flohr, *Land*, 98; 1949, "Hans Kohn: 'Zionism Is Not Judaism.'"
95. Mendes-Flohr, *Land*, 196; 1947, "Two Peoples in Palestine."
96. Mendes-Flohr, *Land*, 89; 1929, "The National Home and National Policy in Palestine."
97. Mendes-Flohr, *Land*, 22, "Introduction."

was economically capable of supporting" them both.⁹⁸ The wider Zionist movement either disregarded or dismissed. Except for a small minority of Jews, mainstream Zionism saw Arabs as a problem to be solved not a people who had a deep and long relationship to the land.

Tom Segev describes it well:

> He [Ben-Gurion] was entirely at peace with the fact that the Arabs had been displaced—between 500,000 and 600,000 of them at his estimate, according to others about 750,000. That was the price of Jewish independence in the Land of Israel, "a captured land," as he put it. "War is war," he added. His colleagues supported him. One termed the exit of the Arabs a divine miracle, a second remarked that the country's landscape was much finer without them, and Shlomo Lavi said: "The transfer of the Arabs out of the country is in my eyes one of the most just, moral, and correct things that needs to bed done" . . . "There are too many Arabs in the country," Ben-Gurion declared.⁹⁹

On the subject of binationalism, Seveg recounts a fascinating exchange between Ben-Gurion and Buber over an ethnic majority in the land. Ben-Gurion on occasion hosted gatherings in his home of writers and artists to discuss a range of issues. Seveg introduces this scene to illustrate the limits of Ben-Gurion's toleration of topics. He comments "His [Ben-Gurion] broadmindedness was limited to the bounds of the Zionist discourse." Seveg goes on to recount "Martin Buber skeptically remarked: 'We said we would redeem the land, and we meant to make it a Jewish land. Why does it have to be Jewish land?' Ben-Guion interrupted. 'To bring forth bread from the earth!' Buber retorted: 'Why?' 'To eat!' Ben-Gurion replied. 'Why?' Buber insisted. 'That's enough,' said Ben-Gurion." Seveg comments after describing the scene, "He [Ben-Gurion] thought that the question 'Why?' was out of place. The correct question was 'How?'"¹⁰⁰

In 1929 in a letter to Hans Kohn, Buber wrote "For twelve years we pretended that the Arabs did not exist and were glad when we were not reminded of their existence."¹⁰¹ He acknowledged the long history of Arab settlement in the Land when he wrote: "These of course are the Arabs, who have dwelt in this Land for something like thirteen hundred years."¹⁰² Aimed at Zionist leadership, Buber sharply said

---

98. Segev, *A State*, 316. Ben-Gurion's comment was in response to the American diplomat William Bullitt's declaration "all the Arabs should be expelled from Palestine and a Jewish state established there." Ben-Gurion's full answer, according to Segev, was "there was no need to deport the Arabs, because the country was economically capable of supporting them all." Segev concludes "From this point forward, Ben-Gurion and Bullitt met frequently."

99. Segev, *A State*, 452.

100. Segev, *A State*, 196.

101. Mendes-Flohr, *Land*, 99; 1929, "Hans Kohn: "Zionism Is Not Judaism."

102. Mendes-Flohr, *Land*, 196 (1947, "Two Peoples in Palestine").

"What distances us from the Arabs is our national arrogance."[103] Likewise, he wrote, "when we returned to our Land after many hundreds of years, we behaved as though the Land were empty of inhabitants—no, even worse—as though the people we saw didn't affect us, as though we didn't have to deal with them, that is, as if they didn't see us.[104] Buber warned that to disregard the Arabs would be to Israel's harm. He wrote, "there is nothing sillier than to be overjoyed because the Arab population has left. One day we will realize that the fellah is the caryatid that holds up the edifice of Eretz Israel." (251). Ramping up even more, Buber wrote,

> As soon as we truly recognize that this [Jewish] nation has no salvation except in creating a covenant and a comprehensive alliance between the two brother nations, we will attain the ability to show the Arabs too that that is the case.[105]

Buber and his small company championed the cause of Jewish cooperation and mutual respect with Arabs. He wanted to eliminate the causes of conflict and build a society in the Land that would transform the Middle East. This desire and activism for Jewish-Arab cooperation is woven through all his writings. One of his essays is titled "We Need the Arabs and They Need Us." Another is "A Protest Against Expropriation of Arab Lands." And a third "Letter to Ben-Gurion on the Arab Refuges." In the first essay, he writes,

> I believe our principle error was that when we first came here, we did not endeavor to gain the Arabs' trust in political and economic matters. Thus, we gave cause to be regarded as aliens, as outsiders who were not interested in befriending the Arabs. To a large measure, our subsequent difficulties are a consequence of this initial failure to achieve mutual trust.[106]

In a passage from the essay "A Protest Against Expropriation of Arab Lands" Buber stated,

> We all know . . . that in numerous cases Land is expropriated not on grounds of security, but for other reasons, such as expansion of existing settlements, etc. These grounds do not justify a Jewish legislative body in placing the seizure of Land under the protection of law. In some densely populated villages two-thirds and even more of the Land has been seized.[107]

Finally, in the third document, a letter, Buber and the *Ichud* give two appeals directed toward the resolution of the Arab refugee crisis:

103. Mendes-Flohr, *Land*, 89; 1929, "The National Home and National Policy in Palestine."
104. Mendes-Flohr, *Land*, 131–32; 1939, "Our Pseudo-Samsons."
105. Mendes-Flohr, *Land*, 142; 1932, "Concerning Our Politics."
106. Mendes-Flohr, *Land*, 264–65; 1954, "We Need the Arabs, They Need Us!"
107. Mendes-Flohr, *Land*, 262; 1953, "A Protest Against Expropriation of Arab Lands."

The *Ichud* therefore address: (1) Both the State of Israel and the Arab states with an appeal to change their present stands as expressed in repeated declarations and agree to a solution of the Arab refugee problem through cooperation and mutual understanding; (2) All the nations of the world with an appeal to extend their help to the parties concerned with all the means at their disposal for the achievement of an agreed solution of the Arab refugee problem as a first step toward a real peace in the Middle East . . .[108]

Perhaps more than any other single statement, this one captures most his view of a Jewish responsibility to the Arabs:

We must have a sympathetic knowledge of our neighbors, which can only be acquired by the study of their language and traditions and, above all, by decisively discarding the invidious feeling of superiority.[109]

In conclusion, a word must be said about Buber's view of the Arabs. In all his advocacy for the Arabs, Buber was not able to see his own prejudices toward them. He, as all Zionists of that time, had a low view of the Arabs, although this was not because he viewed them as an inferior people as some surely did. Buber viewed the Arabs as primitive in need of an introduction to the modern world. Jews would "make the desert bloom" was a famous slogan among Zionists at the time. They believed, of course, the Jewish presence in the Palestine would radically improve conditions for sustaining a people. In a letter to Gandhi in 1939, Buber wrote,

In the present, *helplessly primitive state of the fellah agriculture* the amount of the land needed to produce nourishment for a family is ever so much larger than it otherwise would be. *Is it right to cling to ancient forms of agriculture which have become meaningless*, to neglect the potential of productivity of the soil in order to prevent the immigration of new settlers without prejudice to the old? . . . You are only concerned, Mahatma, with the "right of possession" on the one side; you do not consider the right to a piece of free land on the other side—for those who are hungering for it. But there is another of whom you do not inquire and who in justice, i.e., on the basis of the whole perceptible reality, would have to be asked: this other is the soil itself. *Ask the soil what the Arabs have done for in 1300 years and what we have done for her in 50!* Would her answer not be weighty testimony in a just discussion as to whom this land "belongs"?[110]

I don't doubt the truthfulness of the statement. Jews in the Land of Israel have indeed achieved a startling amount of productivity from the land. But what is

---

108. Mendes-Flohr, *Land*, 295, 1961, "Letter to Ben-Gurion on the Arab Refugees."
109. Mendes-Flohr, *Land*, 77; 1926, "Soul-Searching."
110. Mendes-Flohr, Land, 122; 1939, "A Letter to Gandhi."

troubling is the evident condescension. In addition, Buber's vision was the benefit of both the Arab and the Jew by modern technology. The deeply unfortunate and unassailable fact is Israel's feats of industry, agriculture, and tech has not benefitted both peoples since the founding of the State in 1948. The blame, however, does not fall at Buber's feet.

The Opposition Continues

In retrospect Buber's fight against Zionism's nationalism, militarism, expansionism and the hostile relationship with the Arabs was a colossal defeat. None of the principles Buber advocated influenced mainstream Zionism. However, Buber never doubted the power of truth and the function of light to reveal fallacy. He never resigned himself to the status quo. He never stopped advocating for a different kind of Zionism. He possessed a deep well of optimism in spite of the facts on the ground. In that sense, his fight has not been a failure at all. The cause continues among like-minded Zionists who think the State of Israel can be better than one that is nationalistic, militaristic, expansionistic and discriminatory. This kind of Jewish State is made all the harder, by Arab violent hostility from early in the Jewish resettlement of Palestine until now. The legitimacy of fear for Israel's safety, the failure of the peace process, pessimism or outright failure of the two-state solution, two intifadas, and cultural differences all make an Israeli State of the sort Buber hoped for far out of reach. That may very well be true.

The Vexed Atypical Christian Zionist

For me the State of Israel creates a troubling and irreconcilable bind. I resonate with Martin Buber's Zionism. Although in the words of Ben-Gurion, Buber and his tribe's advocacy for a binational Jewish-Arab state was naïve,[111] the spirit behind the proposal, however, has the potential of being a useful guide in holding together Zionism and the objectionable elements of the Jewish State's conduct and policies. While being an advocate for the legitimacy of the Jewish state, I'm deeply troubled and not a little vexed by the defining characteristics of the State. I am finding Martin Buber's Zionism attractive in negotiating through the landscape of the tensions, contradictions and objections. His fight against maintaining a state "At All Costs,"[112] the unbridled militarism, the unrestrained expansionism and Israel's treatment of the Palestinians in the occupied territories are grievances I have against the State of

---

111. Segev, *A State*, 219.
112. Title of Segev's biograph on Ben-Gurion.

Israel as a Zionist. These criticisms were as true for Buber's time as they are for ours. These categories of issues continue to be problems for Christian Zionism.

Within Israel today, Zionism has turned religiously messianic. After a discussion on the collapse of left-wing Zionism and the transformation of the right, radical religious Zionism (the only kind remaining) has gained much political influence over the Likud party led by Benjamin Netanyahu.

The rightwing collation government is driven by a severe fear which materializes in the high priority on security as well as the demographic problem.[113] Furthermore, it promotes settlements, expropriates Palestinian land indiscriminately and with impunity, feigns interest in the wellbeing of Arab Israelis and Palestinians and makes hollow excuses for the failure to initiate resolution of the conflict. Unfortunately, the doves have been marginalized and have all but disappeared from political influence.

In the 2019 election, there was little-to-no discussion of policies, "particularly concerning Israel's policies toward the Palestinians in the West Bank and Gaza." Instead it is a campaign of personalities according to Dov Waxman of *Time*.[114] There is no political will to take even small steps to resolution.

Recently, Micah Goodman, in his book *Catch-67: The Left, the Right, and the Legacy of the Six-Day War*, writes,

> Israel's decades-long military rule over a civilian population[115] since the Six-Day war represents a religious failure. The prophets' vision of a strong society remaining sensitive towed the weak is betrayed anew every day by the IDF's policing activities at checkpoints across the territories.[116]

In the book, he addresses what he labels "Israel's Catch-67." He is referring to the unforeseen and immediate challenge of governing those occupied in the West Bank and Gaza after the Six Day War: how do you govern five million people? According to Goodman, the question has occupied Israel's politics ever since; it continues to be Israel's primary challenge. Goodman presents two possible routes that would address the challenge, if not solve it. Both of the proposals would elevate a great deal of the Palestinians' current plight and open up the possibility to move forward by reducing the injustices currently experienced by Palestinians every day, though

---

113. The demographic problem refers to the ratio of Jews to Arab Palestinians.

114. https://time.com/5566065/israel-election-palestinian-issue/.

115. "civilian population"—an important nuance of words (civilian population vs territory); Goodman makes a distinction between *the people* and *the territories*. Palestinians are under occupation; the land is not. Goodman's argument for the distinction is fair and convincing. The distinction therefor creates severe moral problem for Israel, one for which I am deeply burdened.

116. Goodman, *Catch-67*, 114.

they fall short of independent statehood. I will sketch the outline of only one of his proposals in conclusion because I think it serves an example of a Buberian Zionism.

Goodman names the proposal the "Divergence Plan." The first plank of the Divergence Plan combines two efforts—diplomatic and territorial:

> The purpose of the diplomatic effort would be to boost the symbolic potency of the Palestinian entity, and the purpose of the territorial effort would be to increase the extent of the Palestinians day-to-day practical freedom. Together, these efforts would offer Palestinians greater separation from Israel with less security risk for Israelis.[117]

With the territorial element Goodman gets very practical. He writes that the Palestinians feel the occupation most when they move from P.A. controlled areas through Area C which is controlled by the Israeli military. Passing through Area C requires a Palestinian to pass through checkpoints and be hassled by occasional patrols. "[Palestinians] find themselves in daily friction with Israeli soldiers."[118] I let Goodman sum up the Divergence Plan proposal:

> The Divergence Plan is based on two parallel, complementary processes. The first is the expansion of the zone of Palestinian self-rule, the enhancement of its powers, and the infrastructural connection of its various areas; and the second is the extension of Israeli residency rights to the Palestinians who live outside the areas of Palestinian self-rule. On the other hand, Areas B and B would be expanded and would almost be a state; on the other, the remaining residents of Area C would almost be citizens of Israeli state. The result would be dramatic contraction of Israel's control over the Palestinians, without a dramatic contraction of Israel's security.[119]

Goodman's plan is but one possible example of a Zionist vision in the spirit of Buber.

Buber is revealing a path for vexed Zionists. His path is no longer wholly unknown to me. I hope perhaps now neither for you. There is reason today to be vexed as a Christian Zionist. That there are problematic aspects of Zionism is incontrovertible. Out of the two passages from Wyschogrod I quoted at the beginning of the essay, both of which I resonate with, I reflected on aspects of his Zionism, my Zionism, that trouble me. I went on to describe what I referred to as Christian Zionist's blind spot and their exegetical Catch-22. The coalescence of (1) the unrecognized or unadmitted moral price Zionism was willing to pay to have a State—the blind spot and (2) the solid exegesis of a Zionist-strong passage from the New Testament—the

---

117. Goodman, *Catch-67*, 156–57.
118. Goodman, *Catch-67*, 159.
119. Goodman, *Catch-67*, 161.

exegetical Catch-22 creates confusion, grief, clarity and ambivalence. Yeah, I'm vexed. But I've become a vexed-atypical Christian Zionist.

PERHAPS THE PATH IS MADE BY WALKING: A RESPONSE TO WILLITTS'S ANALYSIS IN "THE UNKNOWN PATH"

Michael Walker

Dr. Willitts's essay is entitled "The Unknown Path." There, Willitts asserts that Jewish philosopher Martin Buber's Zionism—including his interactions with Jewish nationalism, territorialism, militarism, and the ominous-sounding "Arab question"—"opens a new path, an unknown path, for Christian Zionism." I affirm the content and form of Willitts's contention, and would strengthen many of his arguments, because peace within Palestine and Israel is a vital part of the process of human flourishing under late capitalism. That said, in response, I am compelled to wonder why a Christian Zionist's response to the current turbulence in Israel-Palestine must begin with the ineradicable Jewish right of return. Willitts makes this claim repeatedly, but I don't know whether I can fully accept it. While Willitts adeptly clarifies exactly what Buber stands against—and while he ably and poetically affirms Buber's views—he asserts only that Buber's "biblically Jewish mission and ethic" required that Jews and Arabs coexist and cooperate in socioeconomic harmony, and does not fully clarify what that vision looks like. As a non-Zionist, as a Canadian with spastic cerebral palsy, and as a theologian rather than a biblical scholar, I want to make that vision a little clearer.

So, let me clarify. I affirm Dr. Willitts's deep and broad exploration of Buber's Zionist writings in terms of nationalism, militarism, and territorialism, and even the "Arab question," strikingly similar to the "Jewish question" that motivated the Holocaust. I appreciate, halfway through his paper, when Willitts observes Buber's deep reservations about both the 1917 Balfour Declaration and the 1947 Partition Plan, because as Leviticus 19:33—God's words to Moses about refugees and aliens—makes clear, one of the foundations of a uniquely Jewish response to migration and settlement is love of neighbour. Moreover, Willitts also poses Buber's questions about vigilance to his audience, including, "The battles will cease—but will suspicion cease?" Fair question, Dr. Buber. Peace cannot simply consist in a ceaseless scrutiny of the activities of "the other," or else both sides abrogate the respect that is central to trust.

I also appreciate Willitts's points about territorialism—both his caveats in the first section of his paper, in light of the massacre at Lydda in 1948, and the balanced view that Buber holds in his writing of the right of Jewish return to the land and the Palestinians' concomitant "national aspirations."[1] Willitts makes entirely clear that, as a Christian Zionist, he believes "that Palestinians suffering under Israel's occupation should be of great concern to me, especially for Christian brothers and sisters." I echo, and affirm, Willitts's claim here, because we ought all to be concerned when one group of people causes another to suffer as Israelis are currently oppressing Palestinians.

Plus, those same concerns lead us ineluctably into Willitts's examination of the "Arab question": I appreciate Willitts's clarification of *Ichud's* fervent desire for a bi-national state based on "cooperation and mutual respect," and I too affirm Buber's strenuous efforts to aid Arab refugees in the newly-formed state of Israel, because cooperation and solidarity contribute greatly to peace. I too want to see a state of cooperation and respect exist between Israelis and Palestinians; I'm sure that we all do.

All that said, I have some reservations about Willitts's essay. Those reservations—most of which, for me, are questions—are grounded primarily in Willitts's repeated claim, in his own Christian Zionism, that the Jewish people have "a covenant relationship with the Land," and his underlying argument for an "abiding Jewish presence in the land of Israel." This claim of the inalienable Hebrew right to the land creates a paradox that undercuts Willitts's support of Buber, for the peace that Buber longs for proves elusive simply because many Zionists claim their absolute right to the Land to which they have returned. In the time that remains, I'll name three questions about that same set of reservations, and suggest responses.

The first question, for me, is both simple and complex: how can I accept the massacre in Lydda, especially in light of the claim that Jewish folks have an enduring right to the land? The answer too is simple and complex: I can't, any more than Willitts does. Let me be clear . . .

Whenever I read of Jerusalem in any western news source, I hear the explosions of bombs with nails inside them, and the cries of innocent people who do not deserve to die. When that happens, I hear sociologist of religion Nancy Eiesland's claim, as a Lutheran woman in a wheelchair, that war creates disability.[2] Describing

---

1. Paul Mendes-Flohr, *A Land of Two Peoples: Martin Buber on Jews and Arabs* (Chicago: University of Chicago, 2005) 22, in Willitts.

2. Nancy L. Eiesland, *The Disabled God: Toward a Liberatory Theology of Disability* (Nashville: Abingdon, 1994) 115.

the Eucharist, the Christian ritual of bread and wine that recalls the Jewish Passover, Eiesland claims, "Often the Eucharist institutes a glorification of suffering, rather than a repudiation of injustice . . . Acts of injustice are inscribed on the bodies of many people with disabilities. War and malnutrition as major causes of disability underscore the role of injustice in creating disabled bodies" (115).

How many Palestinians, and others, have had the acts of war inscribed on their bodies by people who would use violence to establish their claim on the land? How can a Jewish right of return to Zion be irrefutable, when its refutation is written in the corpses of thousands of slaughtered and marginalized Palestinians? Putting that differently, it's also relevant here that I'm a person with serious spatial disabilities. I can't make my way from here to Lake Michigan unaided, because I experience constant spatial disorientation. I would therefore add to Eiesland's claims that war is not simply destructive. It's disorienting. That disorientation makes our desires for peace much less accessible, if not impossible, if we also hold Zionist Jewish claims on the land as true. Thus, as a theologian with disabilities, and as a scholar of religion and disability, I contend that I can neither accept Lydda, nor affirm any massacre that echoes it in our own day.

A second, even more pressing, question in light of Willitts's fascinating essay: where are the Palestinian sources whose insight would surely reinforce his affirmation of Buber's yearning for a state founded on mutual cooperation and respect between Israelis and Palestinians? Where is Dr. Isaac's paper, that provided us with such open-ended discussion yesterday? What could Palestinian Christian Father Naim Ateek's "Palestinian liberation theology," or Palestinian-American critic Edward Said's thorough *Question of Palestine*, add to Willitts's admiration for Buber?[3] For instance, Said asserts that Palestinians have been silenced by Zionist Israelis (37–45) and later enumerates several literary works by Palestinian authors that offer glimpses into the tenuous and tortured state of Palestinians inside modern Israel (150–57). How could Palestinian sources like those help Willitts to further explore the question of the land that may be standing in the way of Israeli-Palestinian peace?

A third and final question: how can Buber's own philosophical work aid Willitts's continued investigations of the impact of Zionism on the nation-state of Israel? In *I and Thou*, Buber proposes a profoundly relational ethic for human beings. For instance, he claims,

"The basic word I-You can be spoken only with one's whole being. The concentration and fusion into a whole being can never be accomplished by me, can never

---

3. Naim Ateek, *Justice and Only Justice: A Palestinian Theology of Liberation* (Maryknoll: Orbis, 1989) and Edward W. Said, *The Question of Palestine* (New York: Vintage, 1992).

be accomplished without me. I require a You to become; becoming I, I say You. / All actual life is encounter."[4]

In light of Buber's claim, could it be that Jewish Israelis—especially those who espouse Zionism as a philosophical system—refuse to say "You" with their whole beings to the Palestinians in their midst, and to call them neighbors and friends? Thus, I wonder how Willitts's argument could be augmented by a sustained examination of Buber's contemplative and philosophical work on human relationships.

Because of all these claims, I want to restate that I appreciate Dr. Willitts's essay, and I affirm its basic claim that Buber's Zionism was, and remains, a model for the present and future in the Middle East. That said, I wish to ask, in the same breath, whether that model is best followed by dissociating Zionism from an irrefutable right of Israel's return to the land. Since one of the desires that this group of scholars shares is peace and cooperation in the modern state of Israel, it may in fact be true—to quote twentieth-century Spanish poet Antonio Machado—that "the path is made by walking."[5] Perhaps only by walking in peace and neighborliness can Israelis and Palestinians truly create peace, and perhaps the beginning of that peace is the surrender of an immutable right to the state of Israel. Thank you.

---

4. Martin Buber. *I and Thou*. Edited and translated by Walter Kaufman (New York: Touchstone, 1971) 62.

5. Antonio Machado, *Border of a Dream: Selected Poems* (New York: Copper Canyon, 2003) 14.

RETURNING TO THE HEART OF THE GOSPEL:
A PRACTICAL EVANGELICAL THEOLOGY OF LIBERATION AND CALL TO ACTION FOR CHRISTIANS ENGAGED IN PEACEBUILDING IN ISRAEL AND PALESTINE

Mae Elise Cannon

Introduction

I am entering into this conversation about the theological interpretation of Scripture and Biblical perspectives related to Contemporary Conflicts in the Holy Land coming off of a ten-day speaking tour in five different cities across the United States. I am both exhausted and excited and I have come to believe the conversations we have been having both across the country, and here at this symposium have never been more important.

The tour is a twice-yearly program of the nonprofit I lead called Churches for Middle East Peace (CMEP). We've called the tour Pilgrimage to Peace (P2P). P2P seeks to engage with primarily U.S. Christians—but also American Jews and Muslims—to talk about theologies, politics, and practical tools of what pursuing peace and justice in the Holy Land might look like. We travel with Israelis and Palestinians. We travel with rabbis and secular Jews. We travel with Muslims from different theological and political perspectives. Our guest speakers from Israel and the Palestinian territories have included religious actors, secular political activists, and people from across the theological and political spectrum.

One of the most significant goals of the Pilgrimage to Peace tours is to expand the dialogue about Israel and Palestine in the U.S. Christian context. Far too often our churches are ill-informed about what is happening in the conflict, and U.S. media outlets tend to exacerbate the already growing divides between political conservatives and political liberals; and between Christians who adhere to theologically orthodox evangelical beliefs and progressive evangelicals. These divides are a significant part of the problem and impose barriers that only make a just peace more elusive.

This paper looks at some of the current divisions in the United States around questions of evangelical theology about the Holy Land, while calling us to some best practices of how we can most constructively move forward in this time of stark political and theological divides. I sought to use the Scriptures as my guide and to further develop an evangelical theology of liberation and justice that is Good News for those of us who choose to follow Jesus, but also good news to both Jews and Palestinians living in Israel and the occupied Palestinian territories.

Divisions in the United States around Evangelical Theologies related to the Holy Land

It will not come as news to any of you that the American Church, specifically the evangelical church, is divided about questions related to Israel. Some American Christian Zionists adhere to a theological understanding that demands an understanding of Scripture "that God will bless or judge people based on how they treat his people Israel (Gen 12:3; Isa 60:12; Zech 2:8–9; Joel 3:1–3)."[1] Many Christian Zionists like Susan Michael do not differentiate between the modern nation-state of Israel and the Jewish people or the Israelites written about in the Hebrew Scriptures.

On the other hand, more progressive American Christians, many who reside in mainline Protestant liberal churches or denominations, do not self-identify as evangelical and have a viewpoint that because—from their vantage point—the Scriptures are not the inerrant word of God, the promises of God to Abraham and his descendants (Gen 12:2–3) can be discarded.

The reading and hermeneutical study of these promises in Genesis 12 is quite different for those of us who uphold the Scriptures and esteem the Bible as not only historical and moral guidelines for our religious life, but also as being the living and Spirit breathed "Word of God." We in the Evangelical Covenant Church (ECC) identify the "Centrality of the Word of God" as one of our core missional beliefs while believing that the Bible is the "perfect rule for faith, doctrine, and conduct."[2] It is from that vantage point of esteeming the Scriptures that I enter into my hermeneutical approach.

It is appropriate here to pause and intentionally take a moment to look further at the text from Gen 12:2–3, which is lauded by many as the central text of American Christian Zionism. God says to Abram, "I will make you into a great nation, and I will bless you; I will make your name great, and you will be a blessing. I will bless those

---

1. Susan Michael, "Across the Israel Divide," in *A Land Full of God: Christian Perspectives on the Holy Land*, edited by Mae Elise Cannon (Eugene, OR: Cascade, 2017) 135.

2. The Evangelical Covenant Church. "10 Healthy Missional Markers." https://covchurch.org/vitality/healthy-missional-markers/centrality-of-the-word-of-god/.

who bless you, and whoever curses you I will curse, and all peoples on earth will be a blessing through you." While many conservative evangelicals would interpret this passage and its promises to specifically be highlighting God's promises to Abraham's Jewish decedents, Dr. Tony Maalouf, Distinguished Professor of World Christianity and Middle Eastern Studies at Southwestern Baptist Theological Seminary, offers a very different interpretation in his book *Arabs in the Shadow of Israel: The Unfolding of God's Prophetic Plan for Ishmael's Line*. Maalouf asserts that it was "clear that the Lord elected Isaac—whose birth fits the symbolism of the supernatural redemption of Christ—to a special role in redemptive history, from which Ishmael was to a certain degree excluded."[3] At the same time, Maalouf challenges the often held notion by conservative American evangelicals that Ishmael was cursed. Maalouf explains,

> A clear favor given to Ishmael is uttered by Yahweh in Genesis 17, where the plan for Isaac is revealed (Gen 17:15–17, 19). Abraham pleaded before the Lord that Ishmael might live "before" him (Gen 17:18) and God told him that Isaac's line would be the one fulfilling the covenantal promises in history (Gen 17:19). Nevertheless, the Lord listened to Abraham's intercession on behalf of his firstborn (Gen 17:20). As a result, Ishmael will be blessed by God, multiplied exceedingly, and made a "great nation." "He too is to walk [before the Lord] as one of Yahweh's children."[4]

Maalouf goes on to write in great detail about the relationship between Abraham and both of his descendants, Isaac and Ishmael. He concludes, "Only when those who claim Abraham as ancestor follow his moral example, and sacrifice the temporal for the sake of the eternal that they will be able to love instead of hate, and forgive instead of retaliate, in a land that is deeply yearning for a display of these spiritual virtues."[5]

This very brief and incomplete exegesis of the text of Genesis 12 provides one example of how a conservative hermeneutical approach can be utilized to read the text in a way that shows God's desire to bless both Isaac and his descendants, while also blessing Ishmael and his descendants.

I believe it is fundamentally possible to read and study both the Hebrew Scriptures and New Testament from a conservative evangelical theological perspective that allows for all of the verses about the chosenness of the Jewish people (Deut 7:6) to be reconciled with an action-oriented call for justice toward all people in the Holy Land, particularly Palestinians who have lived for more than 50 years under military

---

3. Tony Maalouf, "The Holy Land and the Larger Family of Abraham," in *A Land Full of God: Christian Perspectives on the Holy Land,* edited by Mae Elise Cannon (Eugene, OR: Cascade, 2017) 58.

4. Maalouf, "The Holy Land," 60.

5. Maalouf, "The Holy Land," 65.

occupation. Unfortunately, a detailed biblical study of the relevant verses at hand is beyond the scope of this paper.

A Practical Evangelical Theology toward Liberation and Justice

As a practical theologian who has spent more time in pastoral ministry in the evangelical community and leading ecumenical nonprofits, I would like to present a brief introduction to an evangelical theology of liberation and justice. Evangelical Liberation Theology is a burgeoning movement of mostly evangelicals of color who call the church to uphold the core tenets of evangelicalism as described by historian David Bebbington of conversionism, activism, biblicism, and crucicentrism. As noted by the National Association of Evangelicals (NAE) many evangelicals don't even use that term to describe themselves, but rather focus on the "core convictions of the triune God, the Bible, faith, Jesus, salvation, evangelism, and discipleship."[6] More about *Evangelical Theologies of Liberation and Justice* can be read about in the book I co-edited with Andrea Smith that was published on September 10th of this year by InterVarsity Press.[7]

The main component of an evangelical theology of liberation that is critical for the discussions during this symposium is a reclaiming of the core heart of the Gospel message that the salvation of the soul is only one aspect of the type of liberation that is called for by Christ. Rather, a more holistic evangelical understanding of the Good News of the Gospel is that it must be inclusive of both salvation of the soul *and* liberation for the poor and the oppressed. Yes! Jesus did come to die for our sins so that those who choose to believe in him might be forgiven and have eternal life (John 3:16). He also came to this earth as fully God and fully human so that the world could continue in the process of redemption that was described in Leviticus 25 as the Year of Jubilee. In his very first sermon, Jesus preached the words of the prophet Isaiah, "The Spirit of the Lord is upon me, because he has anointed me to proclaim good news to the poor. He has sent me to proclaim freedom for the prisoners and recovery of sight for the blind, to set the oppressed free, to proclaim the year of the Lord's favor." (Luke 4:18–19).

I am just starting to consider how an evangelical theology of liberation and justice intersects with Jewish liberation theology, often rooted in the exodus of the Jewish people from Egypt (Exod 12:31—15:21) and Palestinian Liberation Theology that has its roots in the progressive Anglicanism of Naim Ateek. For now, the most

---

6. "What is an evangelical?" National Association of Evangelicals (NAE). https://www.nae.net/what-is-an-evangelical/.

7. Mae Cannon and Andrea Smith, eds., *Evangelical Theologies of Liberation and Justice* (Downers Grove: InterVarsity, 2019).

important thing to understand is that I believe it is absolutely possible to maintain an orthodox evangelical theological framework while also calling for practical application of our beliefs through a theology of liberation and justice.

Praxis and Best Practices in Applied Evangelical Liberation Theology

How might this evangelical theology of liberation and justice be applied in praxis and best practices in questions related to the geopolitical realities of the Israel-Palestinian conflict? And how can we apply our theology in a way that is also honoring to our Jewish and Palestinian counterparts? Over the course of the next several minutes, from the lens of an evangelical theological rubric, I identify several practices that we should avoid and "must not do," and then conclude with a positive call to action and suggested actions for constructive intervention of what we "must do."

I do not believe that to pursue an evangelical justice-oriented framework toward the Israeli-Palestinian conflict that we need to discard the Gospel; in fact, quite the opposite! In fact, the Scriptures from the Hebrew texts of the Old Testament to the Gospels of Jesus and Paul's epistles call us to a theological interpretation of Scripture that demands equality, justice, and the pursuit of the type of peace that will dismantle systems of oppression—both within the occupied Palestinian territories and in Israel proper as well.

Best Practices: What We Must Not Do

We Must Not Have a Binary Approach to the Conflict

First, we must not succumb to the false binaries and zero-sum-game mentality that is constantly presented about the Israeli-Palestinian conflict. In the United States today, both in politics and in theology, there are staunch lines that when crossed, one becomes completely disregarded by members of the opposing community. This false bifurcation is present across the United States in religious circles, in politics, and in the media. In fact, in February 2019, the Public Religion Research Institute (PRRI) issued a report entitled "Americans Deeply Divided by Party on Ideals of Religious and Ethnic Pluralism."[8] PRRI concluded that Americans remained optimistic about overcoming divides, except for divisions in politics. This false dualistic approach and animosity toward people of different political persuasions is one of the most

---

8. Ian Hainline, "Americans Deeply Divided by Party on Ideals of Religious and Ethnic Pluralism." February 21, 2019. https://www.prri.org/press-release/americans-deeply-divided-by-party-on-ideals-of-religious-and-ethnic-pluralism/

significant barriers toward discussions about the Israeli-Palestinian conflict in the United States today.

As an ordained minister in an evangelical denomination, I was raised by the church to love Israel and to love the Jewish people. I continue to do so. At the same time, I have come to believe that we cannot truly love the Jewish people, many of whom make up 80 percent of the current citizens of Israel, unless we also love their Palestinian neighbors. Palestinians currently make up approximately 20 percent of the citizens of Israel and also reside in East Jerusalem, the West Bank, Gaza, refugee camps in the Arab world, and in the diaspora.[9]

The idea that American evangelicals have to "choose a side" does not set anyone up for success. And as discussed previously, it is possible to maintain a conservative theological Christian interpretation of the Scriptures, while still not "choosing a side" as it relates to the conflict between Israelis and Palestinians.

We must come to understand that the work that must be done within the Christian community is to stop choosing one side "over" the other. If we truly care for justice for Palestinians and an end of the occupation for the Palestinian people, we must also care for peace and security for their Jewish Israeli neighbors and Palestinian citizens of Israel as well. As Churches for Middle East Peace's (CMEP) policy positions state, a just and durable resolution to the Israeli-Palestinian crisis must be one where both Israelis and Palestinians are able to realize the vision of a just peace, which "illuminates human dignity and cultivates thriving relationships" for all people living in Israel and the Palestinian territories.[10]

There is a growing movement of Christians across the United States who are coming to understand that the only lasting resolution to the Israeli-Palestinian conflict will be one that creates space for the narratives of both Israelis and Palestinians, while honoring that the Holy Land is also sacred to the three Abrahamic traditions of Judaism, Christianity, and Islam.

We Must Reject the False Equivocation Between Legitimate Critiques of the State of Israel and Anti-Semitism

On Capitol Hill in Washington DC, there has been quite the debate about what constitutes anti-Semitism versus legitimate critique of Israeli policies about the occupation of the Palestinian people. On March 7, 2019, Churches for Middle East

---

9. Henriette Chacar, "No matter how many Palestinians vote in Israeli elections, we still can't win." *Washington Post.* September 20, 2019. https://www.washingtonpost.com/outlook/2019/09/20/no-matter-how-many-palestinians-vote-israeli-elections-we-still-cant-win/

10. Churches for Middle East Peace (CMEP) Policy Positions. Updated July 18, 2017. https://cmep.org/about/policypositions/.

Peace (CMEP) published a statement called "Weaponizing Anti-Semitism Harms Free Speech." Here are a few highlights from that statement:

> Churches for Middle East Peace (CMEP) unequivocally condemns anti-Semitism and recognizes the ways in which the Christian church has contributed to anti-Jewish ideology. Over the past few years, we have seen a disturbing rise in anti-Semitic attacks and a resurgence in neo-Nazi activities. CMEP is committed to standing alongside our Jewish neighbors to confront those who perpetrate hateful acts against Jews and all communities who have faced increased threats and violence.
>
> As Congress considers a resolution condemning anti-Semitism, CMEP calls on leadership not only to repudiate all forms of bigotry, but to be clear in differentiating between actual hate speech and critiques of policy. While we affirm the desire to denounce anti-Semitism, Congress cannot speak with integrity on this issue if it does not also make clear its opposition to Islamophobia and racism as well. If Congress fails to distinguish between anti-Semitism and valid critiques of the government of Israel, they are playing into the hands of forces who wish to weaponize anti-Semitism. Doing so harms everyone by suppressing free speech and undermining open debate about a major U.S. foreign policy issue; and by singling out, as in recent instances, people of color and vulnerable populations while remaining silent when privileged others express clearly bigoted sentiments.
>
> Leveling accusations of anti-Semitism when actually motivated by political gain and not concern for the Jewish community only serves to embolden those responsible for the recent rise in anti-Jewish and white supremacist activity. Tolerance of weaponizing anti-Semitism allows for the possibility that anti-Jewish words and deeds will be lost in the barrage of attacks that are meant not to protect Jews, but to protect long-held political positions. We owe it to all victims of anti-Semitism and bigotry to do better and deal with such serious issues with moral clarity and integrity.[11]

American Christians must reject the false equivocation between legitimate critiques of the State of Israel and at the same time acknowledge legitimate anti-Semitism and work to eradicate it.

I wrote about this issue in a recent article published by Religious News Service (RNS) called "Anti-Semitism Versus Legitimate Critique of the State of Israel." While I don't have time to go into all of the details of differentiation, and I believe this specific question could warrant many articles and books being written about the topic, here are a few highlights of my argument.

---

11. Churches for Middle East Peace (CMEP) "Weaponizing Anti-Semitism Harms Free Speech." March 7, 2019. https://cmep.salsalabs.org/3719publicstatement.

We need to listen to what the Jewish community says about anti-Semitism. While the Jewish community certainly isn't monolithic, there are many commonalities between even liberal and conservative Jewish perspectives about anti-Semitism. In May 2018, Rabbi Jill Jacobs, executive director of Tru'ah an organization committed to human rights in the U.S., Israel, and the occupied Palestinian territories, published a perspective piece in the Washington Post asserting the difference between the legitimate criticism of Israel and the not infrequent actions or statements that "cross the line" into anti-Semitism. Jacobs highlighted how to tell the difference by identifying five markers: seeing Jews as insidious influencers behind the scenes of world events, using "Zionist" as code for "Jew" or "Israeli," denying Jewish history, dismissing the humanity of Israelis, and assuming that the Israeli government speaks for all Jews.[12]

A few months later, in July 2018, 36 "far left" Jewish groups from around the world signed a statement condemning the conflation of anti-Semitism with what they viewed as legitimate criticism of the State of Israel, while also asserting the right of the international community to engage in boycott, divestment, and sanctions (BDS). The Israeli newspaper *Haaretz* wrote about the statement in an article called "Jewish Groups Defend Israel Critics From 'False Accusations of anti-Semitism'" and said, "These attacks too often take the form of cynical and false accusations of anti-Semitism that dangerously conflate anti-Jewish racism with opposition to Israel's policies and systems of occupation and apartheid."[13]

A third resource from the Jewish Council for Public Affairs (JCPA) includes a 2013 statement called "Elevating the Discussion to Advance Peace: Distinguishing Between Criticism of and Bias against Israel." The paper was co-authored by Rabbi Yehiel Poupko, Judaic Scholar, Jewish Federation of Metropolitan Chicago, and one of the speakers at this symposium.[14]

These few sources from very divergent perspectives provide Jewish definitions of anti-Semitism that can help American Christians better understand the commonalities of how Jewish conservatives and liberals mutually agree in their definitions of anti-Semitism. The JCPA article concludes, "Lest anyone in reading this document think that the above-mentioned criteria are meant to stifle or mute criticism of

---

12. Jill Jacobs, "How to Tell When Criticism of Israel Is Actually Anti-Semitism: Calling out Human Rights Violations Shouldn't Stray into Bias against Jews." *Washington Post*, May 18, 2018. https://www.washingtonpost.com/outlook/how-to-tell-when-criticism-of-israel-is-actually-anti-semitism/2018/05/17/cb58bf10-59eb-11e8-b656-a5f8c2a9295d_story.html.

13. JTA. "Jewish Groups Defend Israel Critics From 'False Accusations of Anti-Semitism.'" *Haaretz*, July 18, 2018.

14. Jewish Council for Public Affairs (JCPA). "Elevating the Discussion to Advance Peace: Distinguishing Between Criticism of and Bias against Israel." *Distinguishing Anti-Semitism from Criticism of Israel* (blog) December 24, 2013.

Israel, that is not the case. Among the issues that are legitimate topics for discussion are: land for peace, the status of Jewish settlements over the 1949 Armistice Line, future borders of a Palestinian State, Jerusalem, and treatment of Palestinians. These are appropriate topics of debate, both within the Jewish community and general society. When the debate is undertaken and is free of the above stated concerns then a respectful hearing is gained."[15]

Sorting through some of the contradictory claims of conservative Jewish perspectives and their more liberal Jewish counterparts about anti-Semitism is a much larger project, but these resources help us to understand some of the very clear commonalities of anti-Semitism across the board.

In our attempts to eradicate anti-Semitism, we must acknowledge that Jews, just as Palestinians, have a right to self-determination just as every other people group. We must acknowledge the historic ties of the Jewish people to Jerusalem and the land of Israel and historic Palestine. This does not negate the legitimate ties of Palestinian Arabs who have also been present in the land for thousands of years. Christians might need to be reminded that Arabs also lived in Jerusalem at the time of Pentecost (Acts 2:11). We must also acknowledge the reality that anti-Semitism in the United States and around the world has increased in recent years, and continues to do so. With the rise of neo-Nazis, white nationalists, and other hate groups, significant threats to the Jewish community exist. Christians and those of other belief systems must stand firmly in our solidarity with the Jewish community in response to anti-Semitism and its devastating effects. The recent killings at the Pittsburgh synagogue manifest this reality in its worst form. Anti-Semitism is real and deadly.

We Must Not Demonize and Dehumanize Those with Whom We Disagree

My third and final prohibition in order for Christians to constructively engage in questions related to the Israeli-Palestinian conflict is that we must not demonize and dehumanize those with whom we disagree. The internet, news articles, social media, and the general public are rife with accusations and mudslinging from one side to the other on a regular basis. The bombastic accusations of the "other" have the intention of causing humiliation and harm. This tactic has certainly been applied on all sides of the conflict, and I personally have been the recipient of more libelous statements than I care to confess.

---

15. Jewish Council for Public Affairs (JCPA). "Elevating the Discussion to Advance Peace: Distinguishing Between Criticism of and Bias against Israel." *Distinguishing Anti-Semitism from Criticism of Israel* (blog) December 24, 2013. http://engage.jewishpublicaffairs.org/o/5145/p/salsa/web/blog/public/entries?blog_entry_KEY=7110

For example, during the 2014 war between Israel and Gaza, I was doing some advocacy work at the Israeli Embassy in Washington DC I was working for World Vision at the time and the message I was sent to communicate was calling for an end to the violence because of the devasting effects of the war on Palestinian children living in Gaza. According to UNICEF, by September 2014, 495 Palestinian children were killed by the end of the conflict.[16] In discussing the situation with one of the Israeli ministers, I learned he had two children serving in the Israeli Defense Forces (IDF) in Gaza during the war. I could certainly empathize with what the parent of a child at risk might be experiencing. I thought the conversation went well and that our message had been effectively communicated. However, at the end of our audience, the gentleman turned to me and said, "I know you mean well, but you are inadvertently serving as the handmaiden for Hamas." I was certainly quite taken aback. Particularly because Hamas, deemed a terrorist organization by the United States government, has a military wing that has caused great harm not only threatening Jewish communities in Israel, but toward Palestinians living in Gaza as well.

The Christian Bible certainly has a lot of verses that instruct us on how we are supposed to respond toward people with whom we disagree. We certainly might consider taking the "piece of dust" out of our own eye before we criticize or judge others (Matt 7:1–5). Of course, the most well-known adages of the Scriptures call us not only to love our neighbor (Lev 19:18) but to love our enemy as well. In the Sermon on the Mount (Matt 5:43–44) Jesus tells us "'You have heard it said, 'Love your neighbor and hate your enemy.' But I tell you, love your enemies and pray for those who persecute you." What does that mean in light of questions about U.S. Christian engagement in the Israeli-Palestinian conflict? We consider this question in a discussion of some of the best practices that must be pursued for us to make forward progress while maintaining our evangelical integrity.

Best Practices: What We Must Do

We Must Affirm Beautiful Aspects of Culture and Heritage

First—and these are not necessarily in order of priority or emphasis—we must affirm the beautiful aspects of different cultures and people groups who reside and have historic ties to the Holy Land. Sometimes in our advocacy and affection for one particular people group, we may be unaware of the ways that our language and attachments may be harmful to others.

---

16. "Gaza Crisis: Toll of Operations in Gaza." *BBC News*, September 1, 2014. https://www.bbc.com/news/world-middle-east-28439404.

Palestinians have a rich cultural history that has developed and progressed over centuries of tribal Arabs living in the historic land of Palestine and now the modern nation State of Israel. Rashida Tlaib, representing a district in the Detroit area, was the first Palestinian Muslim woman elected to Congress. During her swearing in, Rep. Tlaib wore a traditional Palestinian dress called a thobe that sparked viral Twitter campaigns around #TweetYourThobe and #MyThobe. In writing for *Elle* magazine, Tlaib said, "It fills me with joy to be able to show aspects of Palestinian culture. When I posted the photo of the thobe I will wear on Instagram, I was overcome with joy at the response I received."[17] This is a beautiful example of affirming the Palestinian culture and history and celebrating it in a positive way today.

Similarly, we must be willing to esteem and praise Jewish aspirations, ingenuity, and contributions in culture and society. The historic longevity and triumphs of the Jewish people over centuries of oppression must not be ignored. Certainly, the survival and the rebuilding of communities after the Holocaust are one great example of how Jewish culture should be celebrated. The Jewish community, like any other, is not monolithic. What might it look like for Christians to learn and study Jewish history, authors, musicians, and artists as a way of building bridges between our communities? Klezmer music, a Yiddish tradition of Ashkenazi Jews of Eastern Europe, can often be heard at weddings or other Jewish events and is one example of the creative aspects of Jewish culture that should be celebrated. The Jewish Orthodox traditions of rabbinical study are also a wonderful starting point for U.S. evangelicals who love and seek to understand the Hebrew Scriptures and *Midrash*.

We Must Learn to Better be able to Love our Neighbors and our Enemies

The affirmation of culture and heritage is only one starting point for ways we will learn to be better able to love our neighbors and our enemies. It is incredibly difficult to love someone you do not know. What does it mean to love our enemies? My Doctor of Ministry focused on this very question: how does one experience spiritual transformation toward love of one's enemy?

Several commonalities were observed and identified over the course of my research about how one might learn to love one's enemies. Vulnerability and willingness to change was one of the first common practices discussed and identified. If someone is not aware of hatred within their own heart, their shadow side, or the enemy within, it is difficult to make progress and to grow, develop, or change.

---

17. Rashida Tlaib, "Rashida Tlaib On Why She's Wearing A Palestinian Gown To Be Sworn Into Congress," *Elle Magazine*, January 3, 2019. https://www.elle.com/culture/career-politics/a25714487/rashida-tlaib-thobe-sworn-into-congress/.

Prayer and submission to the Holy Spirit was also a common practice that was discussed extensively. Transformation does not occur by our willing it to happen, but rather by the work of God within us. Submission and time with God through the practice of spiritual disciplines, like silence, solitude, and prayer, are mechanisms that intentionally allow us to enter into the presence of God as we seek to meet with him and be transformed.

In light of the practicing of spiritual disciplines such as prayer, study of Scripture, silence, solitude, community, and other intentional practices, what does "love of enemy" look like? Jesus teaches and modeled enemy love. One of the attributes of Jesus' love for enemy is rejecting retaliation (1 Pet 2:23). If we want to truly love our enemies, we have to let go of the right to be vindicated and to retaliate when we are wronged. We must also be willing to act kindly toward our enemies (Col 3:12) and to do good for one another (Luke 6:35). We must be willing to show good will to those who persecute us (1 Pet 3:9) and to exercise restraint in judging others (Matt 7:1). Enemy love means that we are willing to forgive (Matt 6:15) even when our enemies may not be asking for forgiveness. We must have the self-control to release our enemies from consequences they may deserve (Matt 10:28). Personal sacrifice can also be a component of enemy love, even to the point of being willing to accept personal harm (Mark 8:34). God calls us to pursue reconciliation with the desire of restoration to community as we also seek to welcome the stranger (Luke 12:58). The most profound lesson learned over the course of this thesis project is that the command to love one's enemy may be the most utterly profound calling of the Christian faith; the one with the greatest demand and the most transformative power.

We Must Not Compromise on Standing in Solidarity with the Oppressed

One of the most beautiful aspects of the Civil Rights Movement was solidarity between Jewish activists and rabbis with the African American community. I have had the privilege of spending significant time in some of the southern cities like Atlanta, Birmingham, Montgomery, and Selma that marked primary destinations of the activities and work of the Civil Rights Movement. Marching across the Edmond Pettus Bridge in Selma, Alabama singing old slave spirituals like "Ain't No Body Gonna Turn Us Around" was a deeply moving spiritual experience for me on my own journey toward reconciliation and justice between whites and blacks in the United States. I was deeply moved when I learned that Rabbi Abraham Joshua Heschel marched with Rev. Dr. Martin Luther King, Jr. on March 21, 1965.[18] That

---

18. Jewish Women's Archive. "Rabbi Abraham Joshua Heschel on the Selma March, March 21, 1965." https://jwa.org/media/abraham-joshua-heschel-on-selma-march-1965.

Rabbi Heschel's mother and sister died in the Holocaust deeply influenced his philosophy as he became one of the most influential 20th century Jewish theologians and activists. Heschel believed that people should act alongside of God to help create a better world. In describing his own activism, Heschel said, "When I marched in Selma, my feet are praying."[19]

In 2019, more than five million Palestinians are living under military control in the occupied Palestinian territories (oPt). The human rights concerns and abuses in the oPt include the hundreds of thousands of Israeli settlers living on land designated to be the future State of Palestine, home demolitions, forced displacement, land confiscation, military detention, and collective punishment being imposed upon the Palestinian people. When looking at what it might take to resolve the Israeli-Palestinian conflict, human rights considerations are not the only issues that are on the table, but they cannot be ignored. At the same time, Jewish—and Palestinian-Israeli citizens have the right to live without fear of attack, suicide bombs, and rocket fire from Gaza. It is not helpful to embrace a framework that asks the question of "who is the most oppressed?" While there are certainly aspects of injustice and oppression on both the Israeli and Palestinian sides of the conflict, the gross differential of power between the modern-day nation state of Israel and the limited access to self-determination and autonomy for Palestinians must be acknowledged.

Rather, if we truly want to pursue a just solution that allows for freedom and equality for both Israelis and Palestinians, we must have an approach that seeks to address the needs and aspirations of both people. Even the Israeli security establishment agrees that the occupation of the Palestinian people is not in the long-term best interests of the State of Israel. At the same time, I hope that we can respond to the current realities affecting the Palestinian community for their own sake—seeing Palestinians, including our Christian brothers and sisters in Palestine, as deserving of human dignity and equality in their own right. As we consider the current plight of Palestinians who have been living under military control in East Jerusalem, the West Bank, and Gaza since 1967, I hope that we might all summon the moral courage of Rabbi Heschel.

We Must Return to the Heart of the Gospel through an Evangelical Theology of Liberation

The framework of this discussion has been the theological assumption of the power of faith in Christ to liberate the soul from the wages and consequences of sin and

---

19. Julie Bressler, "Praying With Your Feet." *ReformJudaism.Org* (blog) https://reformjudaism.org/blog/2009/07/02/praying-your-feet.

brokenness (Rom 10:9). A return to the heart of the Gospel holds onto the belief that Christ is one who sets our souls free, while also calling for the unjust systems of this world to be dismantled and broken down. In our pursuit of justice for Palestinians, we must be diligent to not return to our previous egregious ways of Christian anti-Semitism. We must be vigilant and courageous in calling to account and responding to the human rights abuses we witness in the occupied Palestinian territories. Might American evangelicals become better able to love both our Jewish and Palestinian neighbors and enemies, as we seek to live out the entirety of the Gospel that calls for robust and diligent advocate toward equality, human rights, and justice for Palestinians living under military occupation—and also for their Israeli neighbors? May we continue to walk a narrow path as we pursue these two realities. May it be so.

CHRISTIANS AND PEACEBUILDING FOR PALESTINE-ISRAEL

Robert Hostetter

This is a response to Mae Cannon's paper "Returning to the Heart of the Gospel: A Practical Evangelical Theology of Liberation and Call to Action for Christians Engaged in Peacebuilding in Israel and Palestine." In her introduction, Cannon refers to her participation in a recent speaking tour across the U.S., which included Christian, Jewish, and Muslim speakers, aiming "to expand the dialogue about Israel and Palestine in the U.S. Christian context." However, Cannon narrows the focus of her present paper to examine "some of the current divisions in the United States around questions of evangelical theology about the Holy Land, [and to] develop an evangelical theology of liberation and justice."

My starting points for dialogue with Cannon's paper are the prophetic tradition of the Hebrew prophets and this declaration from Menno Simons and the Protestant Reformation: "True evangelical faith cannot lie dormant. It clothes the naked, it feeds the hungry, it comforts the sorrowful, it shelters the destitute, it serves those who harm it, it binds that which is wounded, it becomes all things to all people."[1] As an ethnographer, rather than a theologian, I share Cannon's commitment to dialogue and to justice. I am currently finishing a book, *Peacemakers in Palestine-Israel: Dialogues for a Just Peace*, based on 75 recorded dialogue with peacemakers, including Mitri Raheb, Sami Awad, Naim Ateek, Jeff Halper, Ilan Pappe, Arik Ascherman, and others. At the end of my Introduction to these dialogues—with both religious and secular peace activists—I develop a platform for a just peace, based on a prophetic paradigm and a universal vision for a just peace in Israel-Palestine.

I also resonate with God's call to Jeremiah to be "a prophet unto the nations," a universal mission. Jeremiah protests, saying he can't speak because he is a "child." God promises to give Jeremiah the words to speak: "I have this day set you over the nations and over the kingdoms, to root out, and to pull down, and to destroy, and to throw down, to build and to plant" (Jer 1:5–10). Gila Svirsky, an ardent Jewish advocate for peace and justice, conveys a similar spirit of resistance and rebuilding:

1. https://sojo.net/articles/voice-day-menno-simons-true-evangelical-faith, September 29, 2006.

> Israel was born in sin, and that is why I'm grateful to the Palestinians for saying, Let's live with that fact. Let's see how we can make peace, with a Palestinian state side by side with an Israeli state. Today, *my* Zionism is manifested, not in grabbing more land in the Occupied Territories, but in working on the character of the state of Israel; in trying to develop the state according to its original vision as annunciated in the Proclamation of Independence for Israel. That includes the vision of the Hebrew prophets. They talk about equality for all and justice for the poor. That vision is what I want very much to work on. For me that is being a Zionist, working on developing the character of Israel to be the kind of state that we envisioned when we founded it.[2]

Svirsky is explicit in her connection to the Hebrew prophets and her vision of justice for all. I believe that Cannon shares this universal, prophetic vision with Svirsky and Jeremiah, though in this paper she takes a narrower focus on a "practical evangelical theology of liberation." This is a worthy goal, but this paper seems to include multiple goals which remain undeveloped:

1. To look "at some of the current divisions in the U.S. around questions of evangelical theology, while calling us to … best practices of how we can most constructively move forward in this time of stark political differences."

2. To "develop an evangelical theology of liberation and justice" using scripture as her "hermeneutical approach."

3. To identify herself as a "practical theologian," and to call for an "evangelical theology of liberation" which is "more holistic"; that is, to include both "salvation of the soul and liberation for the poor and the oppressed."

4. To provide very strong affirmations of both Palestinian and Jewish cultures.

All of these goals are worthy of attention. However, they all deserve more development than Cannon's paper provides. Cannon says she is just starting to consider how an evangelical theology of liberation intersects with Jewish liberation theology and Naim Ateek's Palestinian liberation theology, but she does not pursue this topic with the rigor it deserves. Instead, she reassures us that it is "absolutely possible to maintain an orthodox evangelical theological framework." I'm unclear why Cannon seems anxious to reassure us about this. In any case, Cannon calls herself a practical theologian. So, I wanted very much to hear more about practical, evangelical efforts to enter into dialogue with Palestinian and Jewish liberation writers.

Cannon briefly notes "what we must do," which is to look to the Old Testament, Paul, Jesus, and the Gospels; affirm the beautiful aspects of different cultures and people groups who reside in and have historic ties to the Holy Land; learn to better

---

2. Gila Svirsky, personal dialogue with the author, June 2005.

love our neighbors as well as enemies; practice, spiritual disciplines of prayer and submission to the Holy Spirit; stand in solidarity with the oppressed, and, in the U.S. we must make room for both Palestinian and Israeli narratives. It would be useful for us to hear specific examples of places where this is already happening. It would also be useful for Cannon to remind us how challenging it is for any of us who try to make space for both sets of narratives. Cannon declares, quite rightly, that American Christians, as well as the U.S. Congress, must avoid falsely linking legitimate critiques of the state of Israel with the accusation of anti-Semitism.

Near the end of her paper, Cannon arrives at one of her most compelling insights: we must acknowledge "the gross differential of power between the modern-day nation state of Israel and the limited access to self-determination and autonomy for Palestinians." Indeed, in this context, liberation theology must account for major differences of power between Israelis and Palestinians in terms of culture, political power, financial resources, water, land, military forces, and nuclear weapons. In my dialogues with Jeff Halper, a secular peace activist, and public intellectual, he develops a robust analysis of the Israeli victimhood and will to power. He says:

> The goal of Zionism and the Israeli elite is exclusive control, and exclusive claim to the land, excluding everybody else. How do you do that—militarily, politically, and conceptually? Most Israelis are good people. They don't see themselves as oppressors. So, you've got to legitimize this, provide some kind of ideology for people to hold on to. One of the ways of doing that ... is to cast yourself as the victim. [Israelis say,] "We're the victim, you see." It's ironic that Zionism initially rejected the victim portrayal ... It's the way that Israelis today see themselves, as the victim ... ["They] brought it on themselves. They attacked us; they deserve it. *We're* the victims. This is all security; this is all defense." It's a very dangerous combination. The point is that [Israelis] have a combination of *tremendous power,* and tremendous aggressiveness, no responsibility, and no accountability, because international law doesn't apply to [us]; human rights don't apply to [us]. [We're] the victim. So, if you combine being the ... victim, with being the fourth-largest nuclear power in the world, you've got all the freedom in the world to do anything you want to do to anybody. We see that today—actual impunity, IMPUNITY in capital letters, in their relationship to the Palestinians. There's no responsibility.[3]

Like the prophetic work of Halper and Jeremiah, the work of liberation theologians must enter fully into the massive challenges of the Israeli-Palestinian conflict.

I concur with Cannon's call for American evangelicals to "seek to live out the entirety of the gospel that calls for robust and diligent [advocacy for] equality, human rights, and justice for Palestinians living under military occupation—and also

3. Jeff Halper, personal dialogue with the author, June 2003.

for their Israeli neighbors." I would also welcome a clearer analysis of the challenges of Christian Zionism in the U.S., and the challenges to all of us who pay U.S. income taxes and thereby help to enable the building of illegal Israeli settlements in the West Bank. I urge Cannon, as a practical theologian, to articulate in more extensive ways *how* the gospel calls Christians to be accountable to peacebuilding, and *how* to generate robust dialogues and other strategic practices among all people committed to a just peace in Israel-Palestine.

TEACH US YOUR WAYS, LORD (MICAH 4:1-3)

Jack Y. Sara

The Lord wants to be our teacher in the way of peace. Dear president David Kersten, president of North Park Seminary, fellow professors and lecturers at Bethlehem Bible College, Nazareth Evangelical College, and North Park University; dear presenters and respondents at this symposium; dear friends, brothers and sisters those who come from far and close,

We bring to you warm and special greetings from the church of the Holy Land, the Land that we will be talking about during our gathering. God has honored me to serve with amazing leaders and scholars, whom I appreciate a lot: Drs. Yohana Katanacho, Roula Mansour, and Munther Ishak who join me representing the faculties of Bethlehem Bible College and Nazareth Evangelical College. Also with us are two amazing students: Merna Ishak and Ghada Banoura.

We are honored that you are hosting us all, and we do appreciate the generosity and welcome of North Park and the Covenant Church. We don't take that lightly. At a time when many people want to hush our voices and sometimes block us from speaking about our experience living in the Holy Land, North Park has done the opposite. You have opened multiple opportunities for us to speak and you have partnered with us in making this symposium a platform to share with you our viewpoints, joys and pains—and also our hope.

Thank you, North Park and the Covenant Church.

The Lord declared a blessing over those who are seeking peace and living for peace, when he said in Matt 5:9, "Blessed are the peacemakers for they will be called the children of God." These words that are uttered from the beautiful mouth of our Lord and Savior Jesus are not just his personal wish—as if he wishes for his people to become peacemakers—but rather, it is a mandate. It is a major talent/gift that the Lord wants us to have in our Christian walk with Christ. In *The Peacemaker: A Biblical Guide to Resolving Personal Conflict*, Ken Sande says, "The concept of stewardship is especially relevant to peacemaking. Whenever you are involved in a conflict, God has given you a management opportunity. He has entrusted you with natural abilities and spiritual resources, and his Word clearly explains how he wants you to manage the situation. The more faithfully you follow his instructions, the more likely you are to see a proper solution and genuine reconciliation. Moreover, faithful stewarding will leave you with a clear conscience before God, regardless of what the other people do."

As we are gathered to discuss the Holy Land and look into the scripture, the inspired word of God in its two testaments, we must ask: "How does the word of God speak to our realities today?" I am sure there will be manifold answers related to this question. The Land that we call Holy, the Land that saw a major part of the *Heilsgeschichte*— the salvation history, the story of God's continuous and never-ending interventions in the lives of humanity to work and to fulfil his good plan for the whole world.

As I was praying and meditating on scriptures in regard to our time together this weekend, the Lord pointed my eyes to an amazing pericope in the Bible that sheds light into the issues that we will be discussing and talking about: Mic 4:1–3 (NASB).

> And it will come about in the last days
> That the mountain of the house of the LORD
> Will be established as the chief of the mountains.
> It will be raised above the hills,
> And the peoples will stream to it.
> Many nations will come and say,
> "Come and let us go up to the mountain of the LORD
> And to the house of the God of Jacob,
> That He may teach us about His ways
> And that we may walk in His paths."
> For from Zion will go forth the law,
> Even the word of the LORD from Jerusalem.
> And He will judge between many peoples
> And render decisions for mighty, distant nations.
> Then they will hammer their swords into plowshares
> And their spears into pruning hooks;
> Nation will not lift up sword against nation,
> And never again will they train for war.

I am not a biblical scholar, but I am student of the Bible, and as I began to do some exposition and exegesis, I realized how important this text really is. It is a fitting text to begin our time with. It is important to point out that the Holy Spirit— praise be to him—inspired the same words to two contemporary prophets, Micah and the premier prophet of the old times, Isaiah, in chapter 2:2-4. The words are almost identical. There is only a change of four-to-five words which mainly reflects vocabulary choice.

I know that there is a discussion over who copied whom, since they were contemporary, (although Isaiah lived longer). Did they quote someone else? We can go into that discussion and at the end lose the meaning and the messages that God is giving through both of them, especially if we dive into textual criticism. I am not up for that tonight and neither you. We want God to give us the gist of what he means in these words and since both texts are in alignment with God's salvation plan, then we certainly would be blessed and encouraged and challenged by them, with the hope that it will push us to the forefront in trying to live a life of peace-building wherever we are.

This is my prayer for the American Evangelical church and specifically the Evangelical Covenant Church and those who are present here and listening to us: that you may become a peacemaker, following in the footsteps of our Master Jesus.

And may the prophecy of Jer 3:17 that draws from the same texts in Micah 4 and Isaiah 2 be fulfilled. In fact, the prophet Jeremiah talks about change of heart when the nations come to Jerusalem. "At that time they will call Jerusalem, 'The Throne of the LORD', and all the nations will be gathered to it, to Jerusalem, for the name of the LORD; nor will they walk anymore after the stubbornness of their evil heart" (NASB).

In these texts we see:

1. The Last days: We are living in the last days since Pentecost (Apostle Peter's sermon quoting from Joel 2).

2. The mountain of the house of the Lord: The Kingdom of God, the Church, God's presence, his manifest presence. "From that time Jesus began to preach and say, 'Repent, for the kingdom of heaven is at hand'" (Matt 4:17 NASB). "And heal those in it who are sick, and say to them, 'The kingdom of God has come near to you'" (Luke 10:9 NASB).

3. Many nations will come to the mountain of the Lord: Acts 2 and beyond. It's fulfilled in the life of Jesus: Samaritan, Canaanite, Roman Centurion, inclusivity of the Covenant of God to all Jews and Gentiles (Ephesians 2, Gal 3:28). We are in the last days: "In the last days, God says, I will pour out my Spirit on all people. Your sons and daughters will prophesy, your young men will see visions, your old men will dream dreams" (Acts 2:17 NIV). "For he himself is our peace, who has made the two groups one and has destroyed the barrier, the dividing wall of hostility, by setting aside in his flesh the law with its commands

and regulations. His purpose was to create in himself one new humanity out of the two, thus making peace, and in one body to reconcile both of them to God through the cross, by which he put to death their hostility" (Eph 2:14–16 NIV).

These are amazing texts that tell us about the true peace in Christ. If there is one new humanity, then both backgrounds (Jew and Gentile) who come under the Lordship of Jesus are totally equal in everything and in every promise.

In a few days, the Feast of Tabernacles will begin in Israel. We will see a flood of Christians coming to Jerusalem to celebrate that feast. Sadly, many Christian ministries make it a point to do conferences and events around feast days, beginning with the Jewish New Year, Rosh Hashana, then Sukkot (Tabernacles). Some even teach that it's a mandate to celebrate based on the prophesies of Micah and Isaiah. Now, I don't want to give the impression that these are merely Jewish holidays and have nothing to do with believers nowadays, except to respect them. We learn from these holidays God's intention for people to celebrate and remember. I believe this is a better approach than making these feasts into an eschatological manifestation of fulfilled prophesies that are relating only to certain people, in this case the Jews. You see, as Palestinian Christians, we are frustrated with the so-called Zionist Christians and their agendas to promote such things.

Our people, the Palestinians, have lived through years of conflict and instability with no joyous event or national independence to celebrate. Rather, the Palestinian historical memory has been one shattered hope after another, shaping the identity of Palestinians and the way they view and understand the world around them. Palestinians continue to live within an unpredictable and unstable political environment. Hope that is not realized and expectations that remain unmet serve to increase the level of frustration within Palestinian society. Understanding of their history and perception of hopelessness is important for those who would minister amongst Palestinians as it affects their receptivity to the gospel. The politically-charged environment preoccupies the minds of most. Unique to the Holy Land is one's understanding of biblical Israel in relation to the conflict between modern Israel and Palestine. Biblical references are used by many Christians to favor Israel as a nation over the aspirations of the Palestinians for statehood. A question to raise is how the gospel speaks to the felt needs of Palestinians—how celebrating and focusing on one people group in the Holy Land is portrayed to the other people who live in the land. Many of them have been dedicated followers of Christ for decades. Ministries like Bethlehem Bible College and many other churches and ministries are trying our best to show the peaceful face of Jesus to our people through our love and witness and through activities that we do day and night. But sadly, sometimes an action or position that some of our brethren take, or say, or pronounce over the TV stations, ruins the image of the Prince of Peace before our people.

As someone said, "As Christians, we need to walk the talk in our lives and actions." If we desire to see the "peace of Jerusalem," we need to think hard about what we mean by that phrase. As Christians, we all know that real peace can come only through the Prince of Peace sitting on the throne of our hearts. If a political leader has not experienced that peace, how can he impart what he does not himself possess?

It is my desire to see my city, Jerusalem, and my all my homeland, the Holy Land, Palestine and Israel, come under the Lordship of the Savior who paid the utmost sacrifice on behalf of all creation. I long for the day when we will see the residents of my country, from all religious backgrounds, crying: "Blessed is he who comes in the name of the Lord." Until that happens, may we see our Christian and evangelical brethren live up to their name. May they become true evangelists in the way they live for all of the Holy Land and not a stumbling block for those who are on their way to Jesus. May we re-tune our hearts to the melody of God's salvation for all of the nations in alignment with Micah 4. From now on, when we pray and seek and work hard for the peace of the Holy Land, let us desire that for all—and not just some—of the people who live here.

4. Absence of Conflict: Nation will not lift up sword against nation, And never again will they train for war. John Lennon's song *Imagine* contains a dream based on the goodness of humanity. By contrast, the band Mercy Me offers a different reality in their song *I Can Only Imagine*: a dream based on the goodness of God. We must clarify God's character, especially because we come from a region that blames God for the cause of conflict, whether in the name of fulfilment of promises and prophesies, or the call for jihad in the name of God.

5. God himself will be the center through the manifest presence of Jesus. God will judge between many peoples and render decisions for many. The centrality of Jesus is not a city, not a country or certain people-group. Although the church is where many things should begin in terms of being the true temple of God, still the church is not the center. It's JESUS.

Therefore, what I see here in our region, is an image of God that is not clear. The God that I see is a God who:

- Wants to be with us
- Wants to teach us
- Will never cause war
- Will never act unjustly. God loves all nations and helps those who humbly come to God.
- Is the God of peace that transcends all understanding.

This identity of our God needs to come clear in our context in the Middle East and specifically in the Holy Land. Probably the best way to do that is through our continuous proclamation of God's love for all the people there, and through living a life that portrays that.

God as portrayed in the Bible as a whole is a God of love, who wants to protect his people. God will protect his people and judge his enemies. Who will judge the greed of people? A few days ago, I saw a video of Greta Thunberg. She was scorning the leaders of the world for talking about saving the world and the ecosystems but not doing anything except indulging their greed and making money.

We must stand with needy people. The realization of the kingdom of God means Jesus touching down on earth and blessing people. The lame can't get where they want to go, but God will gather those who can't walk, who have no clear future. Take them to his bosom and love them.

God wants to reveal his love, his peace, through his church, through his people who are carrying his name. So, let's do that as followers of Christ, wherever and with whomever people we mingle, Christians, Jews, Muslims, and others. God's love for them is the same and so should be our love to them, regardless of their background or color or ethnicity. God has no favoritism and so we ought not.

SELECT ANNOTATED BIBLIOGRAPHY ON THE HOLY LAND: BIBLICAL PERSPECTIVES AND CONTEMPORARY CONFLICTS

Ateek, Naim S. *Justice and Only Justice: A Palestinian Theology of Liberation*. Maryknoll, NY: Orbis, 1989. This significant work was the first to articulate the foundations of a specifically Palestinian theology of liberation.

———. *A Palestinian Theology of Liberation*. Maryknoll, NY: Orbis, 2017. This book develops and updates the themes of *Justice and Only Justice*. Ateek's work emphasizes the prioritization of those aspects of Scripture he regards as inclusive and oriented towards justice as opposed to those aspects of Scripture he regards as exclusivist.

Block, Darrell L. and Mitch Glaser eds. *Israel, the Church, and the Middle East: A Biblical Response to the Current Conflict*. Grand Rapids: Kregel, 2018. A volume of essays by US evangelical scholars in celebration of the 70th anniversary of the establishment of the state of Israel. The authors articulate the view that the land of Israel belongs to the Jewish people as a consequence of God's covenants and promises.

Brueggemann, Walter. *The Land: Place as Gift, Promise, and Challenge in Biblical Faith*. OBT. 2nd edition. Minneapolis: Augsburg Fortress, 2002. A classic study which takes the theme of the land as an entry-point to the theology of the Old Testament and also traces lines of development into the New Testament. The lack of awareness in the first edition of the ideological uses of the concept of a promised land is addressed in the introduction to the second edition.

Burge, Gary M. *Jesus and the Land: The New Testament Challenge to Holy Land Theology*. Grand Rapids: Baker, 2010. Burge offers an evangelical critique of Christian Zionism on the basis that the New Testament texts demonstrate a critical distancing by the early Christian movement between itself and any territorial dimension to faith.

———. *Whose Land? Whose Promise? What Christians are not being told about Israel and the Palestinians*. Revised and updated edition. Cleveland, OH: Pilgrim Press, 2013. A study aimed at helping western Christians understand, and engage with, the Middle East conflict from a perspective that regards the Palestinians as victims of significant injustice, and which is sharply critical of Christian Zionism.

Burnett, Carole M., ed. *Zionism through Christian Lenses: Ecumenical Perspectives on the Promised Land*. Eugene, OR: Pickwick, 2013. A volume of essays by authors from various Christian traditions united by their rejection of any legitimate basis in the Bible for the claims of Zionism, whether Jewish or Christian.

Cannon, Mae E., ed. *A Land Full of God: Christian Perspectives on the Holy Land*. Eugene, OR: Cascade, 2017. A volume of essays by authors seeking to move Western Christians beyond adopting stances that are simply either pro-Israeli or pro-Palestinian towards theological principles and attitudes consistent with peace in the land.

Davies, W. D. *The Gospel and the Land: Early Christianity and Jewish Territorial Doctrine.* Berkeley: University of California Press, 1974. This book moved the theme of the land to prominence within New Testament Studies in a new way. Davies took as his starting point the need to explain the apparent lack of concern within the New Testament with the relationship between God, the people, and the land.

Ellis, Marc H. *Toward a Jewish Theology of Liberation: The Challenge of the 21st Century.* 3rd edition. Waco, TX: Baylor University Press, 2004. Influenced by Latin American Liberation Theology, Ellis critiques what he regards as the use of Zionist theology to justify repressive violence by the state of Israel. He believes that the future of Jewish theology begins with a call for justice for the oppressed Palestinian people.

Goldman, Shalom. *Zeal for Zion: Christians, Jews, and the Idea of the Promised Land.* Chapel Hill, NC: University of North Carolina Press, 2009. A history of Zionism by a Jewish scholar that integrates the stories of Jewish Zionism and Christian Zionism, arguing that each cannot be adequately understood except in the context of the other.

Gregerman, Adam. "Old Wine in New Bottles: Liberation Theology and the Israeli-Palestinian Conflict," *Journal of Ecumenical Studies* 41.3-4 (2004) 313-40. Gregerman has written several important essays about the Holy Land and the Israeli-Palestinian conflict from the perspective of one who is deeply engaged in Jewish-Roman Catholic dialogue and strongly concerned to help the church avoid supersessionism in its interpretation of Scripture.

———. "Comparative Christian Hermeneutical Approaches to the Land Promises to Abraham," *Cross Currents* 64.3 (2014) 410-25. See entry above for the same author.

———. "Is the Biblical Land Promise Irrevocable? Post-Nostra Aetate Catholic Theologies of the Jewish Covenant and the Land of Israel," *Modern Theology* 34.2 (2018) 137-58. See entries above for the same author.

Habel, Norman. *The Land is Mine: Six Biblical Land Ideologies*, OBT. Minneapolis: Augsburg Fortress, 1995. A now classic study of attitudes towards the land found in the Old Testament texts. Habel's work forcibly makes the point that the Old Testament contains not a single theological perspective on the gift of the land to Israel but multiple and varied ones.

Halevi, Yossi Klein. *Letters to my Palestinian Neighbor.* New York: Harper Collins, 2018. A text by an Israeli journalist conducting an imagined dialogue with a Palestinian neighbor that includes both reflections upon personal identity and attempts to narrate key historical events. Halevi regards religion not only as a source of conflict but also as a potential resource for peace.

Isaac, Munther. *From Land to Lands: From Eden to the Renewed Earth.* Langham Monographs: Carlisle, 2015. This study traces the theme of land through the Bible, analysing it through the theological categories of holiness, covenant, and kingship. Isaac argues that in Christ the land has been "universalized."

———. *The Other Side of the Wall: A Palestinian Christian Narrative of Lament and Hope.* Downer's Grove, IL: IVP, 2020. A personal perspective from a scholar on his life experiences as a Palestinian Christian and on the biblical and theological issues involved in the Israeli-Palestinian conflict.

Jabbour, Elias. *Sulha: Palestinian Traditional Peace-making Process.* Montreat, NC: House of Hope, 1993. This book seeks to make available as a resource for peace-making a communal process of overcoming feuds between families and moving from revenge to forgiveness that is sanctioned by tradition within Palestinian culture.

Katanacho, Yohanna. *The Land of Christ: A Palestinian Cry.* Eugene, OR: Pickwick, 2013. Katanacho articulates a Palestinian evangelical biblical theology of the land, in the process commenting upon the theology of the land expressed in the Palestinian *Kairos* document.

———. *Reading the Gospel of John through Palestinian Eyes.* Carlisle: Langham Preaching Resources, 2020. This study of the Fourth Gospel from a Palestinian Christian perspective argues that the text reinterprets the history of Judaism in light of an inclusive Christ, who establishes a new identity for the people of God no longer based on race or nationality.

Kinzer, Mark S. *Jerusalem Crucified, Jerusalem Risen: The Resurrected Messiah, the Jewish People, and the Land of Promise.* Eugene, OR: Cascade, 2018. Kinzer offers a case for a Messianic Jewish Zionism to which Christ is central, based upon a theological interpretation of Luke-Acts.

Lewis, Donald M. *The Origins of Christian Zionism: Lord Shaftesbury and Evangelical Support for a Jewish Homeland.* Cambridge: Cambridge University Press, 2010. This historical study shows that, long before it became influential in the United States, Christian Zionism played a significant role in shaping attitudes among British evangelicals and British colonial policy in the Middle East.

Loden, Lisa and Salim J. Munayer., eds. *The Land Cries Out: Theology of the Land in the Israeli-Palestinian Context.* Eugene, OR: Wipf & Stock, 2011. A volume of essays resulting from dialogue between Palestinian Christian and Messianic Jewish scholars, articulating some fundamental differences in interpreting the biblical promises of the land.

Lux, Richard. *The Jewish People, The Holy Land, and the State of Israel: A Catholic View.* New York: Paulist Press, 2010. This study tells the history of the very significant changes in Roman Catholic attitudes towards Judaism since the Second Vatican Council. Lux regards the Holy Land in sacramental terms and discerns an equivalence between the role of the state of Israel for all Jews and the role of the Catholic church for all Christians.

Mansour, Rula K. *Theology of Reconciliation in the Context of Church Relations: A Palestinian Christian Perspective in Dialogue with Miroslav Volf.* Carlisle: Langham Monographs, 2020. Reflecting upon conflicts within Palestinian evangelical churches this study attempts a critical synthesis of Volf's theology and traditional Palestinian peace-making processes. Mansour's work yields significant insights for those seeking peace and reconciliation across as well as within communities.

Select Annotated Bibliography

McDermott, Gerald., ed. *The New Christian Zionism: Fresh Perspectives on Israel and the Land*. Downer's Grove, IL: IVP, 2016. A collection of essays defending the biblical and theological basis of Christian Zionism. It represents something of a landmark because the contributors seek to sever any necessary tie between commitment to Zionism and premillennial dispensationalism.

Pappé, Ilan. *A History of Modern Palestine: One Land, Two Peoples*. 2nd edition. Cambridge: Cambridge University Press, 2006. Pappé is a revisionist Israeli historian who left Israel because of his increasingly unpopular views, which include his contention that the displacement of 700,000 Palestinians in 1948 was not decided on an *ad hoc* basis but resulted from a plan for ethnic cleansing. In this study he provides a general history of Palestine from the mid-nineteenth century to the early years of the twenty-first century.

Raheb, Mitri. *Faith in the Face of Empire: The Bible through Palestinian Eyes*. Maryknoll, NY: Orbis Books, 2014. Written by a Palestinian Lutheran theologian, this study attempts to interpret the Bible in the context of the history of the domination of the Holy Land by various imperial projects. The Israeli-Palestinian conflict is viewed as an aspect of European colonial history.

Ravitsky, Aviezer. *Messianism, Zionism, and Jewish Religious Radicalism*. Chicago: University of Chicago Press, 1996. This study by a Jewish philosopher explores the widely divergent range of attitudes within Orthodox Judaism towards the existence of the state of Israel and the relationship between these attitudes and traditional affirmations that the Jewish exile will end with the coming of the Messiah.

Shavit, Ari. *My Promised Land: The Triumph and Tragedy of Israel*. New York: Spiegel & Grau, 2015. A history of the state of Israel by a left-wing Jewish journalist that both celebrates Israel and empathizes with the consequences of its establishment for the Palestinian people.

Soulen, Kendall R. *The God of Israel and Christian Theology*. Minneapolis: Augsburg Fortress, 1996. This influential study offered both the first full-scale theological critique of Christian supersessionism and a constructive proposal for an alternative perspective.

Tucker, J. Brian. *Reading Romans after Supersessionism: The Continuation of Jewish Covenantal Identity*. Eugene, OR: Cascade, 2018. One of the first volumes of a series committed to reading the New Testament in a way that avoids supersessionism, this study argues that in Romans Jewish covenantal identity continues in Paul's gospel.

Weaver, Alain E. *Mapping Exile and Return: Palestinian Dispossession and a Political Theology for a Shared Future*. Minneapolis: Fortress, 2014. Weaver is a Mennonite scholar utilizing the biblical theme of exile to oppose Zionist cartographies and to argue for a sharing of the land as a path to peace.

Weber, Timothy P. *On the Road to Armageddon: How Evangelicals Became Israel's Best Friend*. Grand Rapids: Baker Academic, 2005. This historical study traces the paths by which the theological commitments of premillennial dispensationalism led from the 1950s onwards to active support for the state of Israel among US evangelicals.

Wenell, Karen. *Jesus and Land: Sacred and Social Space in Second Temple Judaism*. London and New York: T. & T. Clark, 2007. Wenell seeks both to build upon and move beyond the work of W.D. Davies by considering the theme of Jesus and land in the context of the related categories of social and sacred space.

Willitts, Joel. *Matthew's Messianic Shepherd-King: In Search of the Lost Sheep of the House of Israel*. BNZW 147. Berlin: de Gruyter, 2007. This monograph argues that as part of Matthew's presentation of Jesus as the Davidic Messiah, territorial expectations form a significant component of the Gospel's vision for Israel's restoration.

Wyschogrod, Michael and R. Kendall Soulen, *Abraham's Promise: Judaism and Jewish-Christian Relations*. Grand Rapids: Eerdmans, 2004. This is a book of essays by Wyschogrod, an influential Jewish German-American philosopher of religion, with an introduction by Soulen. The essays cover a wide range of topics and they appeal for Jews and Christians to adopt more empathetic perspectives on each other's faith traditions while recognizing the fundamental nature of key theological differences.

NORTH PARK THEOLOGICAL SEMINARY SYMPOSIUM ON THE THEOLOGICAL INTERPRETATION OF SCRIPTURE

SEPTEMBER 26–28, 2019

The Holy Land: Biblical Perspectives and Contemporary Conflicts

PRESENTERS

Philip Alexander
   Professor Emeritus of Post-Biblical Jewish Studies, University of Manchester

Mae Elise Cannon
   Executive Director, Churches for Middle East Peace (CMEP)

Yohanna Katanacho
   Academic Dean & Professor of Biblical Studies, Nazareth Evangelical College

Rula Mansour
   Director of Peace Studies and Lecturer, Nazareth Evangelical College

Yehiel E. Poupko
   Rabbinic Scholar, Jewish Federation of Metropolitan Chicago

Jack Y. Sara
   President, Bethlehem Bible College

Joel Willitts
   Professor in Biblical and Theological Studies, North Park University

K. Lawson Younger, Jr.
   Professor of Old Testament, Semitic Languages, and Ancient Near Eastern History, Trinity Evangelical Divinity School

RESPONDENTS

Jeff Anderson
Serve GloballyMiddle East/North Africa (MENA) Regional Coordinator, Evangelical Covenant Church

William Andrews
Lecturer: Biblical and Theological Studies, North Park Theological Seminary

Robert Cathey
Professor of Theology, McCormick Theological Seminary

J. Nathan Clayton
Old Testament Teaching Fellow, North Park Theological Seminary

Robert Hostetter
Professor of Communication Arts, North Park University

Madison N. Pierce
Assistant Professor of New Testament, Trinity Evangelical Divinity School

Michael Walker
Theology Teaching Fellow, North Park Theological Seminary

www.ingramcontent.com/pod-product-compliance
Lightning Source LLC
Chambersburg PA
CBHW081350230426
43667CB00017B/2787